PHILIP'S QUICK REFERENCE WORLD ATLAS

P9-DEF-736

Contents

CITY CENTRE MAPS – KEY TO SYMBOLS

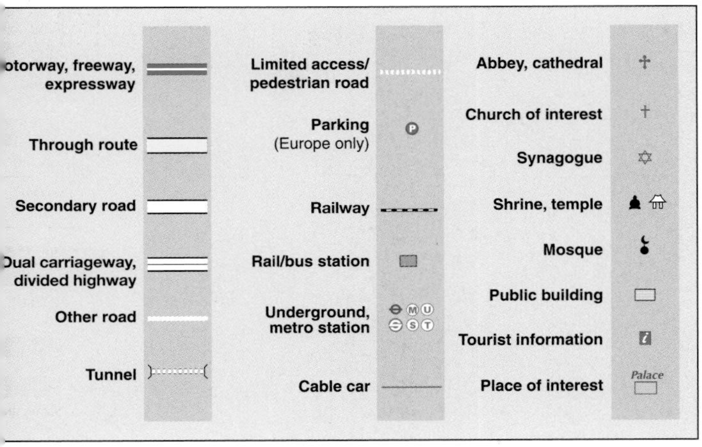

otorway, freeway, expressway		Limited access/ pedestrian road		Abbey, cathedral	✝
Through route		Parking (Europe only)	Ⓟ	Church of interest	†
Secondary road		Railway		Synagogue	✡
				Shrine, temple	♣ 🏯
Dual carriageway, divided highway		Rail/bus station	▢	Mosque	☾
Other road		Underground, metro station	Ⓔ Ⓜ Ⓤ Ⓢ Ⓣ	Public building	▢
				Tourist information	ℹ
Tunnel	) (	Cable car		Place of interest	*Palace* ▢

CENTRE MAPS – Cartography by Philip's

iii, Dublin: The town plan of Dublin is based on Ordnance
ey Ireland by permission of the Government Permit Number
. © Ordnance Survey Ireland and Government of Ireland.

Ordnance Survey® Page iii, Edinburgh, and page iv, London:
This product includes mapping data licensed
Ordnance Survey® with the permission of the Controller
er Majesty's Stationery Office. © Crown copyright 2006.
ghts reserved. Licence number 100011710.

r data: Courtesy of Gräfe and Unser Verlag GmbH,
chen, Germany (city centre maps of Bangkok, Mexico City,
pore, Sydney and Tokyo).

Published in Great Britain in 2006 by Philip's,
a division of Octopus Publishing Group,
2–4 Heron Quays, London E14 4JP

Copyright © 2006 Philip's
Cartography by Philip's

ISBN-13 978–0–540–08911–6
ISBN-10 0–540–08911–7

A CIP catalogue record for this book is available from
the British Library.

Printed in Hong Kong

Details of other Philip's titles and services can be found on our
website at: www.philips-maps.co.uk

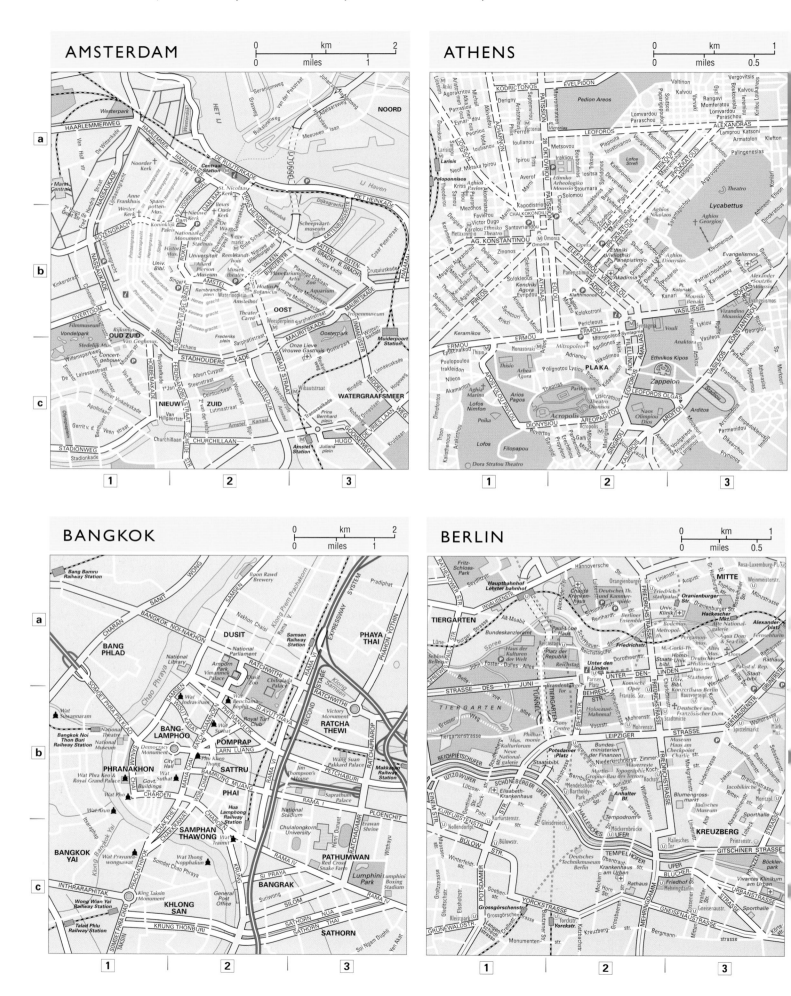

Light Rail (LUAS)

COPYRIGHT PHILIPS

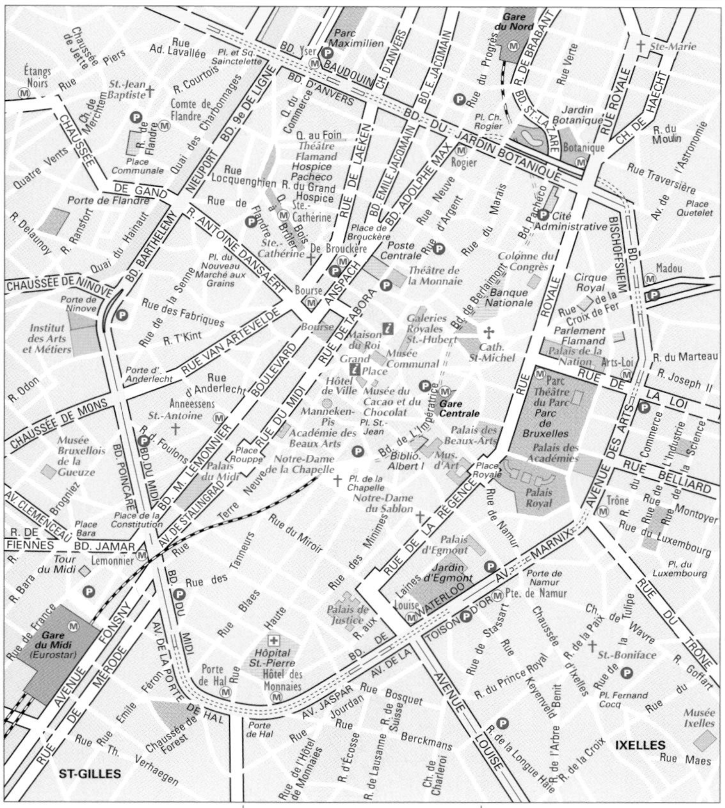

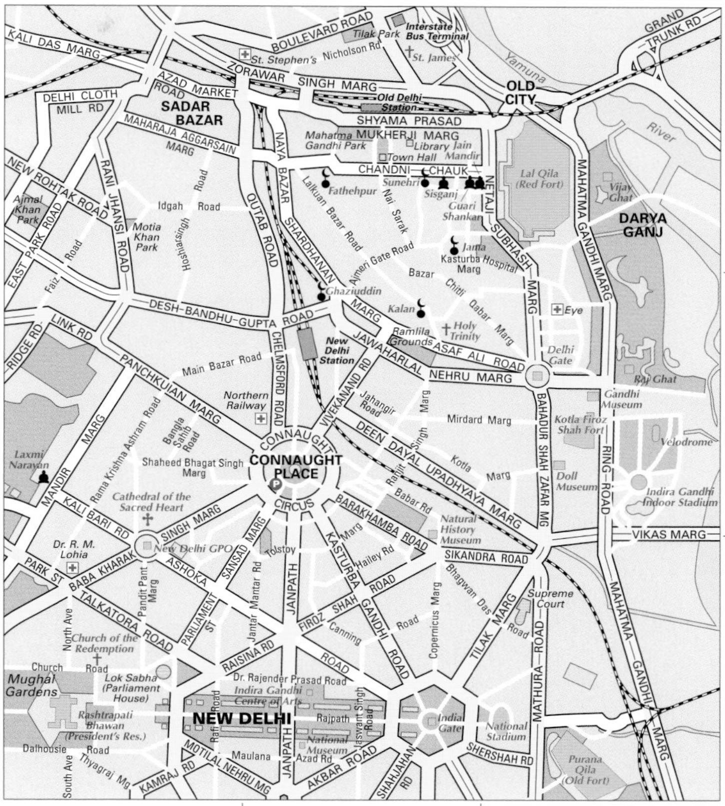

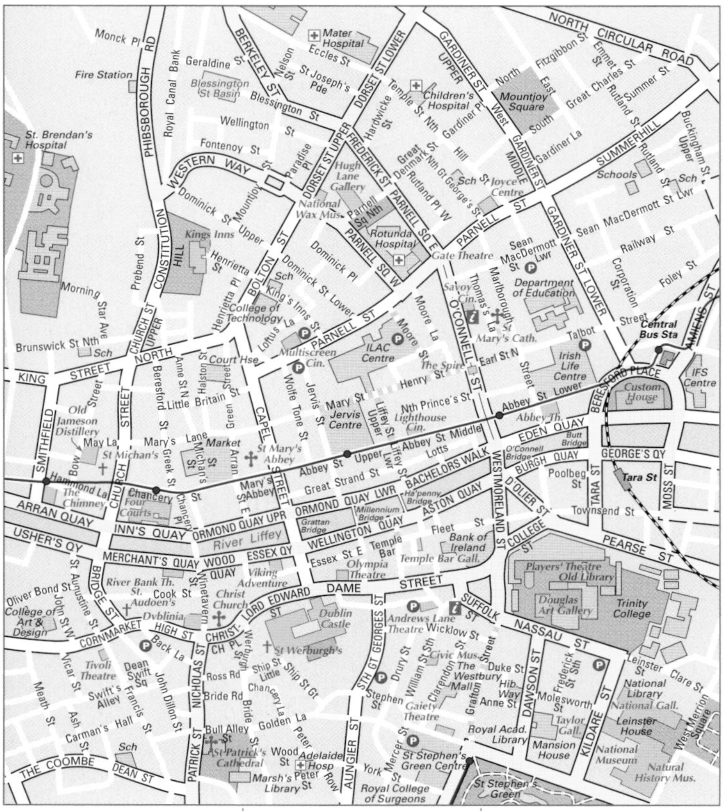

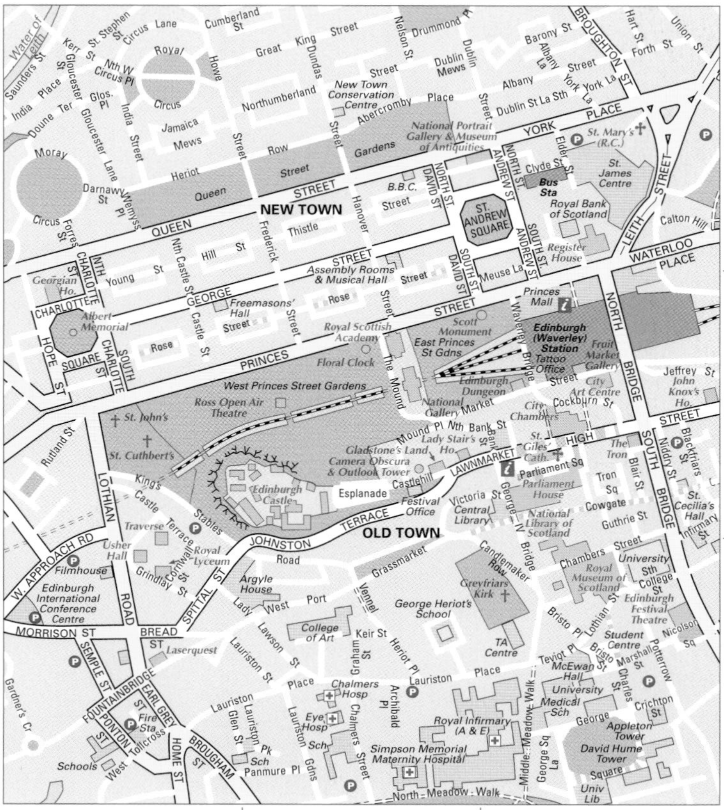

IV LONDON, LISBON, MADRID

LONDON

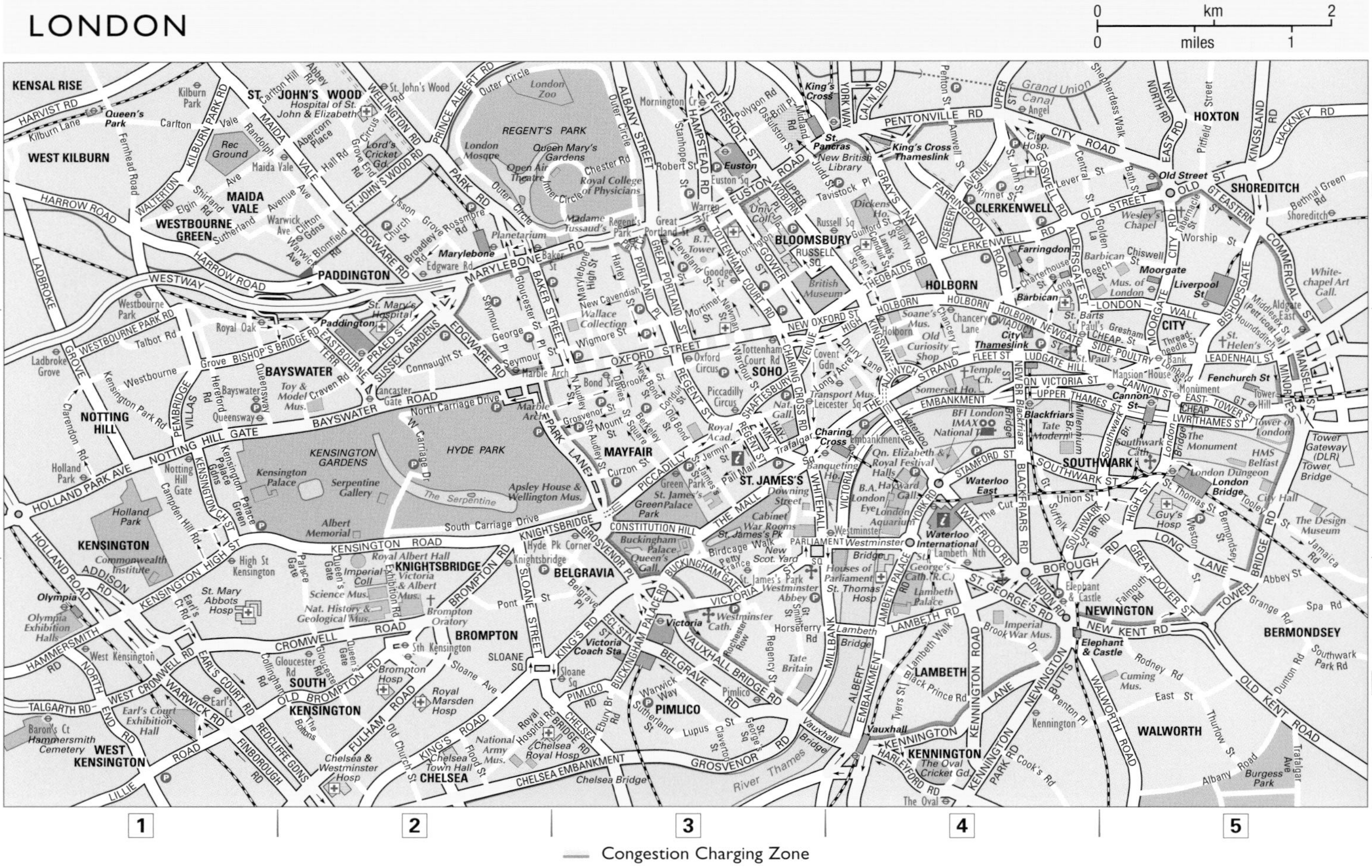

0 km 2
0 miles 1
KENSAL RISE
ST. JOHN'S WOOD
REGENT'S PARK
London Zoo
HOXTON
WEST KILBURN
MAIDA VALE
SHOREDITCH
WESTBOURNE GREEN
BLOOMSBURY
CLERKENWELL
PADDINGTON
HOLBORN
BAYSWATER
SOHO
CITY
NOTTING HILL
HYDE PARK
KENSINGTON GARDENS
MAYFAIR
ST. JAMES'S
SOUTHWARK
KENSINGTON
KNIGHTSBRIDGE
BELGRAVIA
NEWINGTON
BERMONDSEY
BROMPTON
LAMBETH
SOUTH KENSINGTON
PIMLICO
WALWORTH
WEST KENSINGTON
CHELSEA
KENNINGTON
River Thames
a
b
c
1
2
3
4
5
Congestion Charging Zone

LISBON

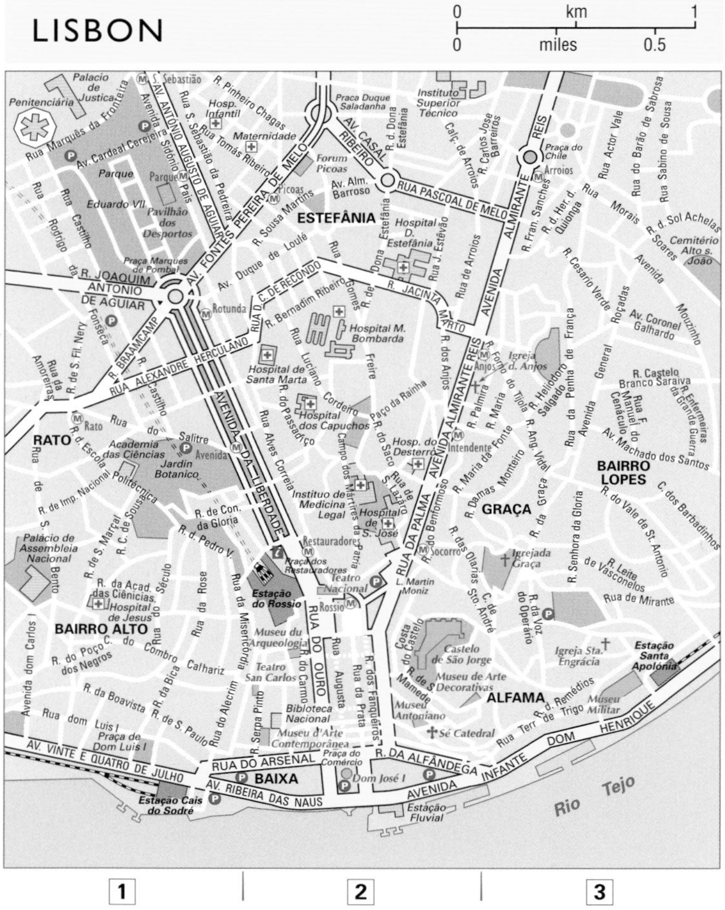

0 km 1
0 miles 0.5
ESTEFÂNIA
RATO
BAIRRO LOPES
GRAÇA
BAIRRO ALTO
ALFAMA
BAIXA
Estação do Rossio
Estação Santa Apolónia
Estação Cais do Sodré
Rio Tejo
a
b
c
1
2
3

MADRID

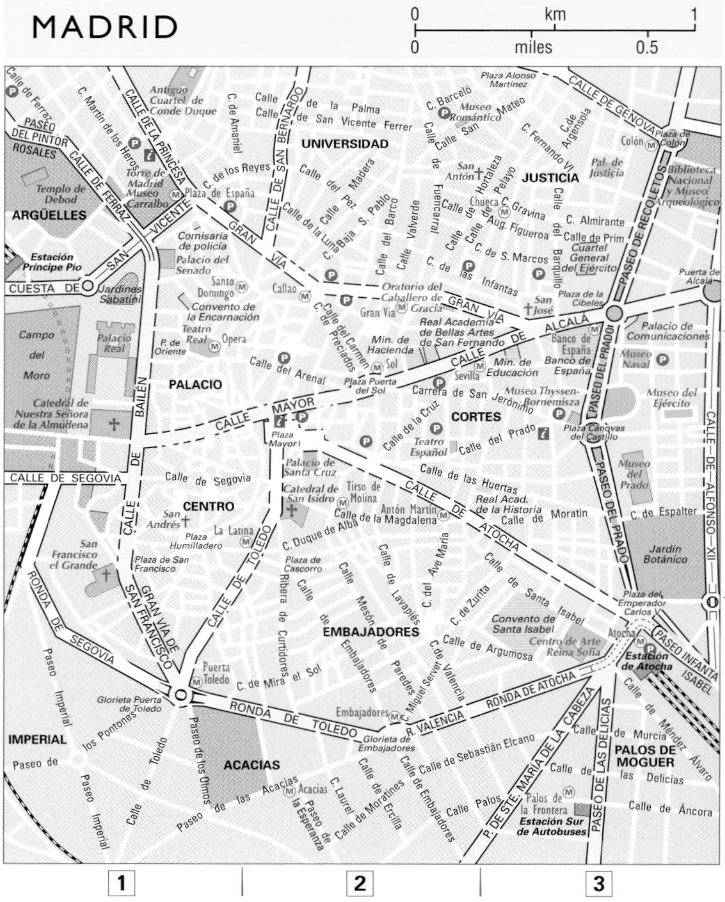

0 km 1
0 miles 0.5
UNIVERSIDAD
JUSTICIA
ARGÜELLES
PALACIO
CORTES
CENTRO
EMBAJADORES
IMPERIAL
ACACIAS
PALOS DE MOGUER
Jardín Botánico
Estación de Atocha
a
b
c
1
2
3

MEXICO CITY

km 0 — 1
miles 0 — 0.5

Sta. Maria
Naranjo
Ciprés
Rosains
J. A. ALZATE
Estación FFCC
Nacionales
Buenavista
Camelia
GUERRERO
Degollado
Héroes
MONUMENTO a Cuitláhuac
Sor Juana Inés de la Cruz
Torres Bodet
A. Nervo
C.J. Menesas
PERAVILLO
SANTA
MARÍA
Guerrero
Mosqueta
Monumento a Gen. San Martín
Ecuador
JESÚS CARRANZA
San Cosme
Zaragoza
Aldama
Rep.
de
Chile
CARRANZA
MDB DE SAN COSME
Museo del Chapo
Mina
Revolución
San Fernando
Monumento a Simón Bolívar
Rep.
Santa Catarina
Honduras
Perú
Santo Domingo
Beisario Domínguez
ARGENTINA
Aztecas
M. Schultz
Herrera
PUENTE ALVARADO
Santa Veracruz
Bellas Artes
AVENIDA HIDALGO
Museo Nacional de Arte
Secretaria de Educación Pública
Carmen
Monumento a la Revolución
Palacio de Bellas Artes
Allende
Templo Mayor
Antonio Caso
DE
Parque Alameda
Iglesia de la Profesa
Catedral Metropolitana
Pl. de la República
D. Guerra
Juárez
Av. 5 de Mayo
Torre Latino-americana
Zócalo (Plaza de la Constitución)
Palacio Nacional
Museo de Artes Industrias Populares
Pal. de Iturbide
CENTRO
Av. Morelos
Monumento a Colón
V. Carranza
Biblioteca Nacional
Museo de la Ciudad de México
Monumento a Cuauhtémoc
Plaza J. M. Morelos y Pavón
Victoria
Isabel la Católica
Salvador
Balderas
Luis Moya
5 de Febrero
20 DE NOVIEMBRE
La Ciudadela
Iglesia de Regina
Isabel la Católica
CHAPULTEPEC
ARCOS
BELEN
Salto del Agua
Iglesia y Fuente Salto del Agua
La Sagrada Familia
Arena México
DR. RIO DE LA LOZA
N. S. de Merceditas
Puebla
Dr. Lavista
Dr. Vertiz
Dr. Navarro
Durango
Dr. Claudio Bernard
Dr. Liceaga
Dr. Barragán
Bolívar
Plaza Taxcoaque
DE MIER
Avenida
Colima
Dr. Velasco
ESPERANZA
Lucas
Alamán
ROMA
Dr. Velasco
Niños Héroes
San Antonio Abad

1   2   3

MUMBAI

km 0 — 2
miles 0 — 1

Haji Ali Tomb
Mahalaxmi Race Course
Causeway
Mahalaxmi Temple
Jijamata Udyan (Victoria Gardens)
BYCULLA
BREACH CANDY
Willingdon Sports Club
MAHALAXMI
R. C. Cathedral
CUMBALLA HILL
Mumbai Central Station
State Road Transport Terminus
MAZAGAON
TARDEO
Jehangir Boman Behram Marg
Dockyard Rd
Kamala Nehru Park (Hanging Gardens)
Mani Bhavan (Gandhi Museum)
Clerk Basin
Babulnath Temple
SARDAR VALLABHBHAI PATEL RD
UMERKHADI
Frere Basin
Malet Shelf
Chowpatty Beach
BHULESHWĀR
MANDVI
Taraporewala Aquarium
KALBADEVI
GIRGAUM
Jama Masjid Mosque
Crawford Market
PYDHUNI
Carnac Basin
Cross Island
Back Bay
Wankhede Stadium
Aibless & Cama Hospital
St. George's Hospital
Chatrapathi Shivaji (Victoria) Terminus
Indira Docks
Mumbai Harbour
Churchgate Sta.
G.P.O.
Brabourne Stadium
The Mint
Custom Basin
West Basin
FORT
Rajabai Twr.
Town Hall
University
Jehangir Art Gallery
Prince of Wales Museum
National Gallery of Modern Art
Nariman Point
National Centre for Performing Arts
COLABA
Gateway of India

a   b   c

1   2   3

NEW YORK

km 0 — 2
miles 0 — 1

HARLEM
QUEENS
To JFK International Airport
WILLIAMSBURG
Central Park
UPPER EAST SIDE
Metropolitan Museum of Art
Guggenheim Museum
Jacqueline Kennedy Onassis Res.
Frick Collection
Queensboro Bridge
GREENPOINT
BROOKLYN
The Lake
American Museum of Natural History
UPPER WEST SIDE
Central Park Zoo
East River
Hudson River
Lincoln Center for Performing Arts
Columbus Circle
Carnegie Hall
St. Patrick's Cathedral
Grand Central Sta.
Chrysler Building
United Nations Headquarters
Queens Midtown Tunnel
LOWER EAST SIDE
Williamsburg Bridge
MANHATTAN
Rockefeller Center
Times Square
Bryant Park
Main Library
Empire State Building
EAST VILLAGE
Tompkins Sq. Park
US Naval Reserve Center
Wallabout Bay
Riverside Park
Port Authority Bus Terminal
Penn Sta.
Madison Sq. Garden
Flatiron Building
Union Square
GREENWICH VILLAGE
Washington Sq. Park
LITTLE ITALY
Manhattan Bridge
BROOKLYN HEIGHTS
CHELSEA
Jacob Javits Convention Center
Greenwich Village
SOHO
CHINA TOWN
Criminal Cts. Bldg.
N.Y. State Ct.
Municipal Bldg.
Brooklyn Bridge
WEEHAWKEN
Intrepid Sea Air & Space Museum
Passenger Ship Terminal
Lincoln Tunnel
LOWER MANHATTAN
South St. Seaport
GUTTENBERG
North Hudson Park
Toll Plaza
Holland Tunnel to Newark
World Financial Center
Ground Zero (Site of former World Trade Center)
Battery Park
Trinity Church
Wall St.
Stock Exch.
Staten Island Ferry
Brooklyn-Battery Tunnel
WEST NEW YORK
Hudson River
HOBOKEN
Ellis I. &
Statue of Liberty
Governors Island
UNION CITY

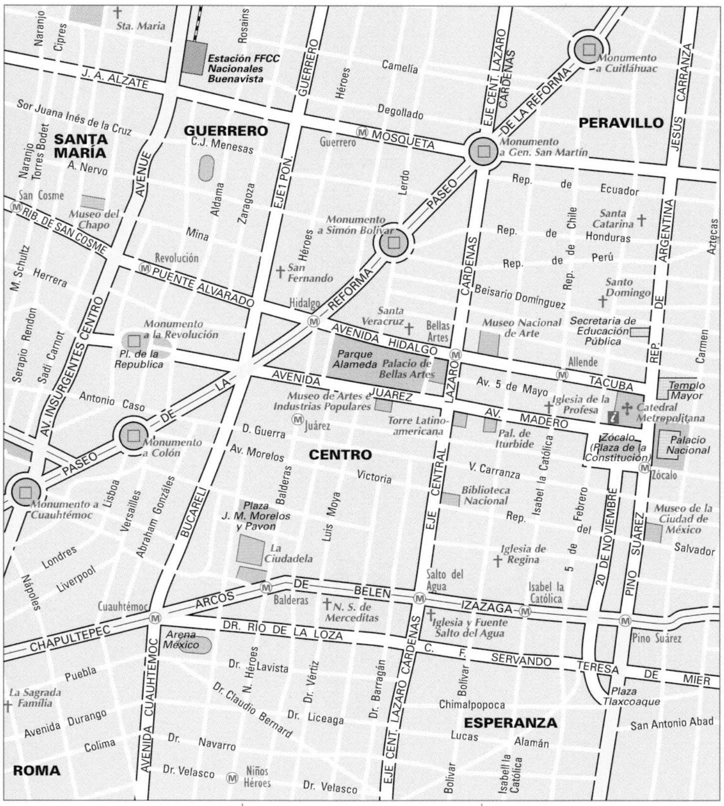

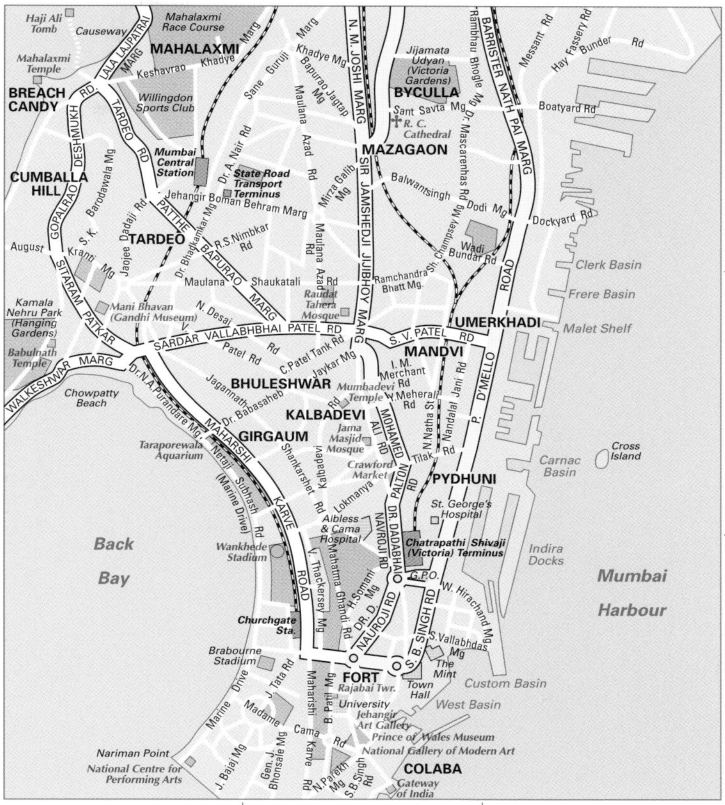

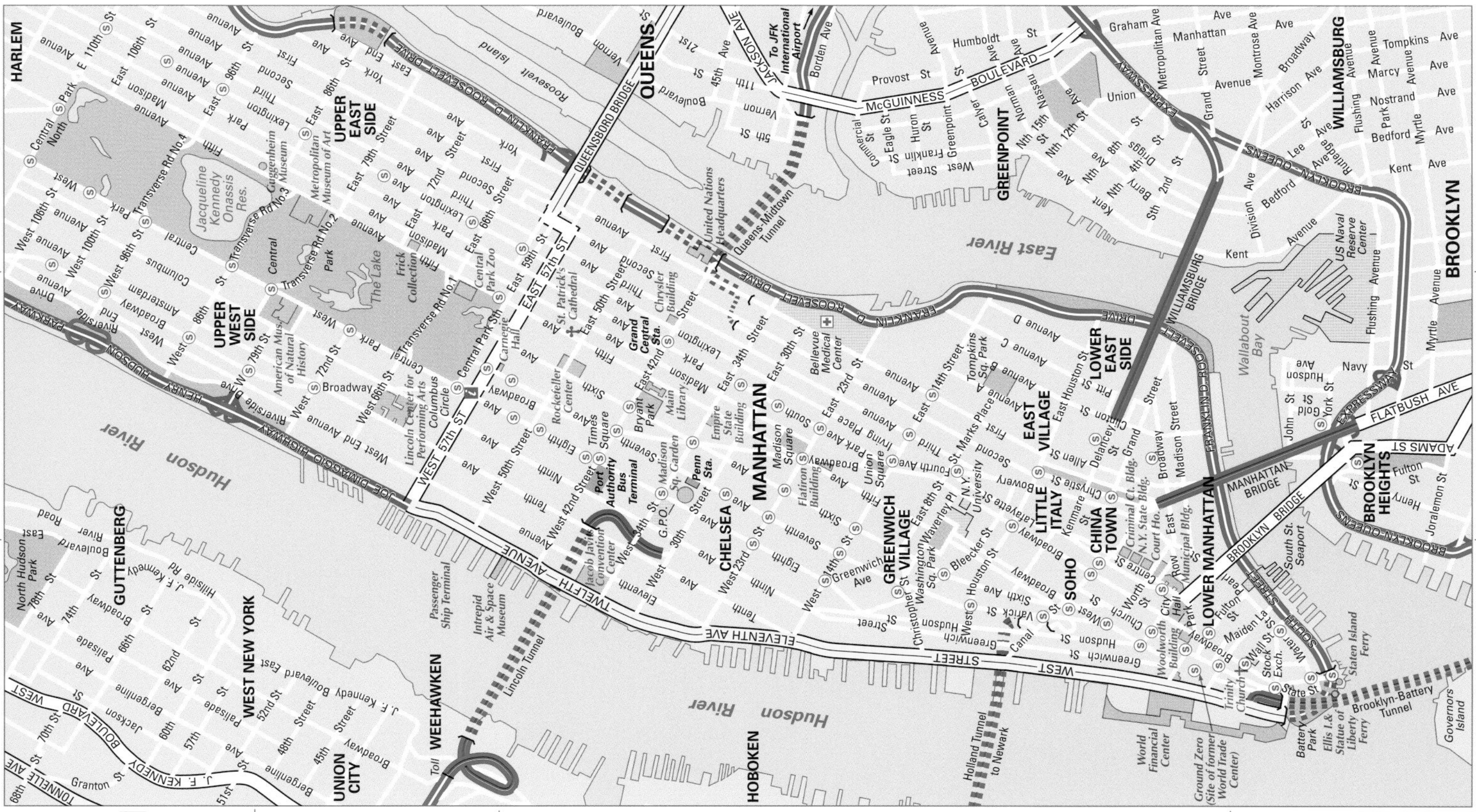

a   b   c   d   e   f

1   2   3

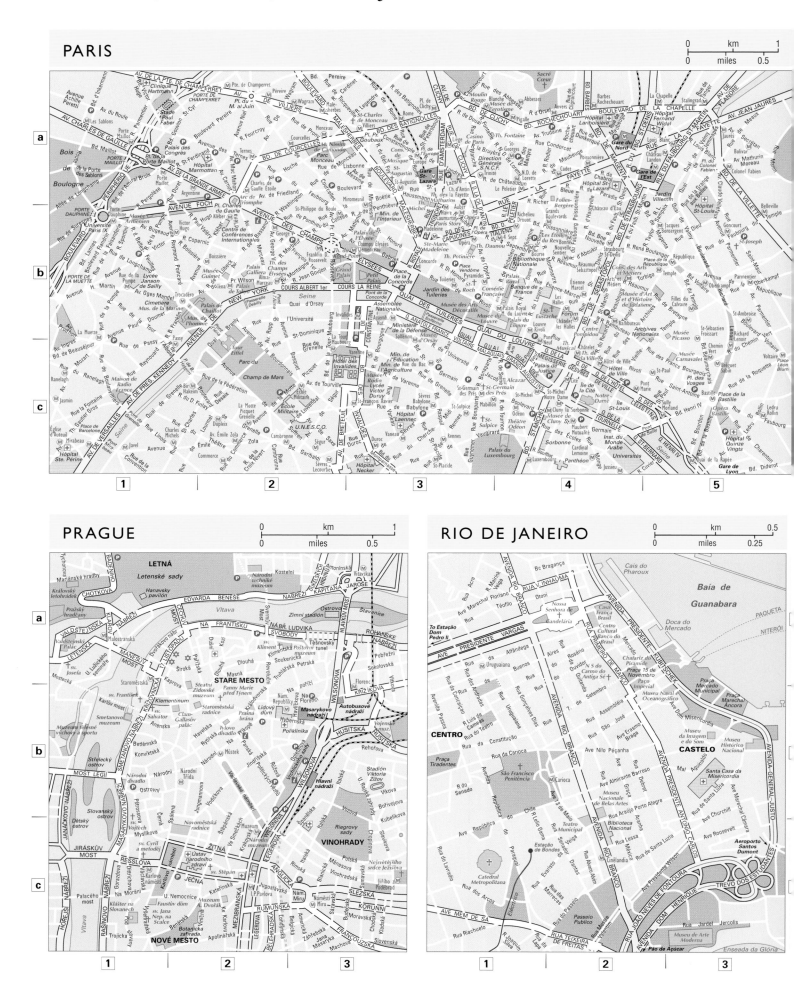

PARIS

PRAGUE

RIO DE JANEIRO

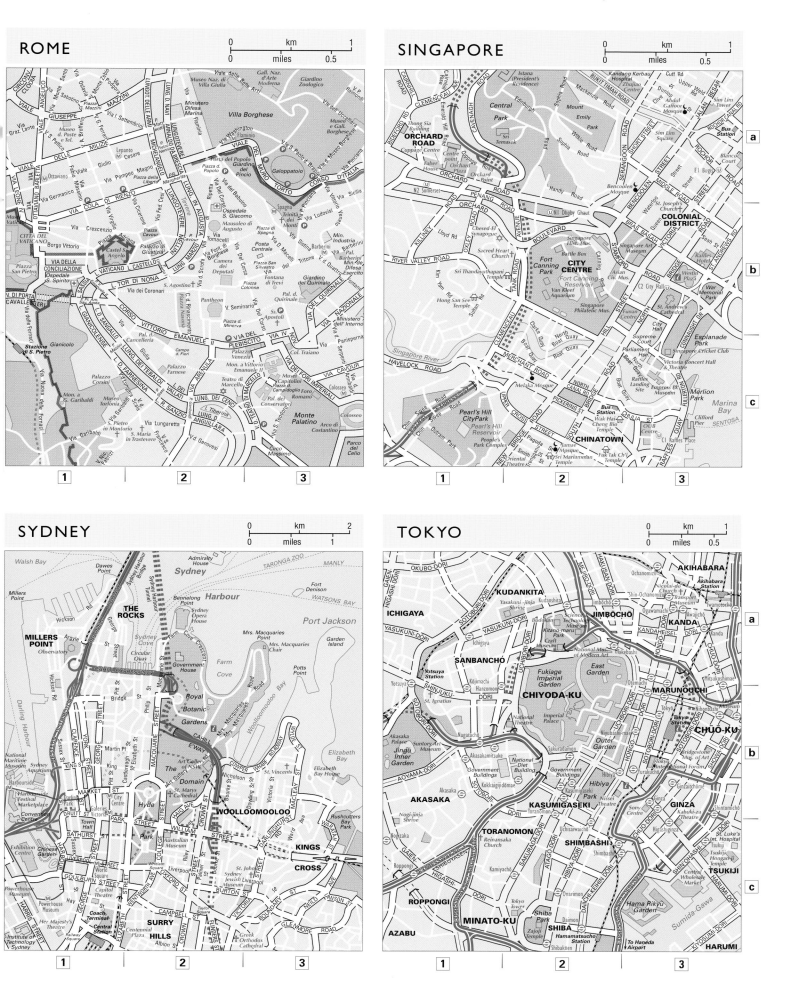

VIII   WORLD CITIES: DISTANCES

The table shows air distances in kilometres and miles between 24 major cities. Known as 'great circle' distances, these measure the shortest routes between the cities, which are used by aircraft wherever possible. The maps show the world centred on six cities, and illustrate, for example, why direct flights from Japan to North America and Europe are across the Arctic regions. The m[aps] have been constructed on an Azimuthal Equidistant project[ion] on which all distances measured through the centre point are [true] to scale. The red lines are drawn at 5,000, 10,000 and 15,000 [km] from the central city.

Distances in the upper-right triangle are in Miles; distances in the lower-left triangle are in Kilometres (Kms).

	Beijing	Bombay (Mumbai)	Buenos Aires	Cairo	Calcutta (Kolkata)	Caracas	Chicago	Hong Kong	Honolulu	Johannesburg	Lagos	London	Los Angeles	Mexico City	Moscow	Nairobi	New York	Paris	Rio de Janeiro	Rome	Singapore	Sydney	Tokyo	Wellington
Beijing	—	2956	11972	4688	2031	8947	6588	1220	5070	7276	7119	5057	6251	7742	3600	5727	6828	5106	10773	5049	2783	5561	1304	6700
Bombay (Mumbai)	4757	—	9275	2706	1034	9024	8048	2683	8024	4334	4730	4467	8700	9728	3126	2816	7793	4356	8332	3837	2432	6313	4189	7686
Buenos Aires	19268	14925	—	7341	10268	3167	5599	11481	7558	5025	4919	6917	6122	4591	8374	6463	5298	6867	1214	6929	9867	7332	11410	6202
Cairo	7544	4355	11814	—	3541	6340	6127	5064	8838	3894	2432	2180	7580	7687	1803	2197	5605	1994	6149	1325	5137	8959	5947	10268
Calcutta (Kolkata)	3269	1664	16524	5699	—	9609	7978	1653	7048	5256	5727	4946	8152	9494	3438	3839	7921	4883	9366	4486	1800	5678	3195	7055
Caracas	14399	14522	5096	10203	15464	—	2502	10166	6009	6847	4810	4664	3612	2228	6175	7173	2131	4738	2825	5196	11407	9534	8801	8154
Chicago	10603	12953	9011	3206	12839	4027	—	7783	4247	8689	5973	3949	1742	1694	4971	8005	711	4132	5311	4809	9369	9243	6299	8358
Hong Kong	1963	4317	18478	8150	2659	16360	12526	—	5543	6669	7360	5980	7232	8775	4439	5453	8047	5984	11001	5769	1615	4582	1786	5857
Honolulu	8160	12914	12164	14223	11343	9670	6836	8921	—	11934	10133	7228	2558	3781	7036	10739	4958	7437	8290	8026	6721	5075	3854	4669
Johannesburg	11710	6974	8088	6267	8459	11019	13984	10732	19206	—	2799	5637	10362	9063	5692	1818	7979	5426	4420	4811	5381	6860	8418	7308
Lagos	11457	7612	7916	3915	9216	7741	9612	11845	16308	4505	—	3118	7713	6879	3886	2366	5268	2929	3750	2510	6925	9643	8376	9973
London	8138	7190	11131	3508	7961	7507	6356	9623	11632	9071	5017	—	5442	5552	1552	4237	3463	212	5778	889	6743	10558	5942	11691
Los Angeles	10060	14000	9852	12200	13120	5812	2804	11639	4117	16676	12414	8758	—	1549	6070	9659	2446	5645	6310	6331	8776	7502	5475	6719
Mexico City	12460	15656	7389	12372	15280	3586	2726	14122	6085	14585	11071	8936	2493	—	6664	9207	2090	5717	4780	6365	10321	8058	7024	6897
Moscow	5794	5031	13477	2902	5534	9938	8000	7144	11323	9161	6254	2498	9769	10724	—	3942	4666	1545	7184	1477	5237	9008	4651	10283
Nairobi	9216	4532	10402	3536	6179	11544	12883	8776	17282	2927	3807	6819	15544	14818	6344	—	7358	4029	5548	3350	4635	7552	6996	8490
New York	10988	12541	8526	9020	12747	3430	1145	12950	7980	12841	8477	5572	3936	3264	7510	11842	—	3626	4832	4280	9531	9935	6741	8951
Paris	8217	7010	11051	3210	7858	7625	6650	9630	11968	8732	4714	342	9085	9200	2486	6485	5836	—	5708	687	6671	10539	6038	11798
Rio de Janeiro	17338	13409	1953	9896	15073	4546	8547	17704	13342	7113	6035	9299	10155	7693	11562	8928	7777	9187	—	5725	9763	8389	11551	7367
Rome	8126	6175	11151	2133	7219	8363	7739	9284	12916	7743	4039	1431	10188	10243	2376	5391	6888	1105	9214	—	6229	10143	6127	11523
Singapore	4478	3914	15879	8267	2897	18359	15078	2599	10816	8660	11145	10852	14123	16610	8428	7460	15339	10737	15712	10025	—	3915	3306	5298
Sydney	8949	10160	11800	14418	9138	15343	14875	7374	8168	11040	15519	16992	12073	12969	14497	12153	15989	16962	13501	16324	6300	—	4861	1383
Tokyo	2099	6742	18362	9571	5141	14164	10137	2874	6202	13547	13480	9562	8811	11304	7485	11260	10849	9718	18589	9861	5321	7823	—	5762
Wellington	10782	12370	9981	16524	11354	13122	13451	9427	7513	11761	16050	18814	10814	11100	16549	13664	14405	18987	11855	18545	8526	2226	9273	—

MEXICO CITY
19° 26'N 99° 04'W

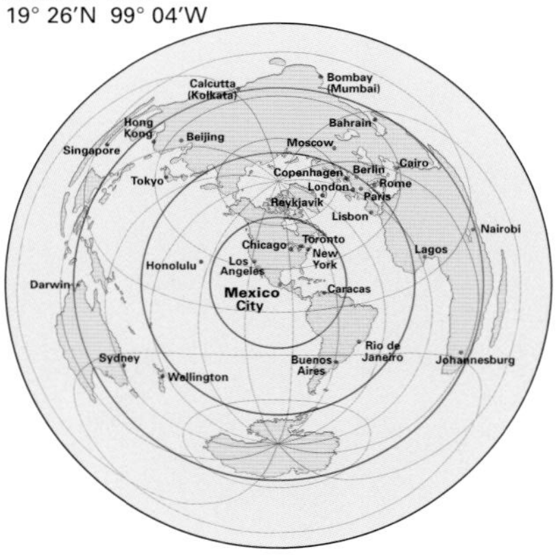

LONDON
51° 28'N 00° 27'W

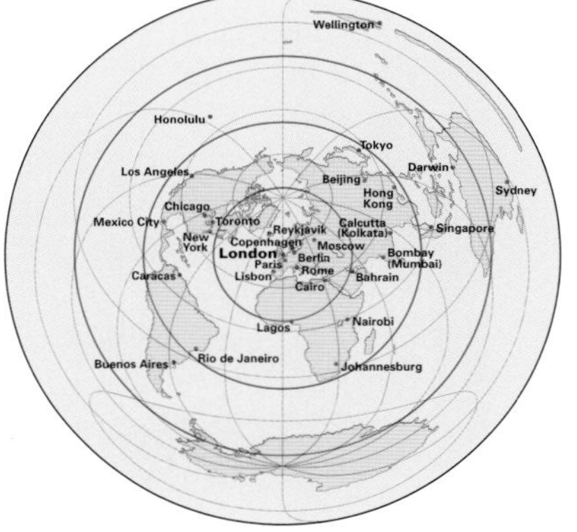

TOKYO
35° 33'N 139° 46'E

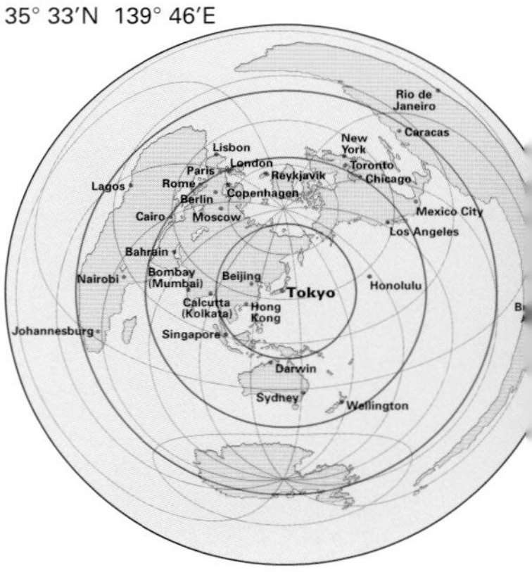

RIO DE JANEIRO
22° 50'S 43° 15'W

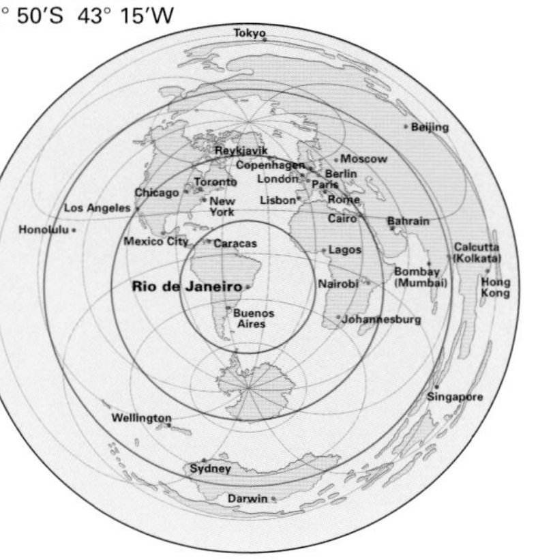

SINGAPORE
1° 21'N 103° 54'E

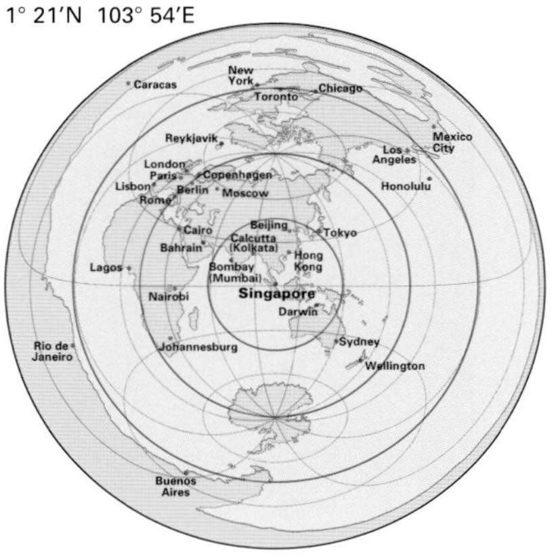

SYDNEY
33° 56'S 151° 10'E

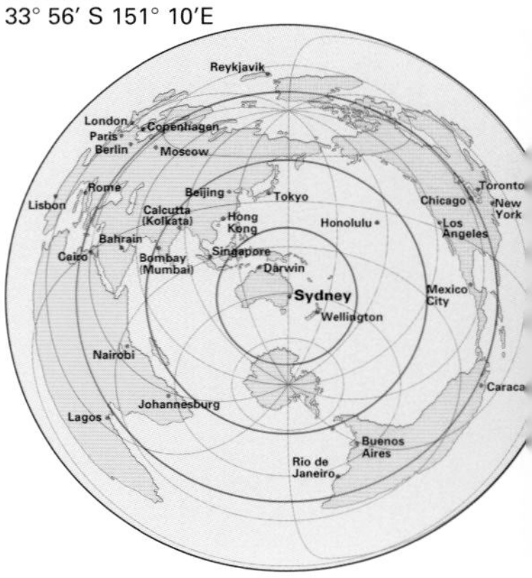

WORLD MAPS

SETTLEMENTS

■ PARIS ■ Berne ◉ Livorno ◉ Brugge ◎ Algeciras ◦ *Frejus* ◦ Oberammergau ○ Thira

Settlement symbols and type styles vary according to the scale of each map and indicate the importance
of towns on the map rather than specific population figures. Capital cities have red infills.

ADMINISTRATION

—·—·— International boundaries
— — — International boundaries (undefined or disputed)
········ Internal boundaries
- - - - - National park boundaries

International boundaries show the *de facto* situation where there are rival claims to territory

COMMUNICATIONS

——— Principal roads
—·—·— Railways
—⊢·—·⊢— Road tunnels
⊁ Passes
——— Principal railways
— — — Railways under construction
⊢·—·⊢ Railway tunnels
·········· Principal canals
⊕ Airfields

PHYSICAL FEATURES

⌁ Perennial streams
- - - Intermittent streams
▱ Perennial lakes
⬭ Intermittent lakes
⬭ Swamps and marshes
▦ Permanent ice and glaciers
▲ 8848 Elevations in metres
▼ 8500 Sea depths in metres
1134 Height of lake surface above sea level in metres

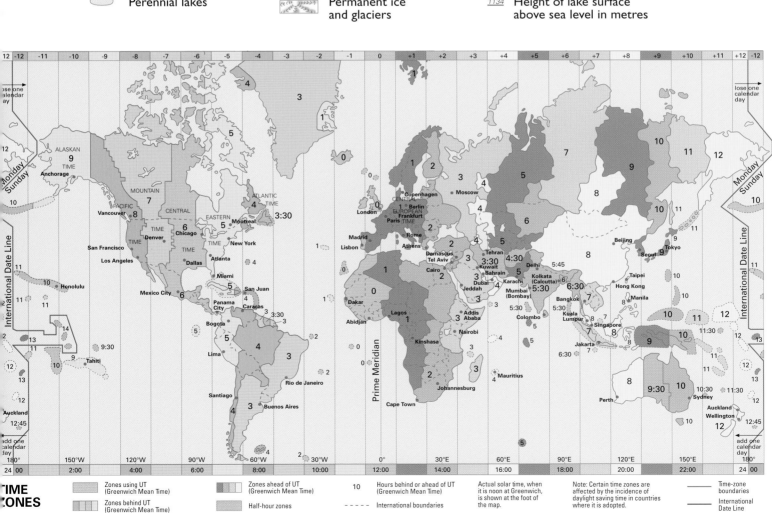

Zones using UT (Greenwich Mean Time)
Zones behind UT (Greenwich Mean Time)
Zones ahead of UT (Greenwich Mean Time)
Half-hour zones
10 Hours behind or ahead of UT (Greenwich Mean Time)
- - - - International boundaries
Actual solar time, when it is noon at Greenwich, is shown at the foot of the map.
Note: Certain time zones are affected by the incidence of daylight saving time in countries where it is adopted.
Time-zone boundaries
International Date Line

Equatorial Scale 1:95 000 000

PHYSICAL COMPARISONS

Continent	Area, '000 km	Coldest place, °C	Hottest place, °C	Wettest place (average annual rainfall, mm)	Driest place (average annual rainf...
Asia	44,500	Oymyakon, Russia -70°C ①	Tirat Zevi, Israel 54°C ⑧	Mawsynram, India 11,870 ⑮	Aden, Yemen 46
Africa	30,302	Ifrane, Morocco -24°C ②	Al Aziziyah, Libya 58°C ⑨	Debundscha, Cameroon 10,290 ⑯	Wadi Haifa, Sudan 2...
North America	24,241	Snag, Yukon -63°C ③	Death Valley, California 57°C ⑩	Henderson Lake, Canada 6,500 ⑰	Bataques, Mexico 3...
South America	17,793	Sarmiento, Argentina -33°C ④	Rivadavia, Argentina 49°C ⑪	Quibdó, Colombia 8,990 ⑱	Quillagua, Chile 0.6
Antarctica	14,000	Vostok -89°C ⑤	Vanda Station 15°C ⑫		
Europe	9,957	Ust'Shchugor, Russia -55°C ⑥	Seville, Spain 50°C ⑬	Crkvice, Serbia & M. 4,650 ⑲	Astrakhan, Russia 1...
Oceania	8,557	Charlotte Pass, Australia -22°C ⑦	Cloncurry, Australia 53°C ⑭	Tully, Australia 4,550 ⑳	Mulka, Australia 10...

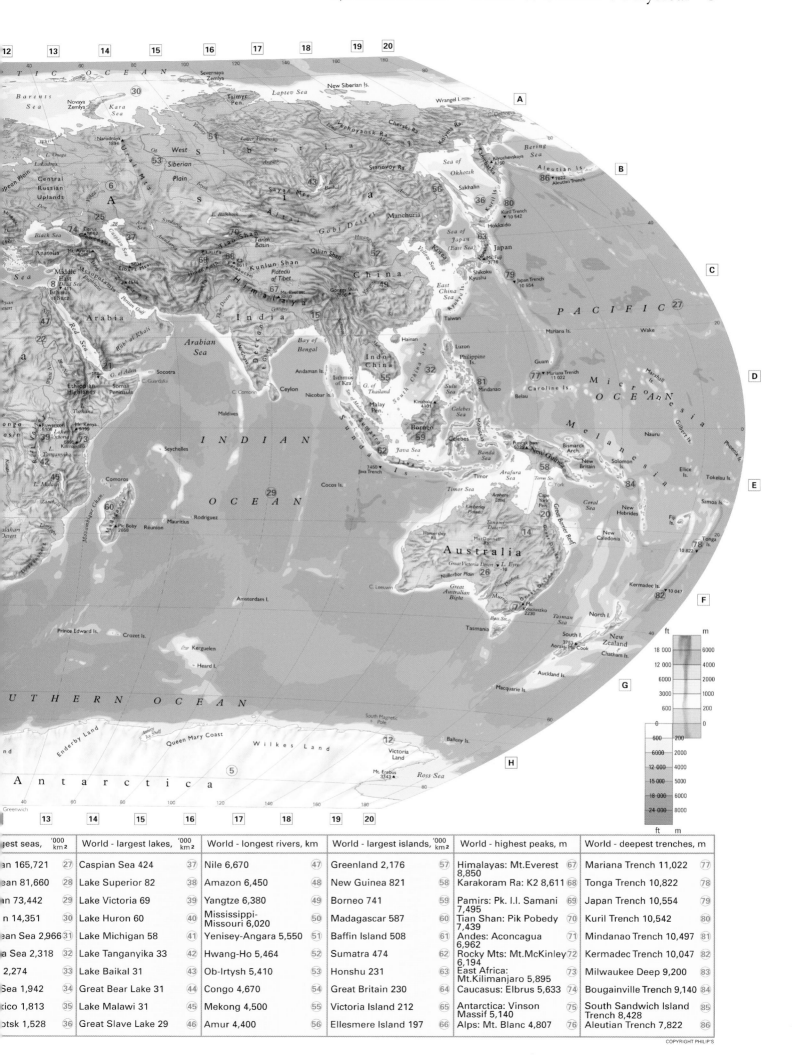

World - largest seas, '000 km²		World - largest lakes, '000 km²		World - longest rivers, km		World - largest islands, '000 km²		World - highest peaks, m		World - deepest trenches, m	
...an 165,721		Caspian Sea 424	37	Nile 6,670	47	Greenland 2,176	57	Himalayas: Mt.Everest 8,850	67	Mariana Trench 11,022	77
...ean 81,660	27	Lake Superior 82	38	Amazon 6,450	48	New Guinea 821	58	Karakoram Ra: K2 8,611	68	Tonga Trench 10,822	78
...an 73,442	28	Lake Victoria 69	39	Yangtze 6,380	49	Borneo 741	59	Pamirs: Pk. I.I. Samani 7,495	69	Japan Trench 10,554	79
...n 14,351	29	Lake Huron 60	40	Mississippi-Missouri 6,020	50	Madagascar 587	60	Tian Shan: Pik Pobedy 7,439	70	Kuril Trench 10,542	80
...ean Sea 2,966	30	Lake Michigan 58	41	Yenisey-Angara 5,550	51	Baffin Island 508	61	Andes: Aconcagua 6,962	71	Mindanao Trench 10,497	81
...a Sea 2,318	31	Lake Tanganyika 33	42	Hwang-Ho 5,464	52	Sumatra 474	62	Rocky Mts: Mt.McKinley 6,194	72	Kermadec Trench 10,047	82
...2,274	32	Lake Baikal 31	43	Ob-Irtysh 5,410	53	Honshu 231	63	East Africa: Mt.Kilimanjaro 5,895	73	Milwaukee Deep 9,200	83
...Sea 1,942	33	Great Bear Lake 31	44	Congo 4,670	54	Great Britain 230	64	Caucasus: Elbrus 5,633	74	Bougainville Trench 9,140	84
...ico 1,813	34	Lake Malawi 31	45	Mekong 4,500	55	Victoria Island 212	65	Antarctica: Vinson Massif 5,140	75	South Sandwich Island Trench 8,428	85
...otsk 1,528	35	Great Slave Lake 29	46	Amur 4,400	56	Ellesmere Island 197	66	Alps: Mt. Blanc 4,807	76	Aleutian Trench 7,822	86

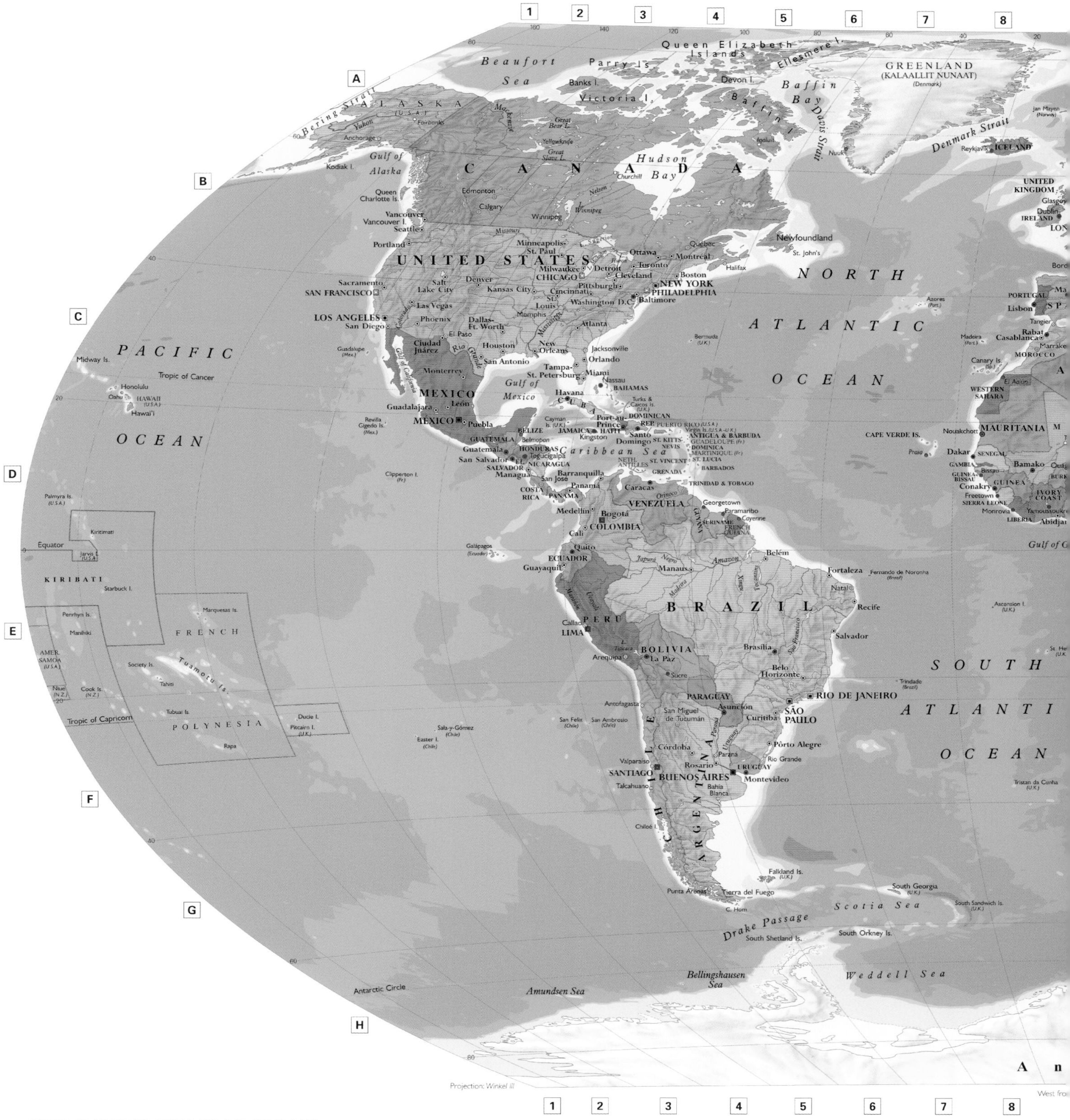

COUNTRY COMPARISONS

Country	Population in thousands 2005 estimate	Area in thous' km²	Country	Population in thousands 2005 estimate	Area in thous' km²	Country	Population in thousands 2005 estimate	Area in thous' km²	Country	Population in thousands 2005 estimate	Area in thous' km²	Country	Pop in tho 2005 e
China	1,306,300	9,597	Mexico	106,200	1,958	France	60,700	552	Argentina	39,500	2,780	Uganda	
India	1,080,300	3,287	Philippines	87,900	300	United Kingdom	60,400	242	Poland	38,600	323	Uzbekistan	
United States	295,700	9,629	Vietnam	83,500	332	Italy	58,100	301	Tanzania	36,800	945	Saudi Arabia	
Indonesia	242,000	1,905	Germany	82,400	357	South Korea	48,600	99	Kenya	33,800	580	Iraq	
Brazil	186,100	8,514	Egypt	77,500	1,001	Ukraine	47,000	604	Canada	32,800	9,971	Venezuela	
Pakistan	162,400	796	Ethiopia	73,100	1,104	Burma (Myanmar)	47,000	677	Morocco	32,700	447	Malaysia	
Bangladesh	144,300	144	Turkey	69,700	775	South Africa	44,300	1,221	Algeria	32,500	2,382	North Korea	
Russia	143,400	17,075	Iran	68,000	1,648	Colombia	43,000	1,139	Afghanistan	29,900	652	Taiwan	
Nigeria	128,800	924	Thailand	64,200	513	Spain	40,300	498	Peru	27,900	1,285	Romania	
Japan	127,400	378	Congo, Dem. Rep.	60,800	2,345	Sudan	40,200	2,506	Nepal	27,700	147	Ghana	

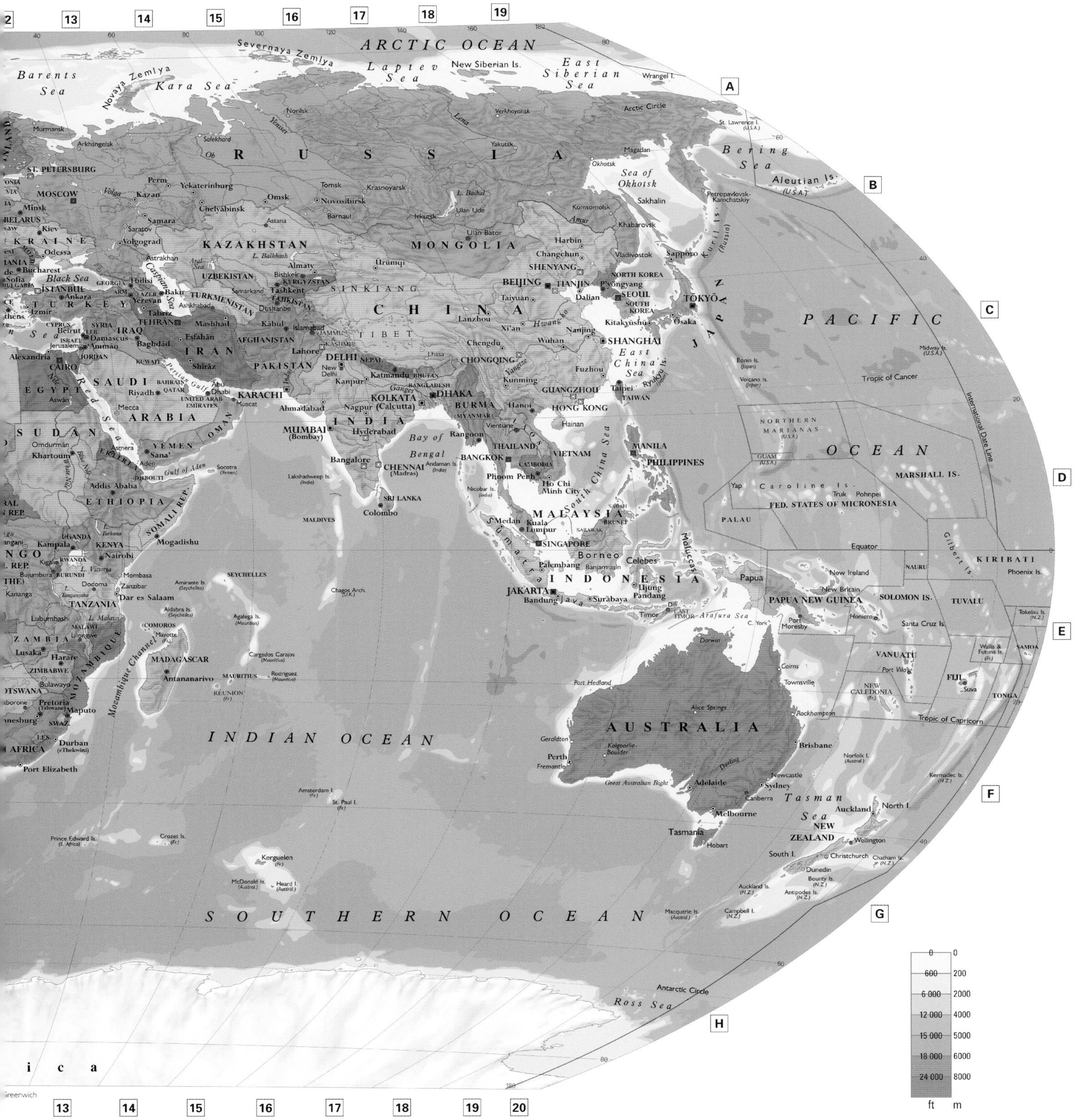

Population in thousands 2005 estimate	Area in thous' km²	Country	Population in thousands 2005 estimate	Area in thous' km²	Country	Population in thousands 2005 estimate	Area in thous' km²	Country	Population in thousands 2005 estimate	Area in thous' km²	Country	Population in thousands 2005 estimate	Area in thous' km²
20,700	528	Kazakhstan	15,200	2,725	Mali	11,400	1,240	Hungary	10,000	93	Azerbaijan	7,900	87
20,100	7,741	Cambodia	13,600	181	Cuba	11,300	111	Chad	9,700	1,284	Burundi	7,800	28
20,100	66	Burkina Faso	13,500	274	Zambia	11,300	753	Guinea	9,500	246	Benin	7,600	113
19,400	802	Ecuador	13,400	284	Serbia & Montenegro	10,800	102	Dominican Rep.	9,000	49	Switzerland	7,500	41
18,400	185	Malawi	12,700	118	Greece	10,700	132	Sweden	9,000	450	Bulgaria	7,500	111
18,000	587	Niger	12,200	1,267	Portugal	10,600	89	Bolivia	8,900	1,099	Honduras	7,200	112
17,300	322	Zimbabwe	12,200	394	Belgium	10,400	31	Somalia	8,600	638	Tajikistan	7,200	143
17,000	475	Guatemala	12,000	109	Belarus	10,300	208	Rwanda	8,400	26	Hong Kong (China)	6,900	1
16,400	42	Angola	11,800	1,247	Czech Republic	10,200	79	Austria	8,200	84	El Salvador	6,700	21
16,000	757	Senegal	11,700	197	Tunisia	10,100	164	Haiti	8,100	28	Paraguay	6,300	407

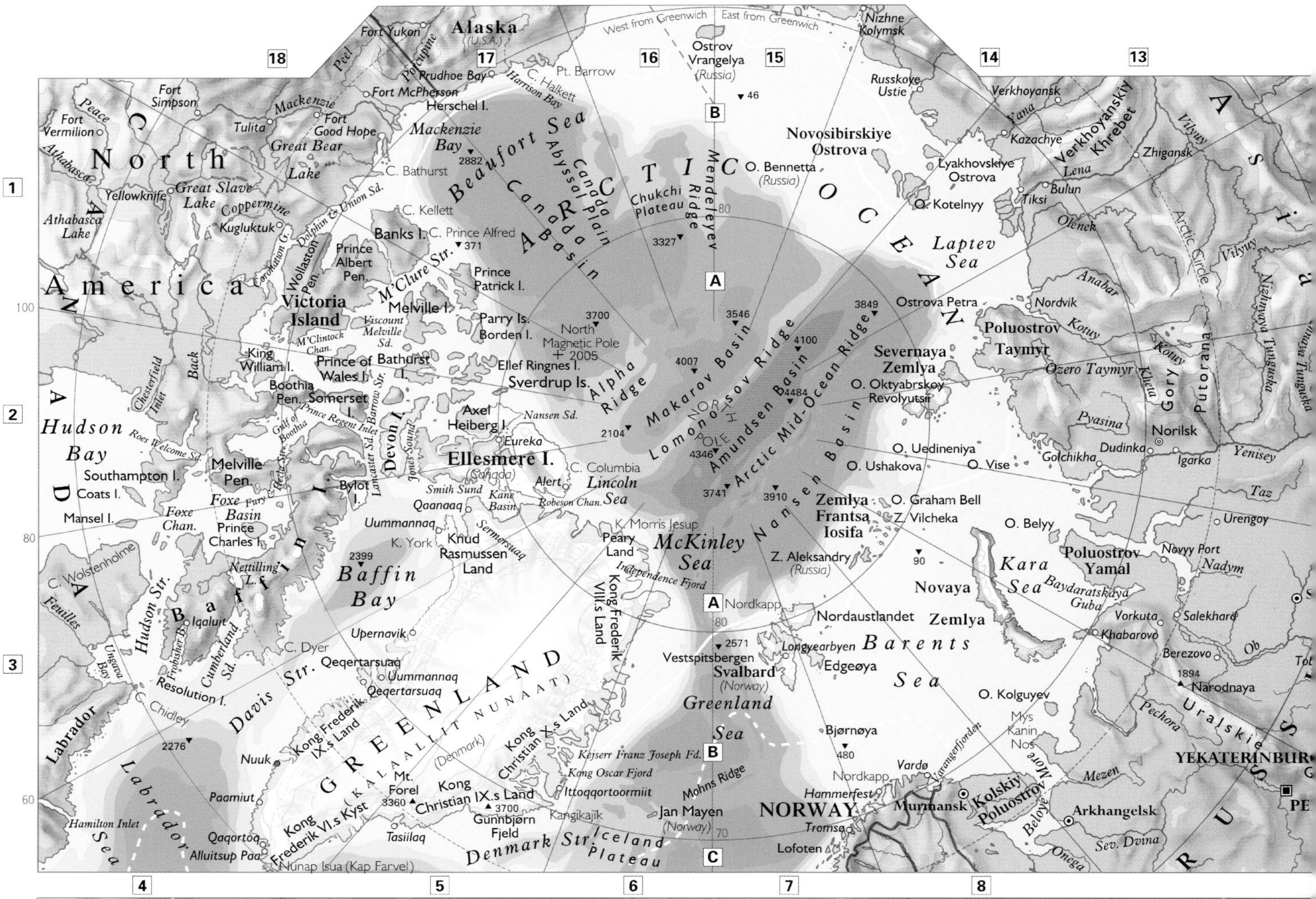

ft / m

9000	3000
6000	2000
4500	1500
3000	1000
1200	400
600	200
0	0
500	1500
1000	3000
2000	6000
3000	9000
4000	12 000
5000	15 000
m	ft

Ice cap

Permanent ice shelf

Maximum extent of sea ice

March (Summer) extent of sea ice

▲ 3488 / 3700   Surface elevation and depth of ice (in metres)

● Stanley (U.K.)   Permanent bases

Projection : Zenithal Equidistant

1:35 000 000

COPYRIGHT PHILIP'S

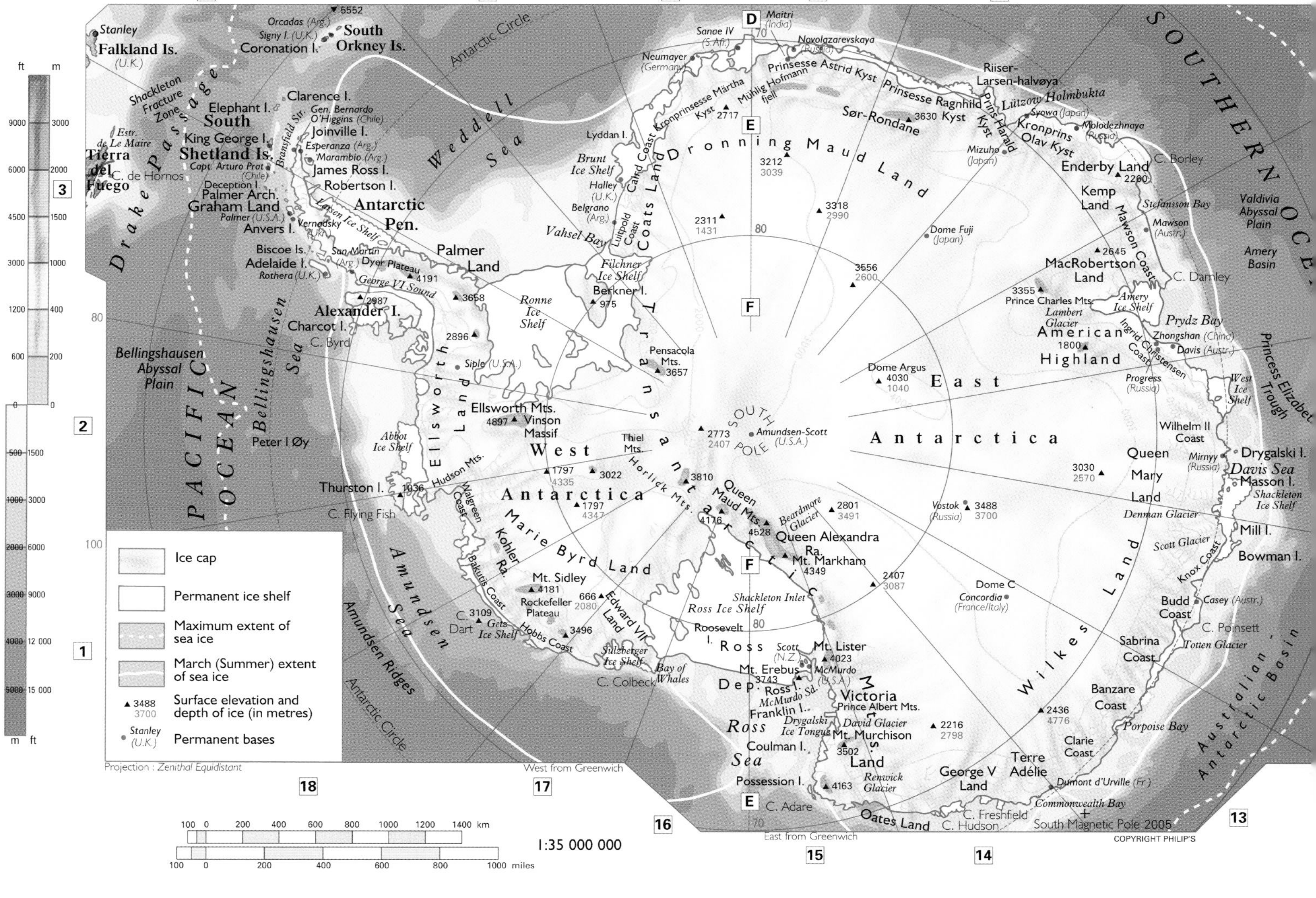

1:10 000 000

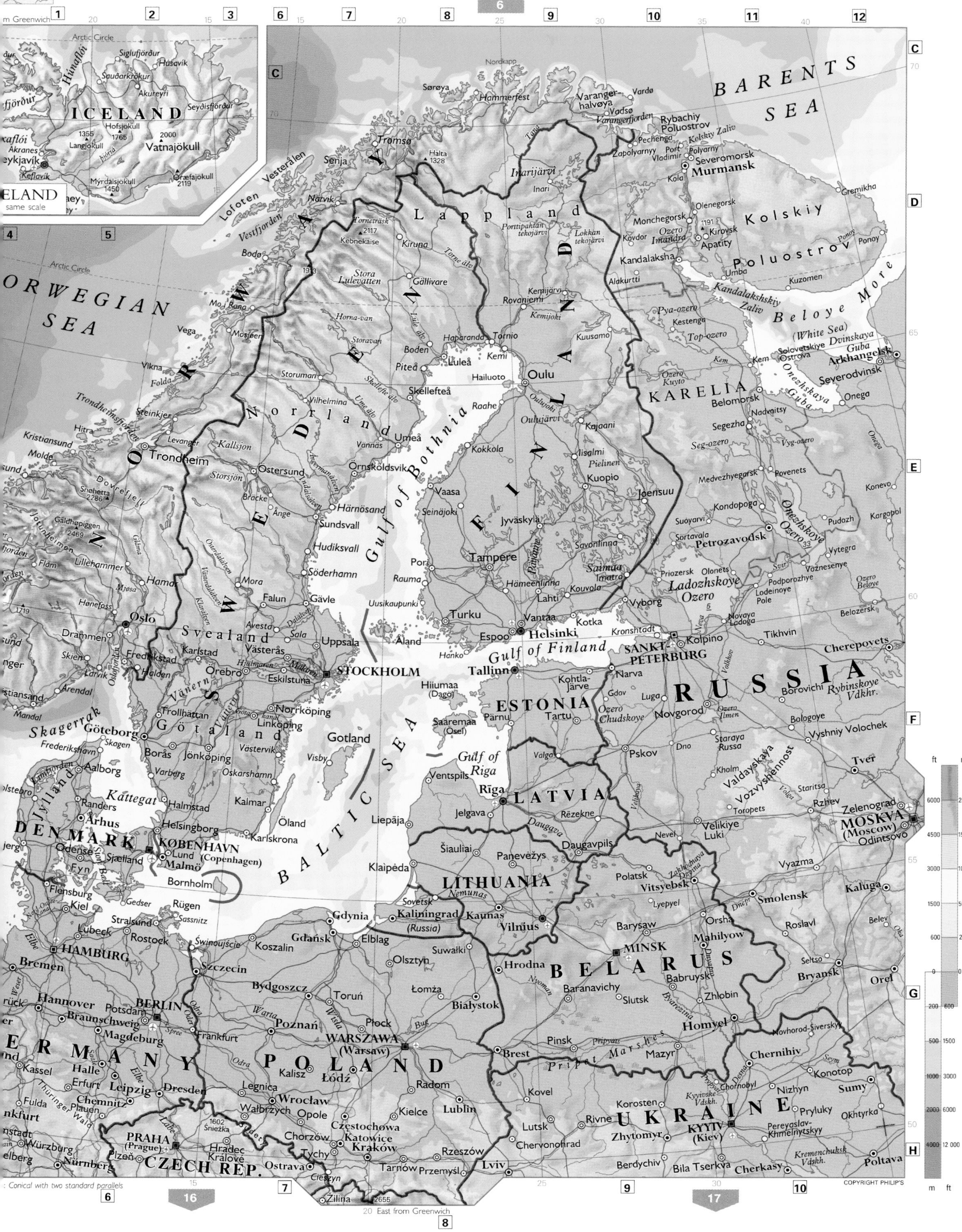

50 0 100 200 300 400 km
50 0 50 100 150 200 250 miles

ICELAND

Húnaflói Siglufjörður Húsavík
Sauðárkrókur Akureyri Seyðisfjörður
Hofsjökull 1355 1765 2000
Langjökull Vatnajökull
Myrdalsjökull Öræfajökull 2119
Akranes Reykjavík Keflavík

ICELAND
same scale

BARENTS SEA

Nordkapp Søroya Hammerfest Varanger-halvøya Vardø Vadsø Varangerfjorden Rybachiy Poluostrov Pechenga
Tromsø Halta 1328 Zapolyarnyy Port Vladimir Polyarnyy Kolskiy Zaliv Severomorsk
Senja Inarijärvi Inari Kola **Murmansk**
Narvik 2117 Kebnekaise Lappland Lokkan tekojärvi Monchegorsk Kovdor Ozero Imandra 1191 Kirovsk Apatity **Kolskiy Poluostrov** Cremikha
Bodø Porttipahtan tekojärvi Kandalaksha Umba Kuzomen Ponoy
Vesterålen Lofoten Stora Lulevatten Kiruna Torne älv Rovaniemi Alakurtti Kandalakshskiy Zaliv **Beloye More** (White Sea)
Gällivare Kemijärvi Kemijoki Pya-ozero Kestenga Kandalakshskaya Dvinskaya Guba
Horna-van Kuusamo Top-ozero Solovetskiye Ostrova Kem **Arkhangelsk**
Haparanda Tornio Luleå Kemi Oulu Ouluärvi Ozero Kuyto Belomorsk Severodvinsk
Storavan Boden Piteå Hailuoto Raahe **KARELIA** Segezha Onega
Skellefteå Kokkola Kajaani Seg-ozero Nadvoitsy Vyg-ozero Konevo
Umeå Vaasa Iisalmi Pielinen Medvezhyegorsk Povenets Ozero
Örnsköldsvik Vännäs Seinäjoki Kuopio **Joensuu** Suoyarvi Kondopoga Onezhskoye Ozero Pudozh Kargopol
Härnösand Jyväskylä Sortavala Petrozavodsk Vytegra
Sundsvall Tampere Savonlinna Saimaa Imatra Priozersk Olonets Voznesenye Ozero Beloye
Hudiksvall Hämeenlinna Kouvola Ladozhskoye Ozero Podporozhye Lodeinoye Pole Belozersk
Söderhamn Pori Lahti Vyborg Novaya Ladoga Tikhvin **Cherepovets**
Mora Falun Gävle Rauma Turku Vantaa **Helsinki** Kotka Kronshtadt Kolpino
Avesta Sala Uusikaupunki Åland Espoo **SANKT-PETERBURG**
Uppsala Hanko **Gulf of Finland** **Tallinn** Kohtla-Järve Narva **RUSSIA** Borovichi Rybinskoye Vdkhr.
Västerås Eskilstuna Hiiumaa (Dago) Gdov Luga Novgorod Vyshniy Volochek
STOCKHOLM Saaremaa (Ösel) Pärnu **ESTONIA** Tartu Ozero Chudskoye Ozero Ilmen Bologoye **Tver**
Norrköping Gotland Valga Pskov Dno Staraya Russa Vyshniy Volochek
Linköping Visby Gulf of Riga Kholm Valdayskaya Vozvyshennost Rzhev Zelenograd
Västervik Ventspils **Rīga** Velikiye Luki Toropets Staritsa **MOSKVA (Moscow)** Odintsovo
Oskarshamn Jelgava Rēzekne **LATVIA** Nevel Vyazma
Kalmar Öland Liepāja Daugava Daugavpils Polatsk Vitsyebsk Smolensk Kaluga
Karlskrona Šiauliai Panevėžys Lyepyel **BALTIC SEA** Kläipeda **LITHUANIA** Nemunas Barysaw Orsha Roslavl Beley Orel
Bornholm Sovetsk Kaliningrad (Russia) Kaunas **Vilnius** **MINSK** Mahilyow Seltso Bryansk
Gdynia Gdańsk Elblag Suwałki Hrodna **BELARUS** Babruysk Zhlobin Orel
Koszalin Olsztyn Łomża Białystok Baranavichy Slutsk Homyel Movhorod-Siversky
Szczecin Bydgoszcz Toruń Płock Pinsk **Pripet Marshes** Mazyr Chernihiv Sumy
Poznań **WARSZAWA (Warsaw)** Brest Pripyats Konotop Nizhyn
POLAND Kalisz Łódź Radom Kovel Korosten Zhytomyr Pryluky Okhtyrka
Legnica Wrocław Opole Kielce Lublin Rivne **UKRAINE** **KYYIV (Kiev)** Pereyaslav-Khmelnytsky Poltava
Wałbrzych Częstochowa Katowice Kraków Rzeszów Lutsk Chervonohrad Lviv Berdychiv Bila Tserkva Cherkasy
Snieżka 1602 Ostrava Tychy Tarnów Przemyśl Zhytomyr Kremenchuksk Vdskh.

PRAHA (Prague) Plzeň Hradec Králové **CZECH REP.** Cieszyn Žilina 2655

NORWEGIAN SEA
Vikna Folda Vega Mosjøen Mo i Rana 1913
Trondheimsfjorden Steinkjer Levanger Kallsjön Norrland Storuman Vilhelmina
Kristiansund Hitra **Trondheim** Östersund Storsjön Bräcke Ånge
Molde Snøhetta 2286 Dovrefjell Indalsälven Ljungan
Galdhøpiggen 2469 Jotunheimen Storvan
Flåm Lillehammer Hamar Mjøsa Mora Falun **SWEDEN**
1719 Hønefoss Drammen **Oslo** Svealand Klarälven Avesta Sala
Skien Fredrikstad Halden Karlstad Örebro Eskilstuna Hjälmaren Uppsala
Arendal Larvik Vänern **Götaland** Norrköping Linköping
Kristiansand Mandal **Skagerrak** Frederikshavn Skagen Göteborg Trollhättan Borås Jönköping Vättern
Kattegat Randers Århus Varberg Halmstad Helsingborg
DENMARK Jylland Odense Fyn Sjælland **KØBENHAVN (Copenhagen)** Lund Malmö
Flensburg Kiel Lübeck Rostock Stralsund Rügen Sassnitz Świnoujście
Bremen **HAMBURG** Schwerin Bremen
GERMANY Hannover Potsdam **BERLIN** Frankfurt Poznań
Braunschweig Magdeburg Halle Leipzig Dresden Chemnitz Plauen
Kassel Fulda Erfurt Würzburg Nürnberg Thüringer Wald

ORWEGIAN SEA **Arctic Circle**

20 East from Greenwich

COPYRIGHT PHILIP'S

Conical with two standard parallels

ft m
6000 2000
4500 1500
3000 1000
1500 500
600 200
0
200 600
500 1500
1000 3000
2000 6000
4000 12 000
m ft

1:2 000 000

10 0 10 20 30 40 50 60 70 80 km
10 0 10 20 30 40 50 miles

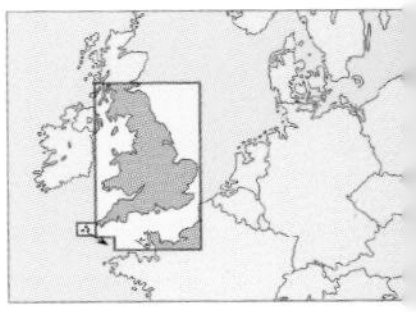

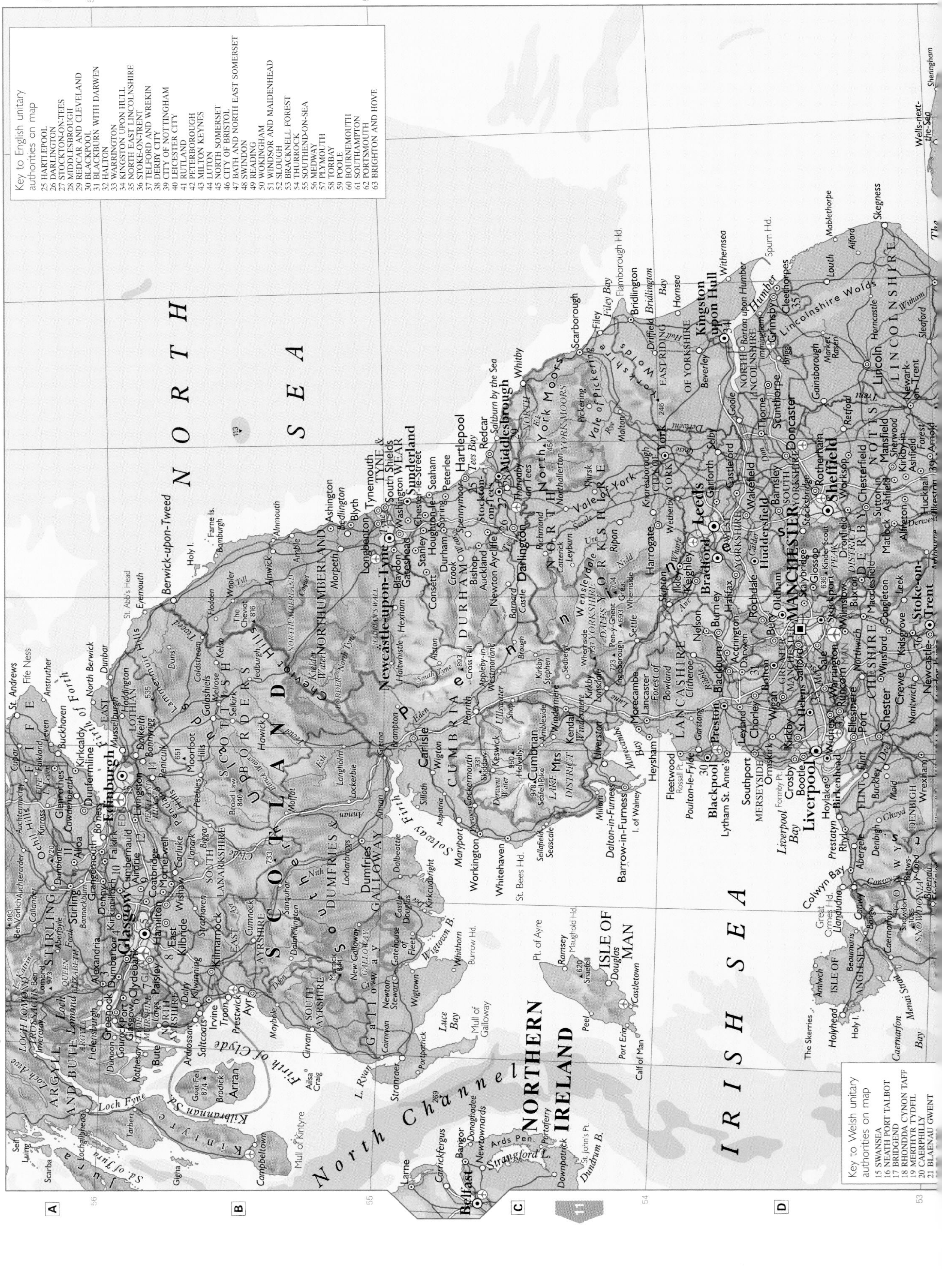

Key to English unitary authorities on map

25 HARTLEPOOL
26 DARLINGTON
27 STOCKTON-ON-TEES
28 MIDDLESBROUGH
29 REDCAR AND CLEVELAND
30 BLACKPOOL
31 BLACKBURN WITH DARWEN
32 HALTON
33 WARRINGTON
34 KINGSTON UPON HULL
35 NORTH EAST LINCOLNSHIRE
36 STOKE-ON-TRENT
37 TELFORD AND WREKIN
38 DERBY CITY
39 CITY OF NOTTINGHAM
40 LEICESTER CITY
41 RUTLAND
42 PETERBOROUGH
43 MILTON KEYNES
44 LUTON
45 NORTH SOMERSET
46 CITY OF BRISTOL
47 BATH AND NORTH EAST SOMERSET
48 SWINDON
49 READING
50 WOKINGHAM
51 WINDSOR AND MAIDENHEAD
52 SLOUGH
53 BRACKNELL FOREST
54 THURROCK
55 SOUTHEND-ON-SEA
56 MEDWAY
57 PLYMOUTH
58 TORBAY
59 POOLE
60 BOURNEMOUTH
61 SOUTHAMPTON
62 PORTSMOUTH
63 BRIGHTON AND HOVE

Key to Welsh unitary authorities on map

15 SWANSEA
16 NEATH PORT TALBOT
17 BRIDGEND
18 RHONDDA CYNON TAFF
19 MERTHYR TYDFIL
20 CAERPHILLY
21 BLAENAU GWENT

NORTH SEA

IRISH SEA

North Channel

NORTHERN IRELAND

SCOTLAND

ISLE OF MAN

Edinburgh
Glasgow
Newcastle-upon-Tyne
Sunderland
Middlesbrough
Hartlepool
Leeds
Bradford
MANCHESTER
Sheffield
Liverpool
Kingston upon Hull
Lincoln
DERBY
Stoke-on-Trent
Chester

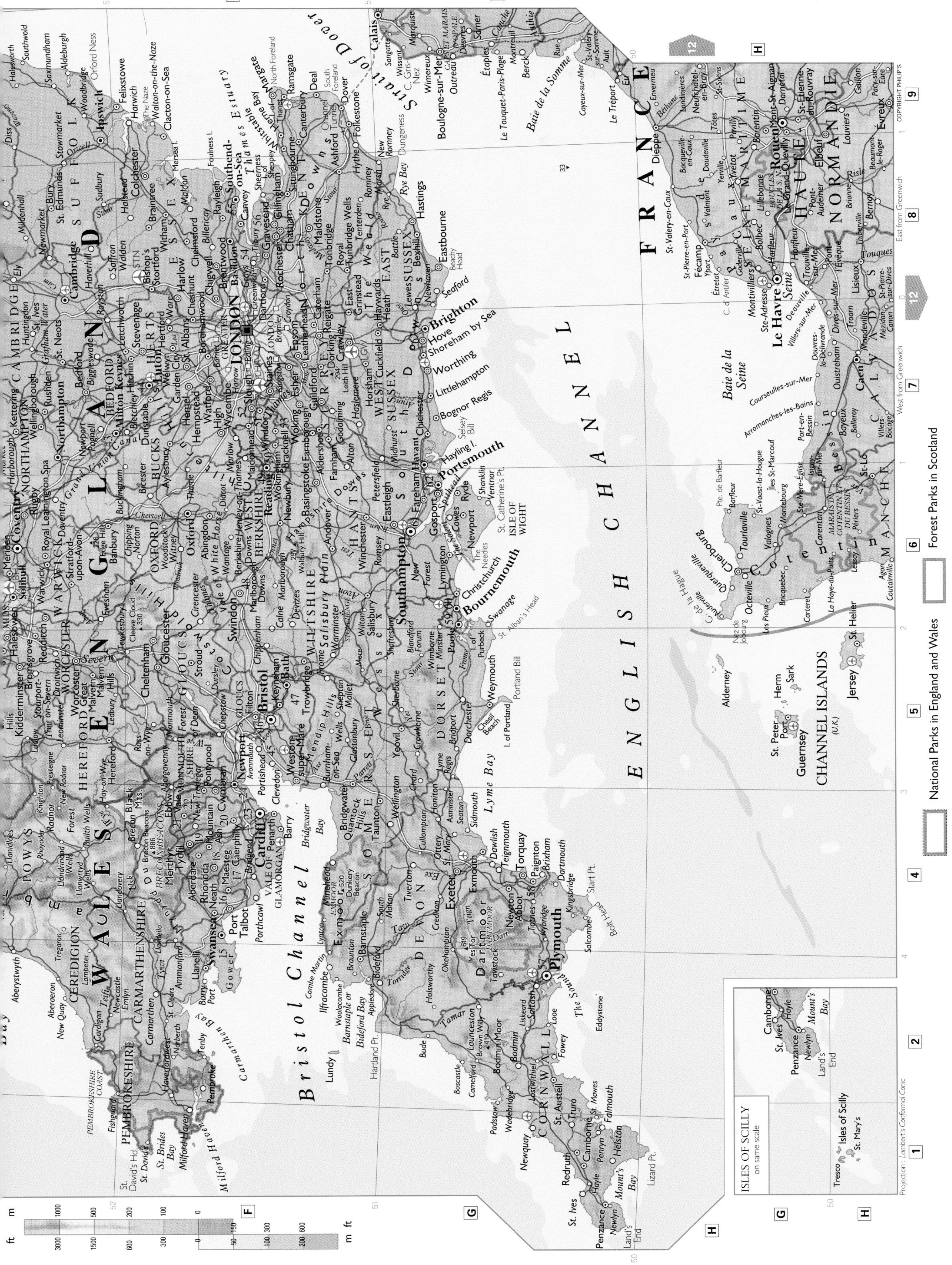

Projection: Lambert's Conformal Conic

ISLES OF SCILLY
on same scale

National Parks in England and Wales

Forest Parks in Scotland

1:2 000 000

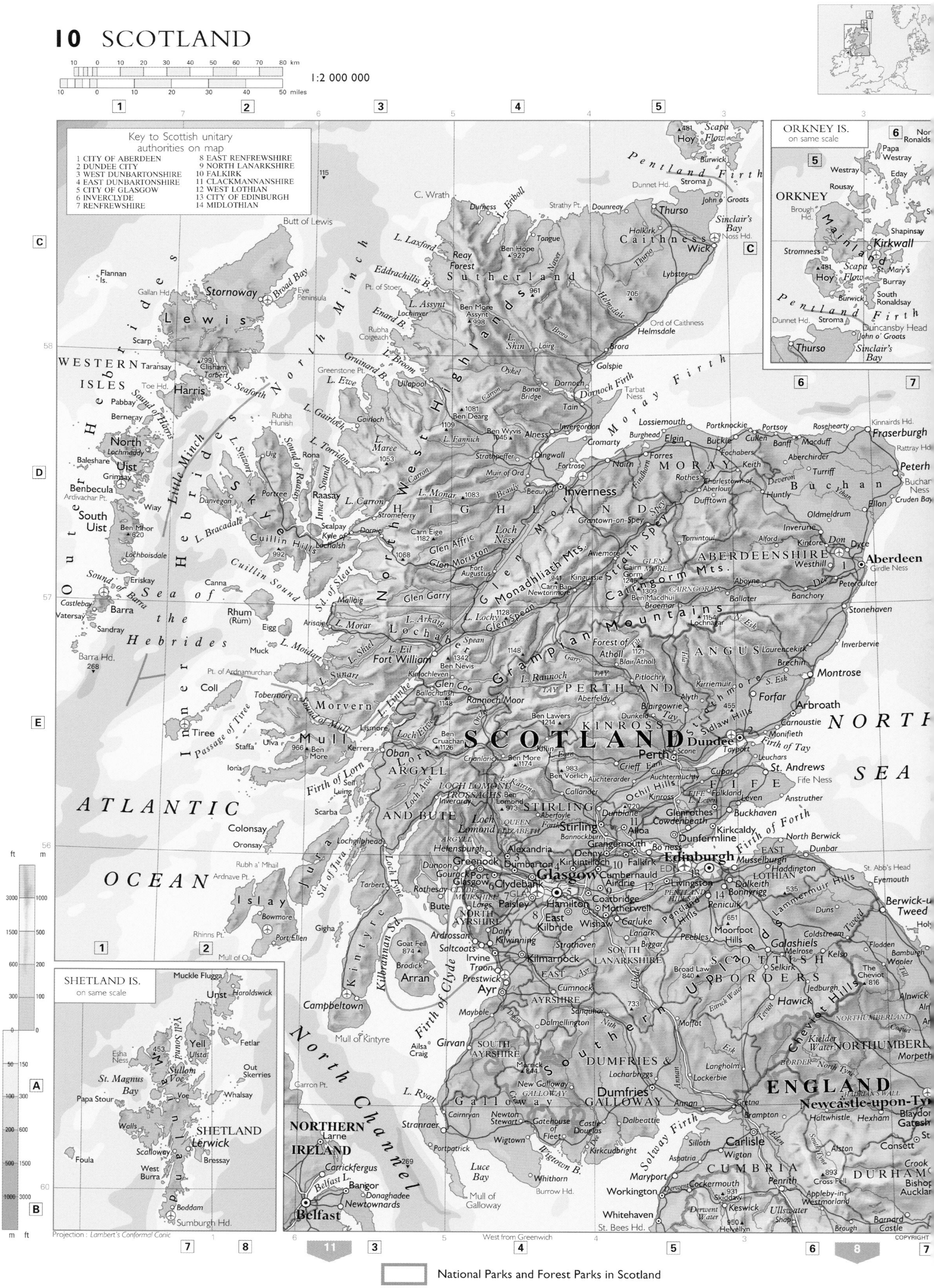

National Parks and Forest Parks in Scotland

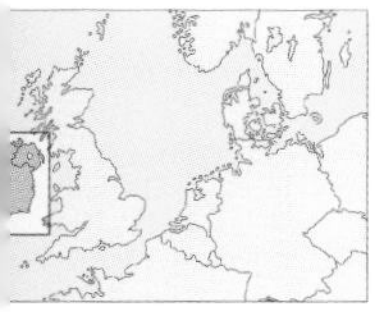

1:2 000 000

National Parks

COPYRIGHT PHILIP'S

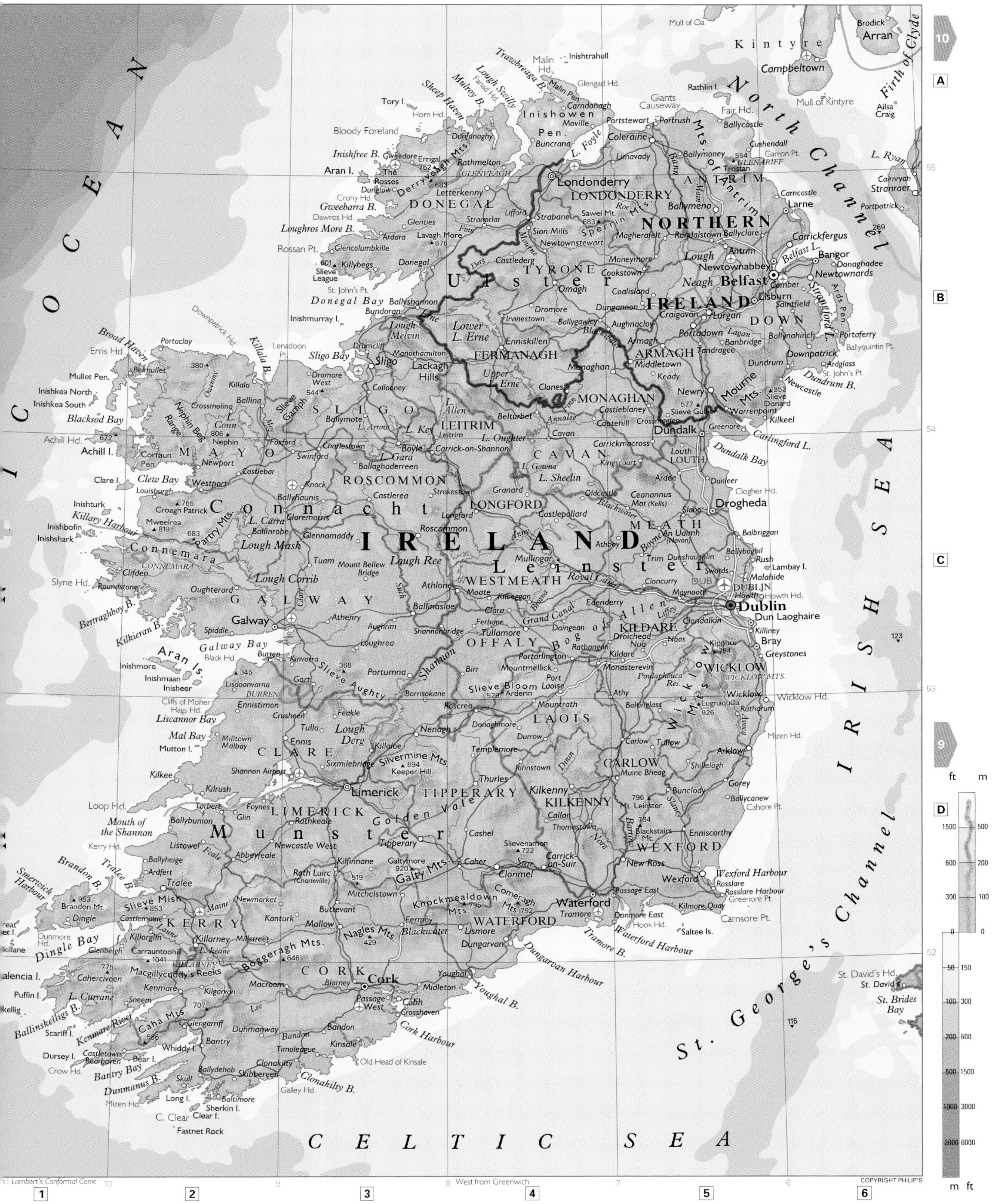

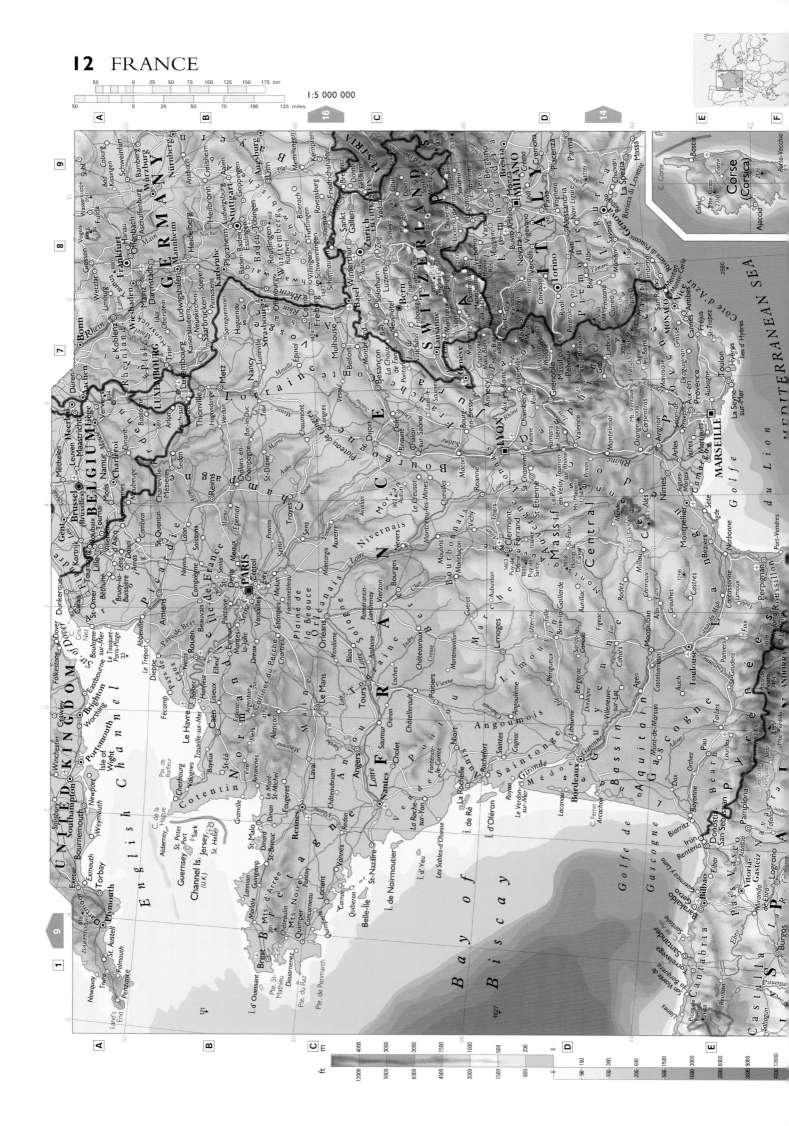

1:5 000 000

National Parks

Projection: Conical with two standard parallels

COPYRIGHT PHILIPS

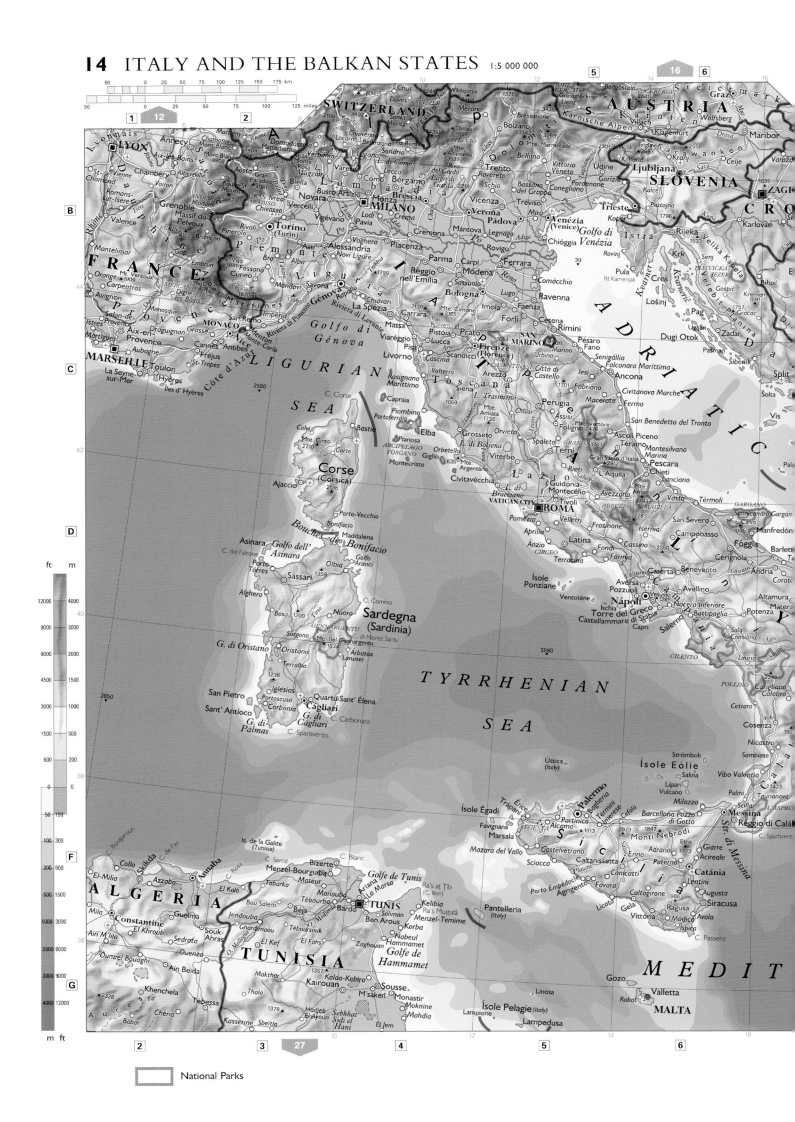

National Parks

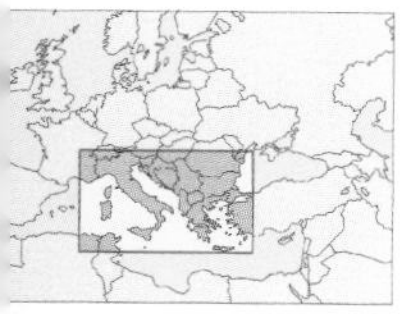

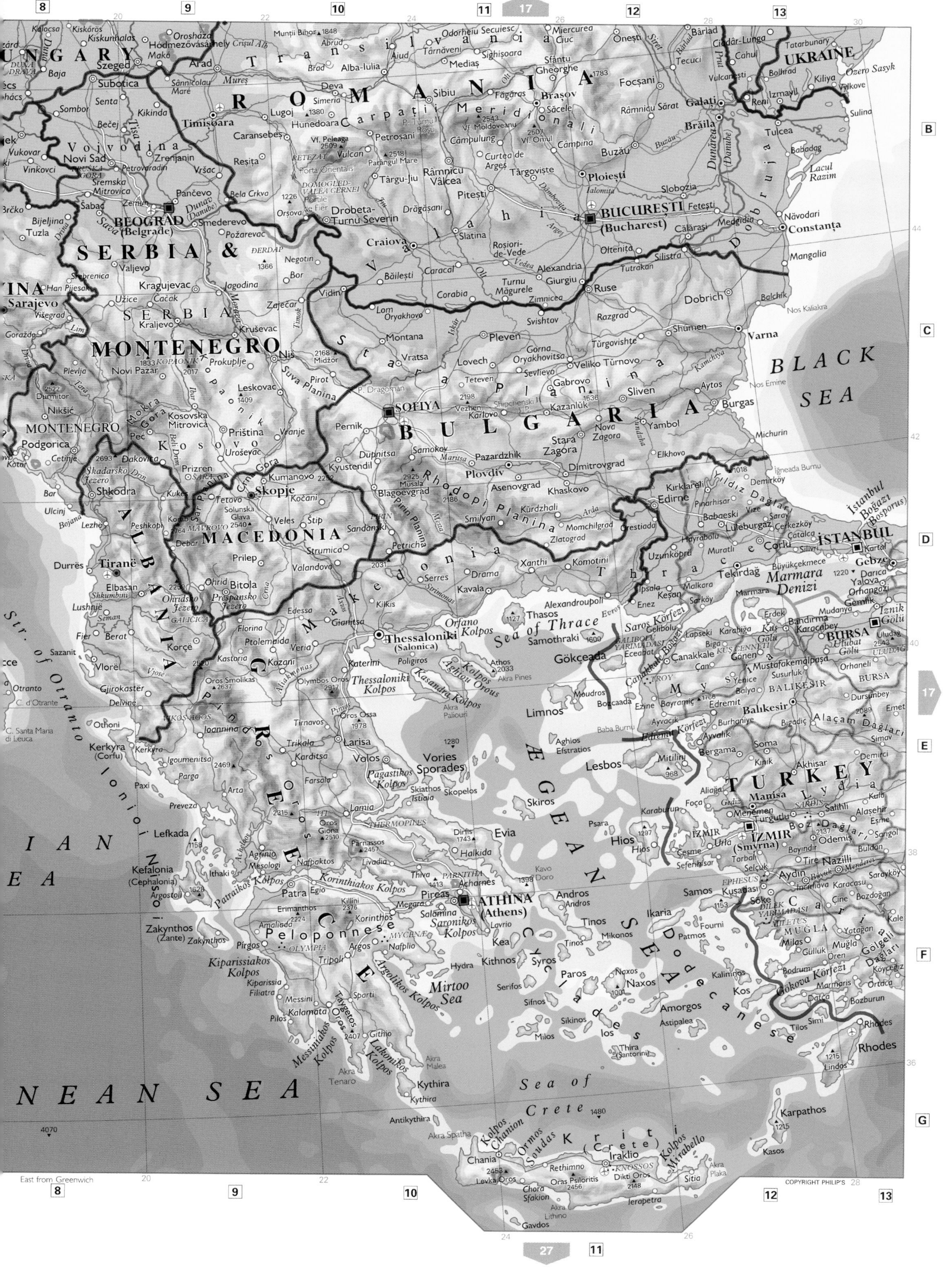
8
9
10
11
17
12
13
B
C
D
E
F
G
HUNGARY
ROMANIA
UKRAINE
SERBIA & MONTENEGRO
SERBIA
MONTENEGRO
Kosovo
Vojvodina
BULGARIA
MACEDONIA
ALBANIA
GREECE
TURKEY
BLACK SEA
Sea of Thrace
AEGEAN SEA
Mirtoo Sea
Sea of Crete
Marmara Denizi
Transilvania
Carpații Meridionali
Valahia
Dobrogea
Stara Planina
Rhodopi Planina
Pirin Planina
Makedonia
Thrace
Peloponnese
Cyclades
Dodecanese
Kriti (Crete)
Lydia
Caria
Str. of Otranto
Ionioi Nisoi
Szeged
Subotica
Novi Sad
Timișoara
Arad
Beograd (Belgrade)
Sarajevo
Podgorica
Skopje
Tiranë
Priština
Niš
Kragujevac
Sofiya
Plovdiv
Varna
Burgas
Ruse
Pleven
Craiova
București (Bucharest)
Constanța
Ploiești
Brașov
Sibiu
Galați
Brăila
Edirne
İstanbul
Bursa
Izmir (Smyrna)
Thessaloniki (Salonica)
Athina (Athens)
Patra
Larisa
Ioannina
Kerkyra (Corfu)
Lesbos
Limnos
Hios
Samos
Rhodes
Naxos
Iraklio
Chania
Gökçeada
Samothraki
Thasos
Evia
Kythira
Karpathos
Kasos
East from Greenwich
COPYRIGHT PHILIP'S
27

1:5 000 000

km
miles

RUSSIA

POLAND

GERMANY

CZECH REP.

SLOVAK REP.

HUNGARY

AUSTRIA

SWITZERLAND

ITALY

FRANCE

LUXEMBOURG

BELGIUM

NETHERLANDS

BALTIC SEA

NORTH SEA

WARSZAWA (Warsaw)

BUDAPEST

WIEN (Vienna)

PRAHA (Prague)

BERLIN

HAMBURG

HANNOVER

MÜNCHEN (Munich)

BREMEN

Łódź

Kraków

Bratislava

Zürich

Bern

Graz

Leipzig

Dresden

Frankfurt

Stuttgart

Nürnberg

Dortmund

Köln

Düsseldorf

Bonn

AMSTERDAM

ROTTERDAM

's-Gravenhage (Den Haag)

Hoek van Holland

Kaliningrad

Gdańsk

Gdynia

Szczecin

Wrocław

Poznań

Kiel

Lübeck

Rostock

Schwerin

Magdeburg

Potsdam

Erfurt

Kassel

Luxembourg

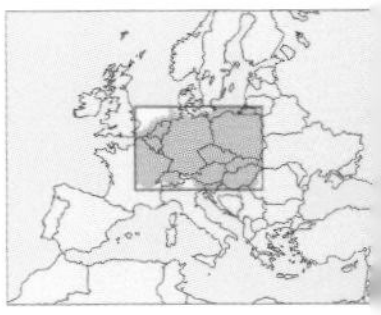

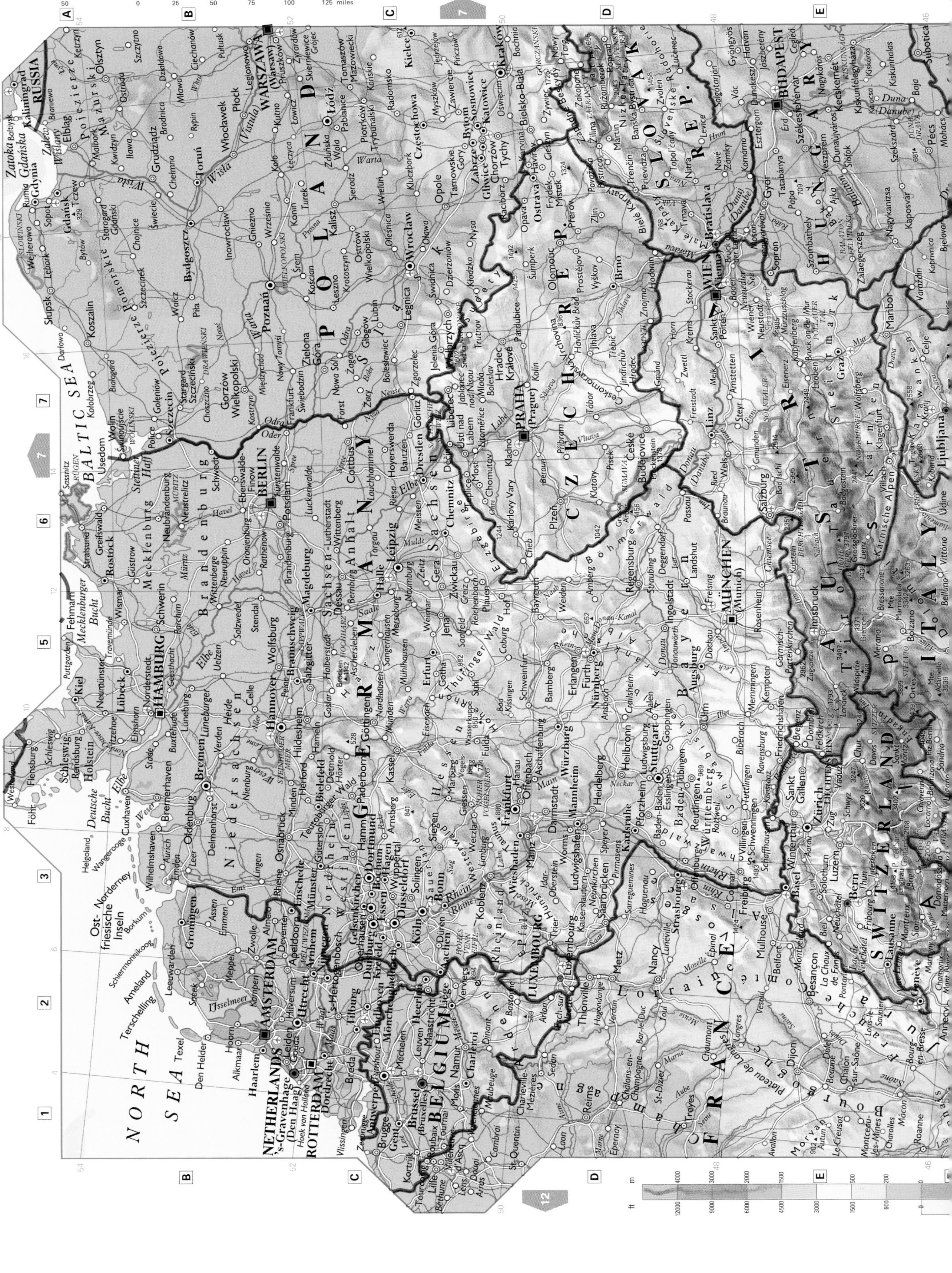

1:10 000 000

50 0 100 200 300 400 km
50 0 50 100 150 200 250 miles

COPYRIGHT PHILIP'S

CASPIAN SEA

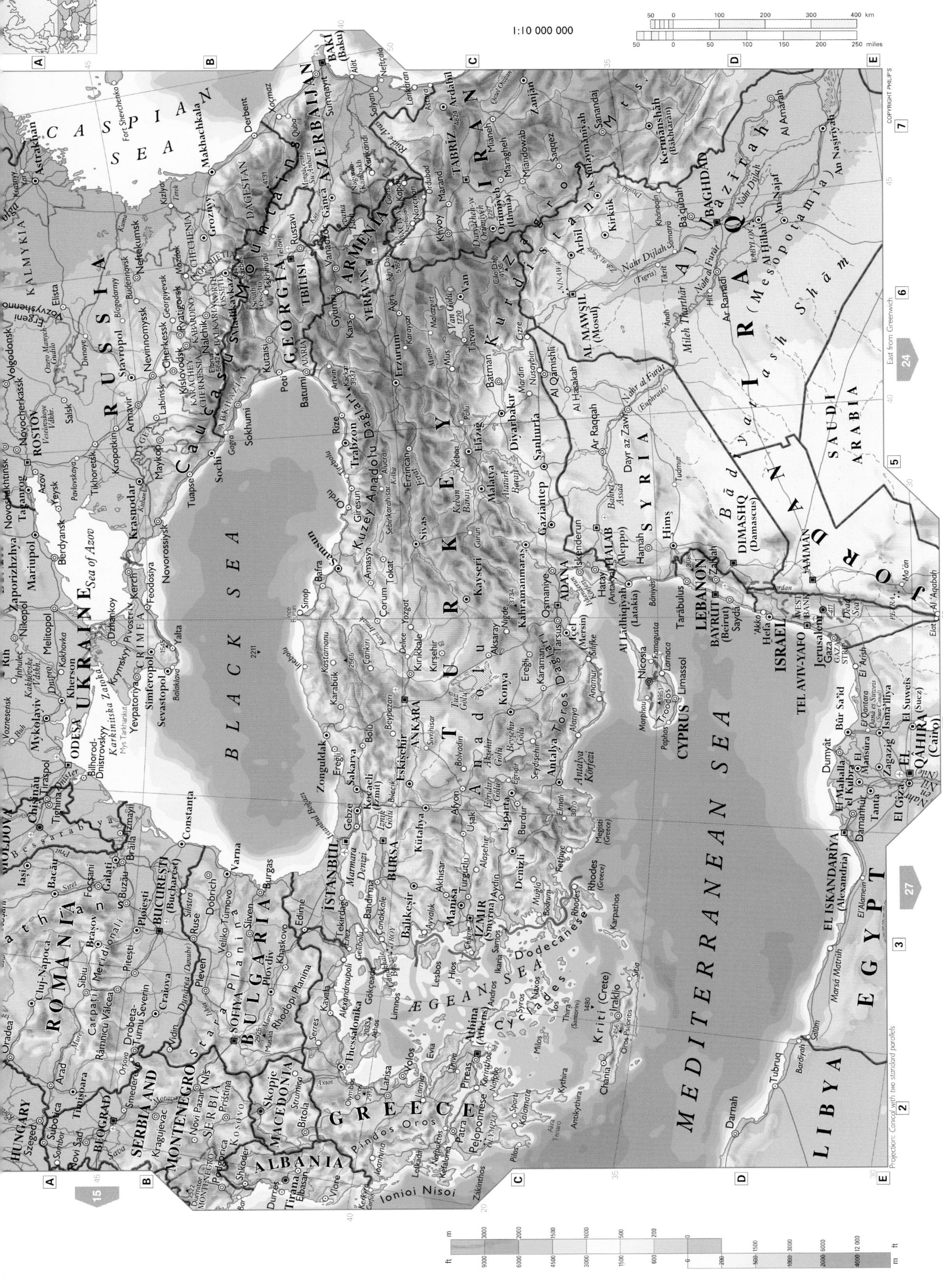

BLACK SEA

MEDITERRANEAN SEA

AEGEAN SEA

Sea of Azov

RUSSIA
KALMYKIA
DAGESTAN
CHECHENIA
KABARDINO-BALKARIA
NORTH OSSETIA
AZERBAIJAN
ARMENIA
GEORGIA
ABKHAZIA
ADZARIA
UKRAINE
CRIMEA
MOLDOVA
ROMANIA
HUNGARY
SERBIA
MONTENEGRO
SERBIA AND MONTENEGRO
MACEDONIA
ALBANIA
GREECE
BULGARIA
TURKEY
IRAN
IRAQ
SYRIA
LEBANON
ISRAEL
JORDAN
SAUDI ARABIA
EGYPT
LIBYA
CYPRUS

Astrakhan
Makhachkala
Groznyy
BAKI (Baku)
TBILISI
YEREVAN
TABRĪZ
Erzurum
ANKARA
İSTANBUL
İZMIR (Smyrna)
BURSA
ADANA
DIMASHQ (Damascus)
BAYRŪT (Beirut)
AMMAN
BAGHDAD
AL MAWSIL (Mosul)
ALEPPO (Ḥalab)
TEL AVIV-YAFO
Jerusalem
EL QAHIRA (Cairo)
EL ISKANDARĪYA (Alexandria)
BUCUREŞTI (Bucharest)
SOFIA
ATHINA (Athens)
Thessaloniki
BEOGRAD
Skopje
Tirana

Rostov
Krasnodar
Sochi
Sevastopol
ODESA
Constanţa
Varna
Burgas
Kriti (Crete)
CYPRUS
Rhodes (Greece)
Dodecanese

Projection: Conical with two standard parallels

East from Greenwich

ft m

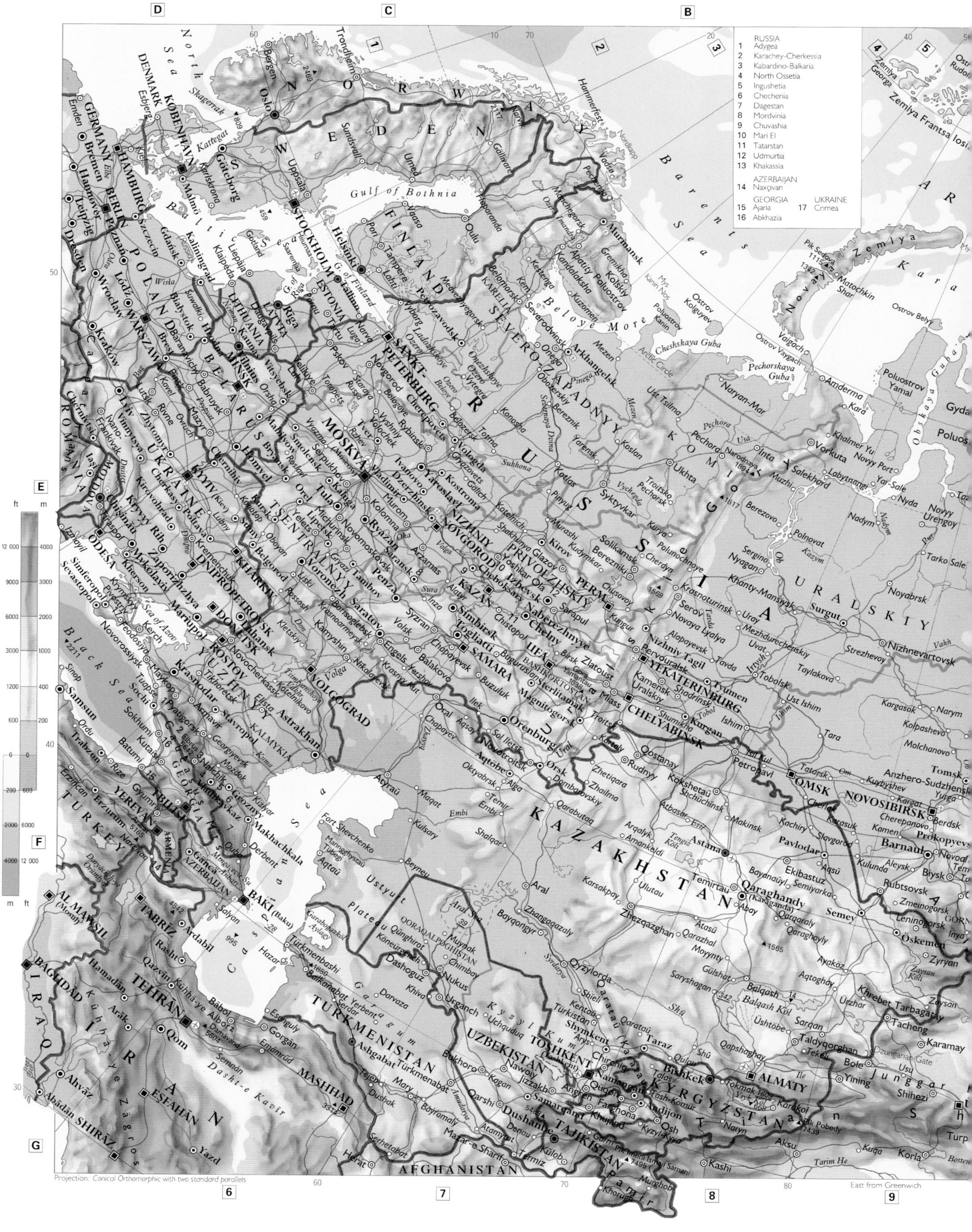

1:20 000 000

	RUSSIA
1	Adygea
2	Karachey-Cherkessia
3	Kabardino-Balkaria
4	North Ossetia
5	Ingushetia
6	Chechenia
7	Dagestan
8	Mordvinia
9	Chuvashia
10	Mari El
11	Tatarstan
12	Udmurtia
13	Khakassia
	AZERBAIJAN
14	Naxçıvan
	GEORGIA
15	Ajaria
16	Abkhazia
	UKRAINE
17	Crimea

Projection: Conical Orthomorphic with two standard parallels

East from Greenwich

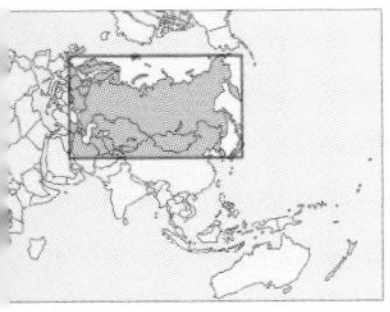

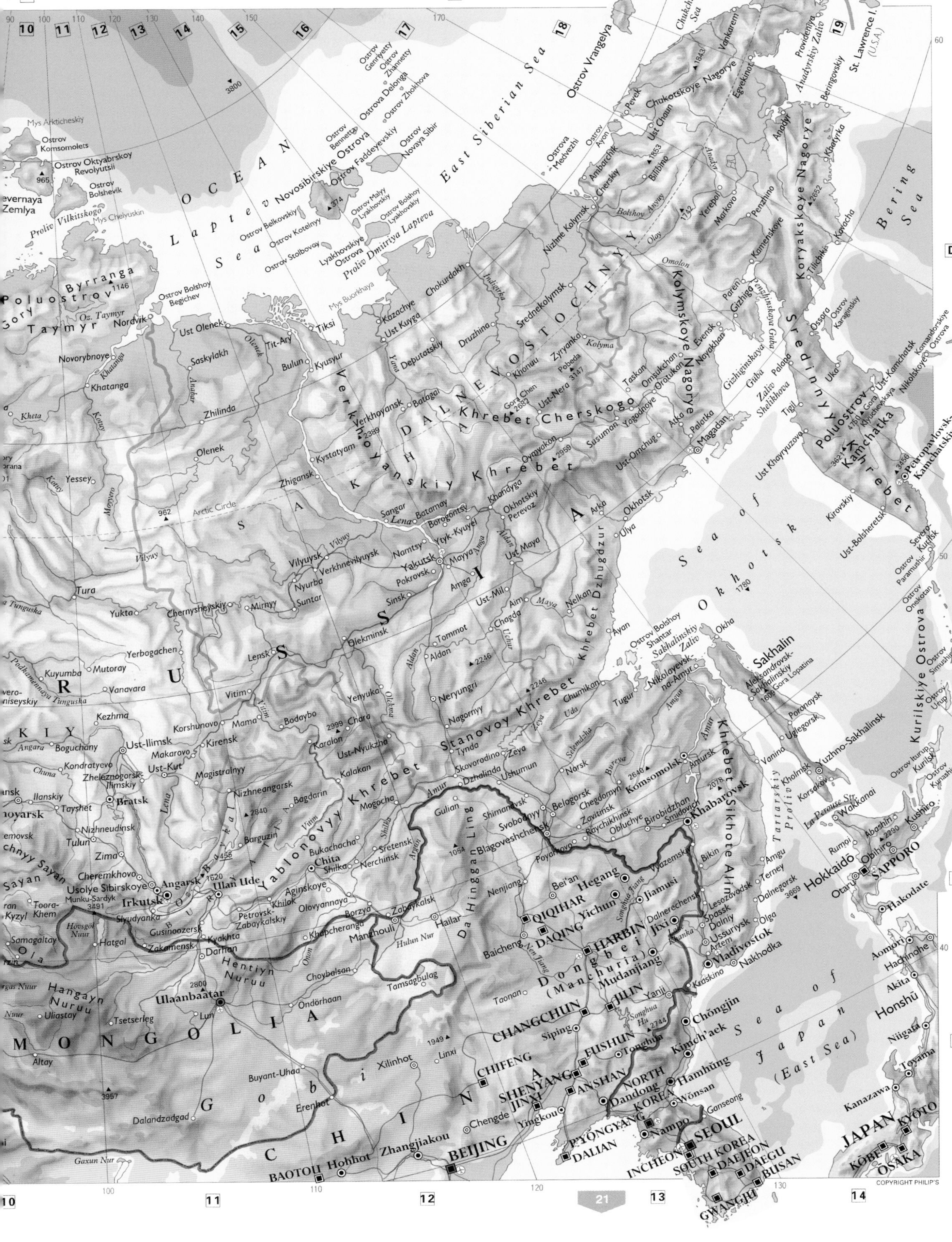
A
B
C
D
E
F
10
11
12
13
14
15
16
17
18
19
RUSSIA
MONGOLIA
CHINA
JAPAN
NORTH KOREA
SOUTH KOREA
OCEAN
Laptev Sea
East Siberian Sea
Chukchi Sea
Bering Sea
Sea of Okhotsk
Sea of Japan (East Sea)
Arctic Circle
Ostrov Vrangelya
Novosibirskiye Ostrova
Poluostrov Taymyr
Gory Byrranga
Severnaya Zemlya
Proliv Vilkitskogo
Mys Chelyuskin
DALNEVOSTOCHNYY
Verkhoyanskiy Khrebet
Khrebet Cherskogo
Kolymskoye Nagorye
Koryakskoye Nagorye
Chukotskoye Nagorye
Poluostrov Kamchatka
Sredinnyy Khrebet
Kurilskiye Ostrova
Sakhalin
Khrebet Dzhugdzur
Stanovoy Khrebet
Yablonovyy Khrebet
Khrebet Sikhote Alin
Da Hinggan Ling
Dongbei (Manchuria)
Gobi
Hangayn Nuruu
Hentiyn Nuruu
Mys Dezhneva (East C.)
St. Lawrence I. (U.S.A.)
Hokkaidō
Honshū
Tiksi
Yakutsk
Magadan
Petropavlovsk-Kamchatskiy
Khabarovsk
Vladivostok
Irkutsk
Ulan Ude
Chita
Bratsk
Ulaanbaatar
HARBIN
CHANGCHUN
SHENYANG
BEIJING
PYONGYANG
SEOUL
SAPPORO
KYOTO
OSAKA
KOBE
BUSAN
DAEGU
DAEJEON
INCHEON
GWANGJU
DALIAN
ANSHAN
FUSHUN
JILIN
QIQIHAR
DAQING
BAOTOU
Hohhot
Zhangjiakou
Chengde
Blagoveshchensk
Komsomolsk
Nikolayevsk-na-Amur
Yuzhno-Sakhalinsk
Okhotsk
Ayan
Lensk
Mirnyy
Vilyuysk
Olekminsk
Neryungri
Tynda
Angarsk
Kyzyl
Hakodate
Aomori
Akita
Niigata
Toyama
Kanazawa
Hamhŭng
Ch'ŏngjin
Wŏnsan
Nampo

21

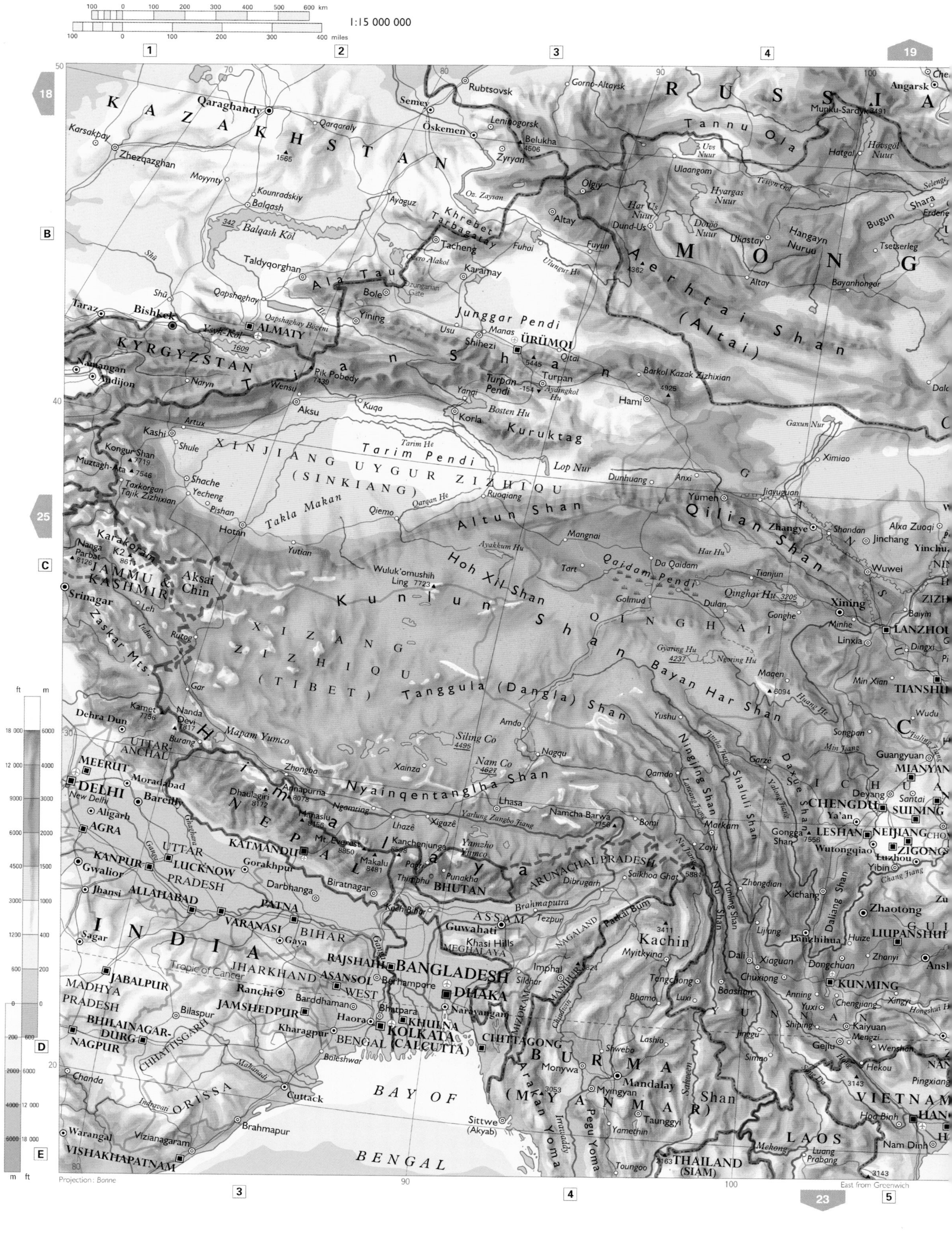

1:15 000 000

Projection : Bonne

East from Greenwich

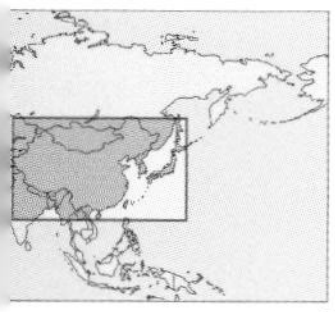

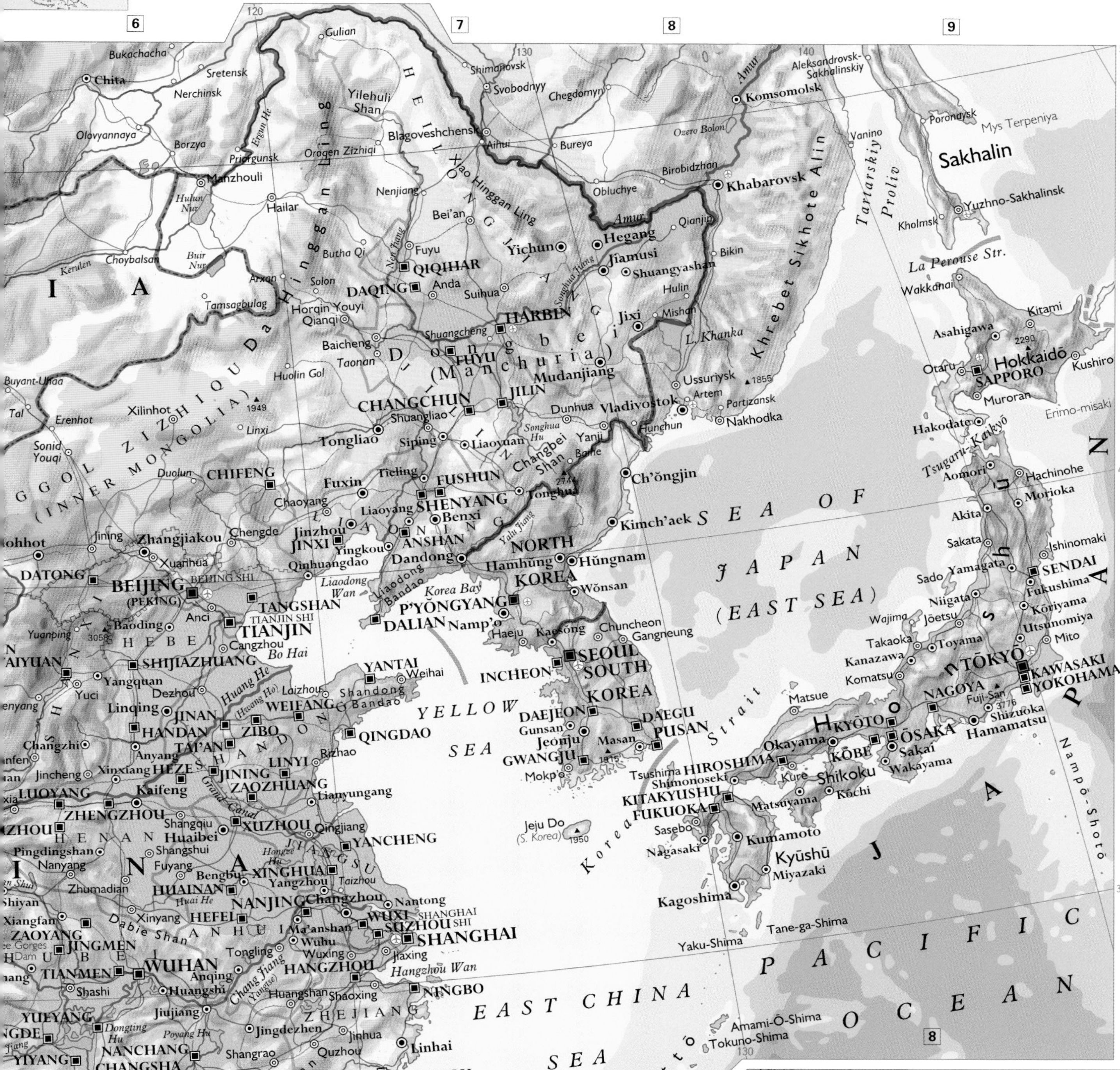

CHINA AND THE FAR EAST

6 7 8 9

Chita
Bukachacha
Sretensk
Nerchinsk
Olovyannaya
Borzya
Manzhouli
Hailar
Choybalsan
Buyant-Uhaa
Tal
Sonid Youqi
Erenhot
Hohhot
DATONG
TAIYUAN
Yuanping
Baoding
BEIJING (PEKING)
BEIJING SHI
TANGSHAN
TIANJIN
TIANJIN SHI
Cangzhou
SHIJIAZHUANG
Yangquan
Yuci
Linqing
Dezhou
JINAN
Weifang
YANTAI
Weihai
Shandong Bandao
HANDAN
ZIBO
TAI'AN
QINGDAO
Rizhao
HEZE
JINING
LINYI
ZAOZHUANG
Lianyungang
LUOYANG
ZHENGZHOU
Kaifeng
Shangqiu
XUZHOU
Qingjiang
YANCHENG
HENAN
Huaibei
Shangshui
XINGHUA
Fuyang
Bengbu
Taizhou
Nantong
HUAINAN
HEFEI
Ma'anshan
Changzhou
WUXI
SUZHOU
SHANGHAI
SHANGHAI SHI
JINGMEN
TIANMEN
WUHAN
Anqing
Tongling
Wuhu
Wuxing
HANGZHOU
Jiaxing
Hangzhou Wan
Huangshi
Huangshan
Shaoxing
NINGBO
YUEYANG
Dongting Hu
YIYANG
NANCHANG
Jiujiang
Jingdezhen
Jinhua
ZHEJIANG
Poyang Hu
Linhai
CHANGSHA
Xiangtan
Shangrao
Quzhou
WENZHOU
PINGXIANG
Ji'an
JIANGXI
Wuyishan
Linchuan
Nanping
Hengyang
Nanping
Sanming
Yong'an
FUZHOU
Ganzhou
Ruijin
Longyan
FUJIAN
Zhangzhou
Xiamen
Meizhou
Chaozhou
SHANTOU
GUANGZHOU (CANTON)
Foshan
SHENZHEN
HONG KONG (XIANGGANG)
Macau
Zhaoqing
Jiangmen
Yangjiang
Maoming
HAINAN

HEILONGJIANG
Gulian
Shimanovsk
Svobodnyy
Chegdomyn
Amur
Aleksandrovsk-Sakhalinskiy
Komsomolsk
Poronaysk
Mys Terpeniya
Sakhalin
Yilehuli Shan
Blagoveshchensk
Aihui
Bureya
Obluchye
Birobidzhan
Khabarovsk
Vanino
Yuzhno-Sakhalinsk
Kholmsk
Priorgunsk
Orogen Zizhiqi
Butha Qi
Yichun
Hegang
Jiamusi
Bikin
Shuangyashan
Hulin
Khrebet Sikhote Alin
La Perouse Str.
Wakkanai
Bei'an
QIQIHAR
DAQING
Anda
Suihua
HARBIN
Shuangcheng
Mudanjiang
Jixi
Mishan
L. Khanka
Ussuriysk
Artem
Asahigawa
Otaru
HOKKAIDO
SAPPORO
Kushiro
Muroran
Hakodate
CHANGCHUN
JILIN
Dunhua
Vladivostok
Nakhodka
Aomori
Hachinohe
Morioka
Akita
Ishinomaki
Sado
Yamagata
SENDAI
Fukushima
P'YONGYANG
DALIAN
Namp'o
Haeju
Kaesong
SEOUL
SOUTH KOREA
INCHEON
Chuncheon
Gangneung
Niigata
Koriyama
Joetsu
Mito
Utsunomiya
TOKYO
KAWASAKI
YOKOHAMA
NAGOYA
KYOTO
OSAKA
KOBE
Sakai
Hamamatsu
HIROSHIMA
KITAKYUSHU
FUKUOKA
Kumamoto
Nagasaki
Kyushu
Miyazaki
Kagoshima

SEA OF JAPAN (EAST SEA)
YELLOW SEA
EAST CHINA SEA
PACIFIC OCEAN
SOUTH CHINA SEA
PHILIPPINES
Babuyan Is.
Batan Is.

TAIPEI
T'aichung
Hsinchu
T'ainan
KAOHSIUNG
TAIWAN (FORMOSA)
Tropic of Cancer

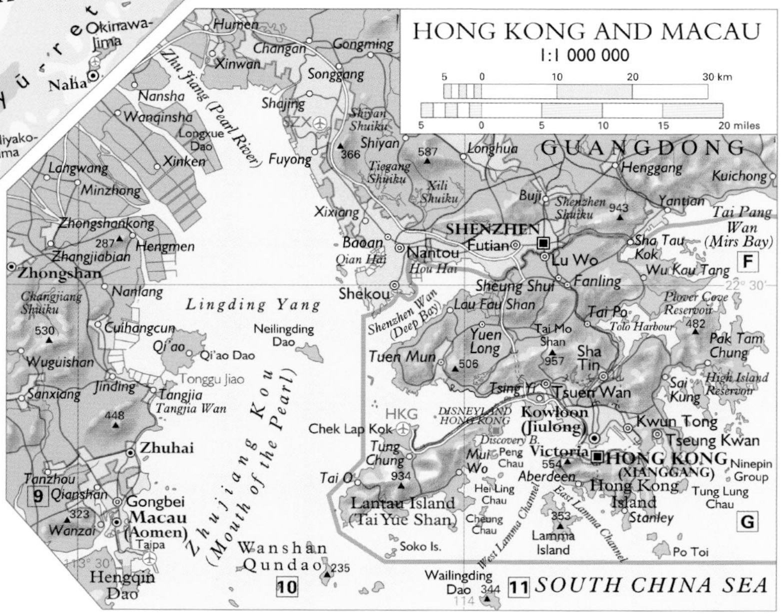

HONG KONG AND MACAU
1:1 000 000

GUANGDONG
SHENZHEN
Futian
HONG KONG (XIANGGANG)
Hong Kong Island
Kowloon (Jiulong)
Victoria
Lantau Island (Tai Yue Shan)
Macau (Aomen)
Zhuhai
Gongbei
Lingding Yang
Zhujiang Kou (Mouth of the Pearl)
SOUTH CHINA SEA

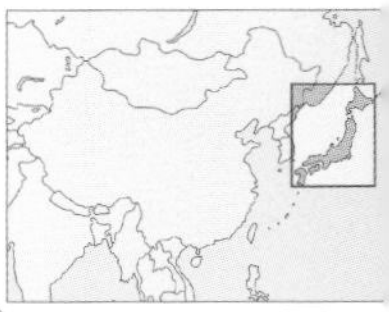

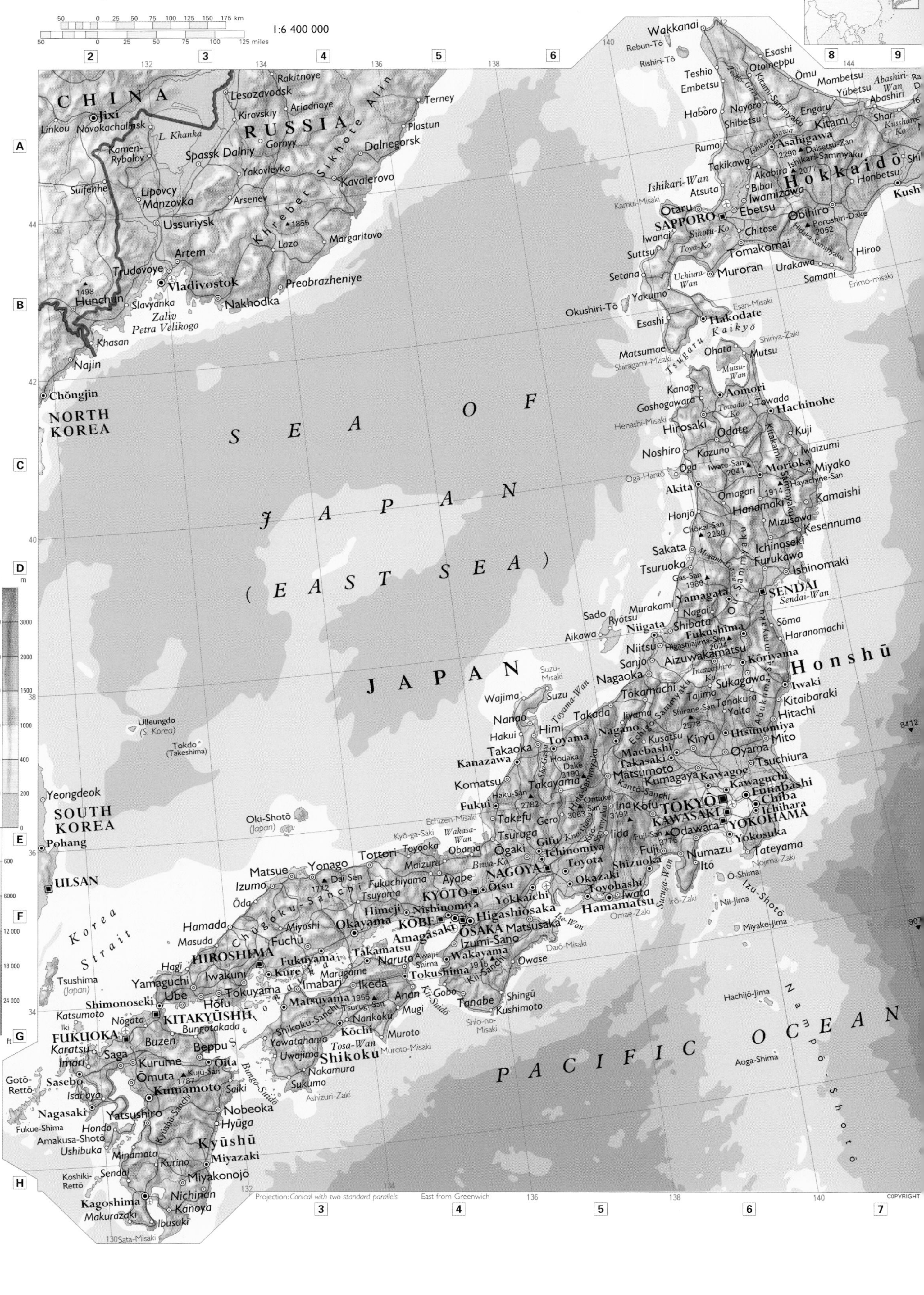

1:6 400 000

50 25 0 25 50 75 100 125 150 175 km
50 0 25 50 75 100 125 miles

CHINA

RUSSIA

Jixi
Linkou
Novokachalinsk
Kamen-Rybolov
Suifenhe
Lipovcy
Manzovka
Ussuriysk
Trudovoye
Hunchun
Slavyanka
Zaliv Petra Velikogo
Khasan
Najin

Lesozavodsk
Rakitnoye
Kirovskiy
Ariadnoye
Terney
Plastun
Dalnegorsk
Kavalerovo
Arsenev
Yakovlevka
Margaritovo
Lazo
Preobrazheniye
Nakhodka
Vladivostok
L. Khanka
Spassk Dalniy
Gornyy
Khrebet Sikhote Alin
1855
1498

NORTH KOREA
Chŏngjin

SEA OF JAPAN

(EAST SEA)

JAPAN

SOUTH KOREA
Yeongdeok
Pohang
ULSAN

Ulleungdo (S. Korea)
Tokdo (Takeshima)

Korea Strait
Tsushima (Japan)
Katsumoto
Iki
Nōgata

Wakkanai
Rebun-Tō
Rishiri-Tō
Teshio
Embetsu
Haboro
Rumoi
Otaru
SAPPORO
Suttsu
Setana
Okushiri-Tō
Yakumo
Esashi
Matsumae
Shiragami-Misaki
Hakodate

Esashi
Otoineppu
Ōmu
Mombetsu
Yūbetsu
Engaru
Kitami
Asahigawa
Takikawa
Bibai
Iwamizawa
Ebetsu
Chitose
Tomakomai
Muroran
Urakawa
Samani
Erimo-misaki

Esan-Misaki
Tsugaru Kaikyō
Shiriya-Zaki
Ohata
Mutsu
Kanagi
Goshogawara
Aomori
Hirosaki
Odate
Noshiro
Akita
Honjō
Sakata
Tsuruoka

Abashiri-Wan
Abashiri
Shari
Hokkaidō
Akabira
Daisetsu-Zan 2290
2077
Obihiro 2052
Hiroo

Hachinohe
Kuji
Morioka
Miyako
Kamaishi
Kesennuma
Ichinoseki
Furukawa
Ishinomaki
SENDAI
Sendai-Wan

Honshū

Niigata
Sado
Ryōtsu
Aikawa
Niitsu
Sanjo
Nagaoka
Fukushima
Yamagata
Aizuwakamatsu
Kōriyama
Iwaki
Kitaibaraki
Hitachi
Mito
Utsunomiya
Oyama
Tsuchiura
Kawaguchi
Funabashi
Chiba
Ichihara
TOKYO
KAWASAKI
YOKOHAMA
Yokosuka
Tateyama

Wajima
Nanao
Hakui
Toyama
Takaoka
Kanazawa
Komatsu
Fukui
Takada
Nagano
Matsumoto
Takayama
Takasaki
Maebashi
Kumagaya
Kawagoe
Kōfu
Numazu
Itō
Ō-Shima

Suzu-Misaki
Toyama-Wan
Haku-San 2782
Hodaka-Dake 3190
Ontake-San 3063
Fuji-San 3776
Shizuoka
Hamamatsu
Iwata
Toyohashi
Okazaki
NAGOYA
Gifu
Ōgaki
Ichinomiya
Toyota
Yokkaichi
Matsusaka
Izumi-Sano
ŌSAKA
Higashiōsaka
KYŌTO
Ōtsu
Nishinomiya
KOBE
Amagasaki
Himeji
Okayama
HIROSHIMA
Fukuyama
Kure
Takamatsu
Marugame
Tokushima
Wakayama
Owase
Kushimoto
Tanabe
Shingū

Tottori
Toyooka
Matsue
Yonago
Izumo
Ōda
Hamada
Masuda
Hagi
Yamaguchi
Ube
Tokuyama
Hōfu
Shimonoseki
Iwakuni
Imabari
Matsuyama
Imari
Anan
Mugi
Kōchi
Muroto
Nakamura
Sukumo

Chūgoku-Sanchi
Dai-Sen 1712
Tsuyama
Miyoshi
Fuchū
Fukuchiyama
Ayabe
Maizuru
Obama
Tsuruga
Takefu
Gero
Iida
Ina
Odawara

Shikoku
Shikoku-Sanchi
Tsurugi-San 1955
Nankoku
Yawatahama
Uwajima
Tosa-Wan
Ashizuri-Zaki

KITAKYŪSHŪ
FUKUOKA
Karatsu
Saga
Kurume
Omuta
Buzen
Beppu
Ōita
Saiki
Nobeoka
Hyūga
Kurino
Kyūshū
Kumamoto
Yatsushiro
Minamata
Miyazaki
Miyakonojō
Kagoshima
Kanoya
Ibusuki
Makurazaki
Sata-Misaki
Nichinan

Nagasaki
Sasebo
Gotō-Rettō
Fukue-Shima
Hondo
Amakusa-Shotō
Ushibuka
Isahaya
Kurino
Koshiki-Rettō

PACIFIC OCEAN

Nampō-Shotō
Hachijō-Jima
Aoga-Shima
Miyake-Jima
Nii-Jima
Izu-Shotō

Projection: Conical with two standard parallels
East from Greenwich

COPYRIGHT

1:20 000 000

| 100 | 0 | 100 | 200 | 300 | 400 | 500 | 600 | 700 | 800 km |
| 100 | 0 | 100 | 200 | 300 | 400 | 500 miles |

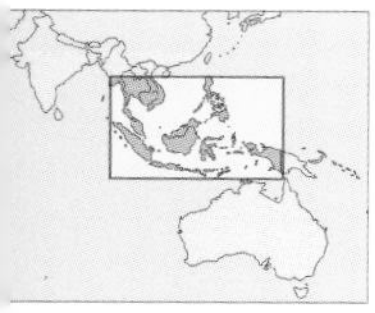

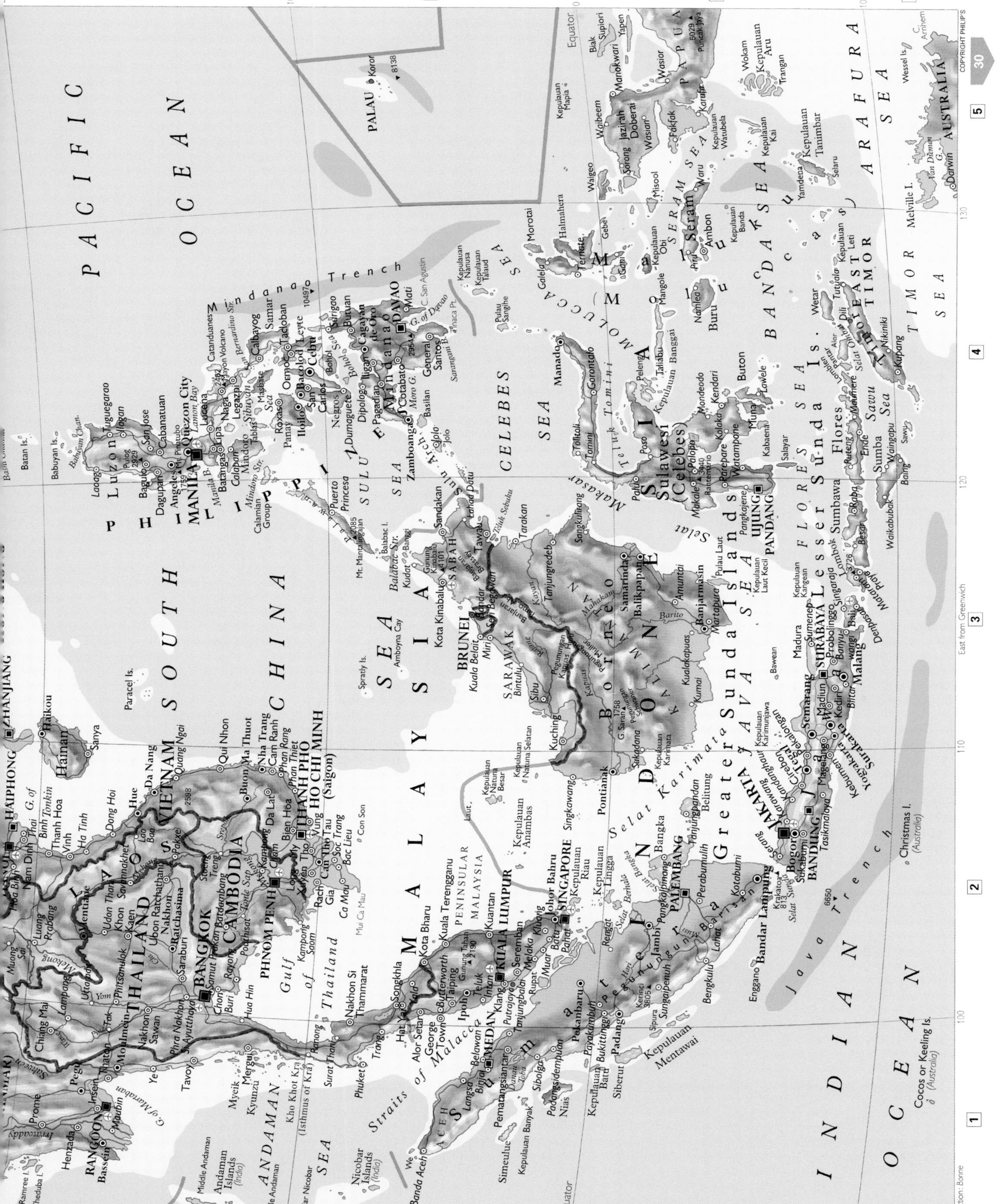

B   C   D   E

PACIFIC OCEAN

Equator

PALAU
Koror ▲8138

8136

Projection: Bonne

East from Greenwich

PAPUA
Puncak Jaya 5029
Biak Supiori Yapen
Manokwari Wasior
Wokam Kepulauan Aru
Trangan
Sorong Jazirah Doberai
Wasian
Waigeo Misool Fakfak
Waru SERAM SEA Kepulauan Wanubela
Obi Kepulauan Watubela Kepulauan Kai
Yamdena Kepulauan Tanimbar
Selaru
Wessel Is. C. Arnhem
Kep. Djaman
Darwin AUSTRALIA
ARAFURA SEA

Ternate MOLUCCA Halmahera Galela Morotai
Gebe
Banda
Ambon BANDA SEA
Buru Nahlee
Mangole Leti
Wetar Alor
TIMOR Dili EAST TIMOR
Kupang
TIMOR SEA
Melville I.

MALUKU

Mindanao Trench
DAVAO Mati
General Santos
Sarangani Is.
G. of Davao

Samar Tacloban Leyte
Catanduanes Catbalogan
Legazpi Masbate Catarman
Naga Calbayog
Lucena Bohol Cebu
Batangas Iloilo Bacolod
Mindoro Negros Dumaguete
Calapan Panay Tagbilaran
Roxas Dipolog
Cagayan
Iligan
Pagadian
Zamboanga
Cotabato
Sulu Archipelago
Jolo
Basilan
Sulu Sea

PHILIPPINE SEA

MANILA Quezon City
Lamon Bay
Luzon
Baguio Angeles
Dagupan Cabanatuan
San Jose
Tuguegarao Ilagan
Vigan Laoag
Batan Is.
Babuyan Is.
Pinatubo 1759
Mayon Volcano 2463
Catanduanes

CELEBES SEA

SABAH Kota Kinabalu
Gunung Kinabalu 4101
Sandakan
Tawau
BRUNEI
SARAWAK
Kuala Belait Miri
Bintulu Sibu
Kuching
Sulawesi (Celebes)
Manado Gorontalo
Palu Poso
Teluk Tomini
Kendari
Watampone
PANDANG UJUNG
Makale
Palopo

BORNEO KALIMANTAN
Samarinda
Balikpapan
Banjarmasin
Pontianak
Tarakan
Ketapang
Barito
Mahakam

INDONESIA

Waingapu SAVU SEA Sumba
Flores FLORES SEA
Sumbawa Lombok
Bali Bima
Raba
Lesser Sunda Islands

JAVA Greater Sunda Islands
JAKARTA Bogor Bandung
SURABAYA Semarang
Yogyakarta Surakarta
Malang
Madura
JAVA SEA
Cirebon

SOUTH CHINA SEA

Paracel Is.
Spratly Is.

VIETNAM
HANOI HAIPHONG
Da Nang
Qui Nhon
Nha Trang
Cam Ranh
Phan Thiet
HO CHI MINH (Saigon)
Vung Tau
Dalat
Hue
Vinh
Dong Hoi
G. of Tonkin
HAIKOU Haikou Sanya
ZHANJIANG
Hainan

LAOS
Vientiane
Luang Prabang
Mekong

THAILAND
BANGKOK
Chiang Mai
Nakhon Ratchasima
Ubon Ratchathani
Khon Kaen
Phitsanulok
Nakhon Sawan

CAMBODIA
PHNOM PENH
Battambang
Tonle Sap

Gulf of Thailand

MALAYSIA
KUALA LUMPUR
Ipoh
George Town
Butterworth
Johor Bahru
Kuantan
Kota Bharu
Kuala Terengganu
Melaka
PENINSULAR MALAYSIA
Gunung Tahan 2190

SINGAPORE

MALACCA Straits of Malacca

Medan
Pematangsiantar
Padang
Pekanbaru
Jambi
PALEMBANG
Bengkulu
Bandar Lampung
SUMATERA

Banda Aceh
ACEH
Nias Kepulauan Mentawai
Siberut
Kepulauan Lingga
Bangka Belitung

ANDAMAN SEA

RANGOON
Bassein
Moulmein
Mergui
Tavoy
Pegu
Prome
Henzada

Nicobar Islands (India)
Andaman Islands (India)
Middle Andaman
Little Andaman
Car Nicobar

INDIAN OCEAN

Cocos or Keeling Is. (Australia)
Christmas I. (Australia)
Java Trench

Equator

| ft | 12 000 | 6000 | 3000 | 1200 | 600 | 200 | 0 |
| m | 4000 | 2000 | 1000 | 400 | 200 | 0 |

COPYRIGHT PHILIP'S

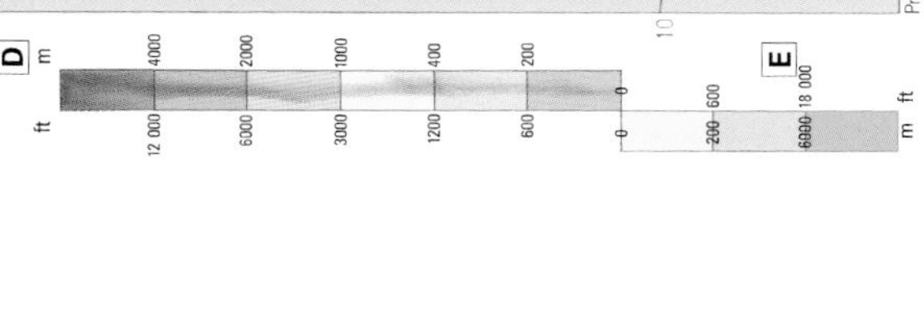

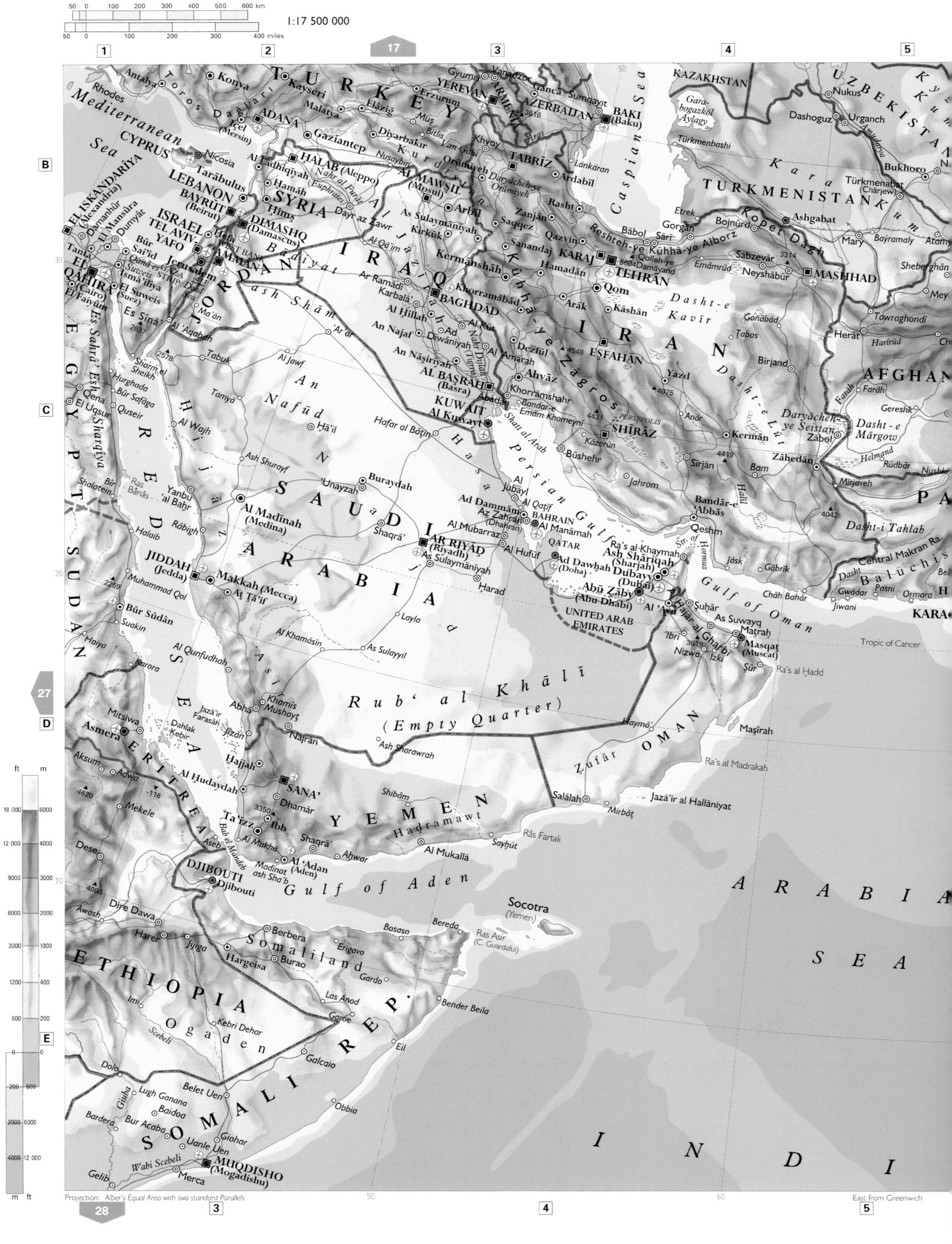

1:17 500 000

Projection: Alber's Equal Area with two standard Parallels

East from Greenwich

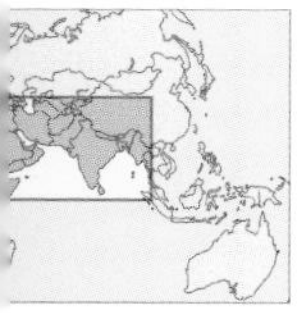

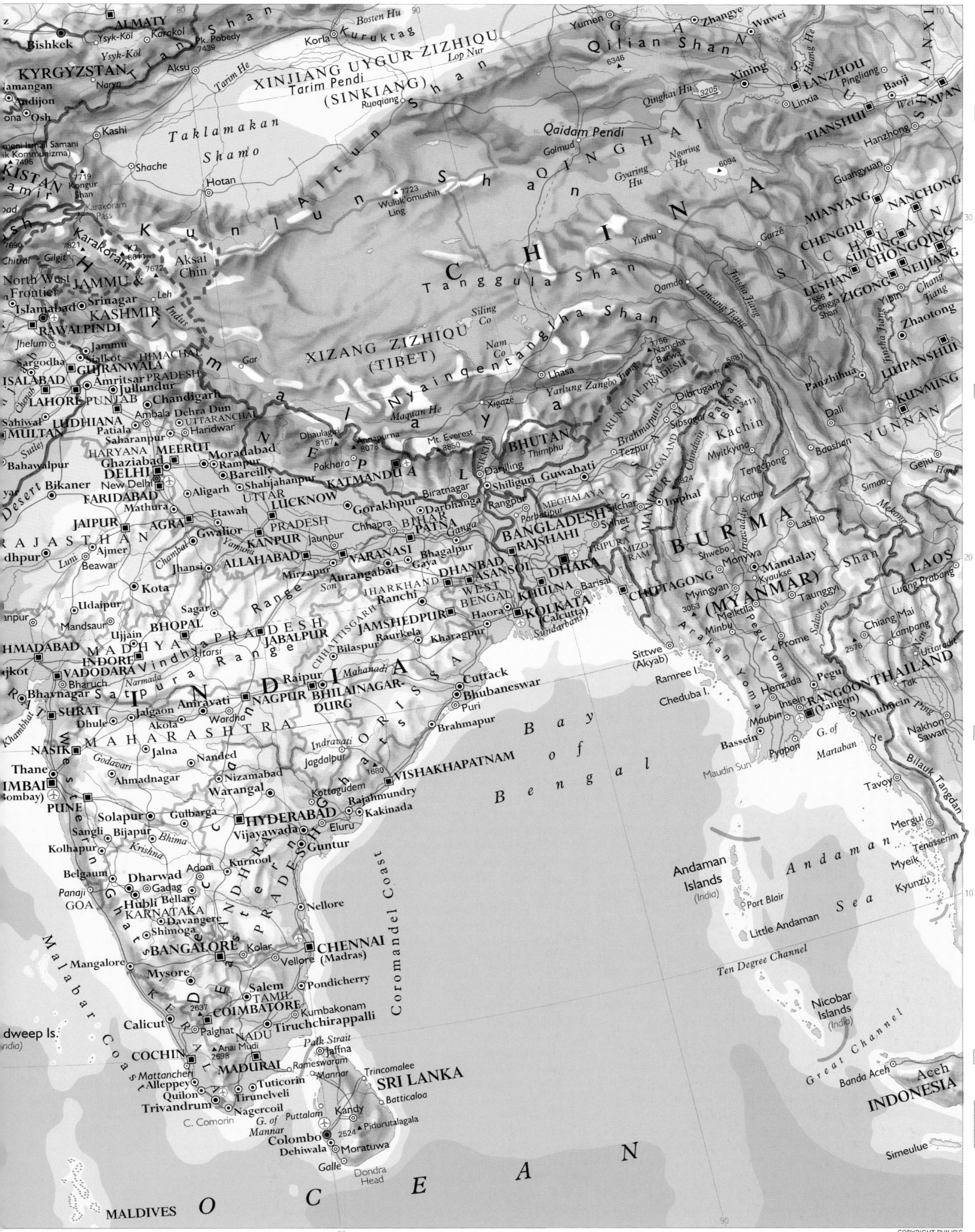

KYRGYZSTAN
Bishkek
ALMATY
XINJIANG UYGUR ZIZHIQU (SINKIANG)
Tarim Pendi
Taklamakan Shamo
Kunlun Shan
Qilian Shan
Qaidam Pendi
QINGHAI
Tanggula Shan
XIZANG ZIZHIQU (TIBET)
Nyainqentanglha Shan
Lhasa
CHINA
SICHUAN
YUNNAN
CHENGDU
CHONGQING
KUNMING
LANZHOU
Xining
JAMMU & KASHMIR
Aksai Chin
Karakoram
K2 8611
Srinagar
Islamabad
RAWALPINDI
LAHORE
PUNJAB
HIMACHAL PRADESH
UTTARANCHAL
HARYANA
DELHI
New Delhi
UTTAR PRADESH
LUCKNOW
KANPUR
RAJASTHAN
JAIPUR
AGRA
NEPAL
KATMANDU
Mt. Everest 8850
Annapurna 8078
Dhaulagiri 8167
BHUTAN
Thimphu
SIKKIM
ARUNACHAL PRADESH
ASSAM
NAGALAND
MANIPUR
MIZORAM
TRIPURA
MEGHALAYA
BANGLADESH
DHAKA
BIHAR
PATNA
JHARKHAND
WEST BENGAL
KOLKATA (Calcutta)
MADHYA PRADESH
BHOPAL
CHHATTISGARH
ORISSA
GUJARAT
AHMADABAD
VADODARA
SURAT
MAHARASHTRA
MUMBAI (Bombay)
PUNE
NAGPUR
INDIA
ANDHRA PRADESH
HYDERABAD
VISHAKHAPATNAM
KARNATAKA
BANGALORE
CHENNAI (Madras)
TAMIL NADU
KERALA
COCHIN
MADURAI
COIMBATORE
Western Ghats
Eastern Ghats
Coromandel Coast
Malabar Coast
SRI LANKA
Colombo
Kandy
Trincomalee
Palk Strait
MALDIVES
BURMA (MYANMAR)
Mandalay
RANGOON (Yangon)
CHITTAGONG
Arakan Yoma
G. of Martaban
THAILAND
LAOS
Andaman Islands (India)
Port Blair
Nicobar Islands (India)
Ten Degree Channel
Great Channel
Andaman Sea
Bay of Bengal
INDIAN OCEAN
INDONESIA
Aceh
Banda Aceh
Simeulue

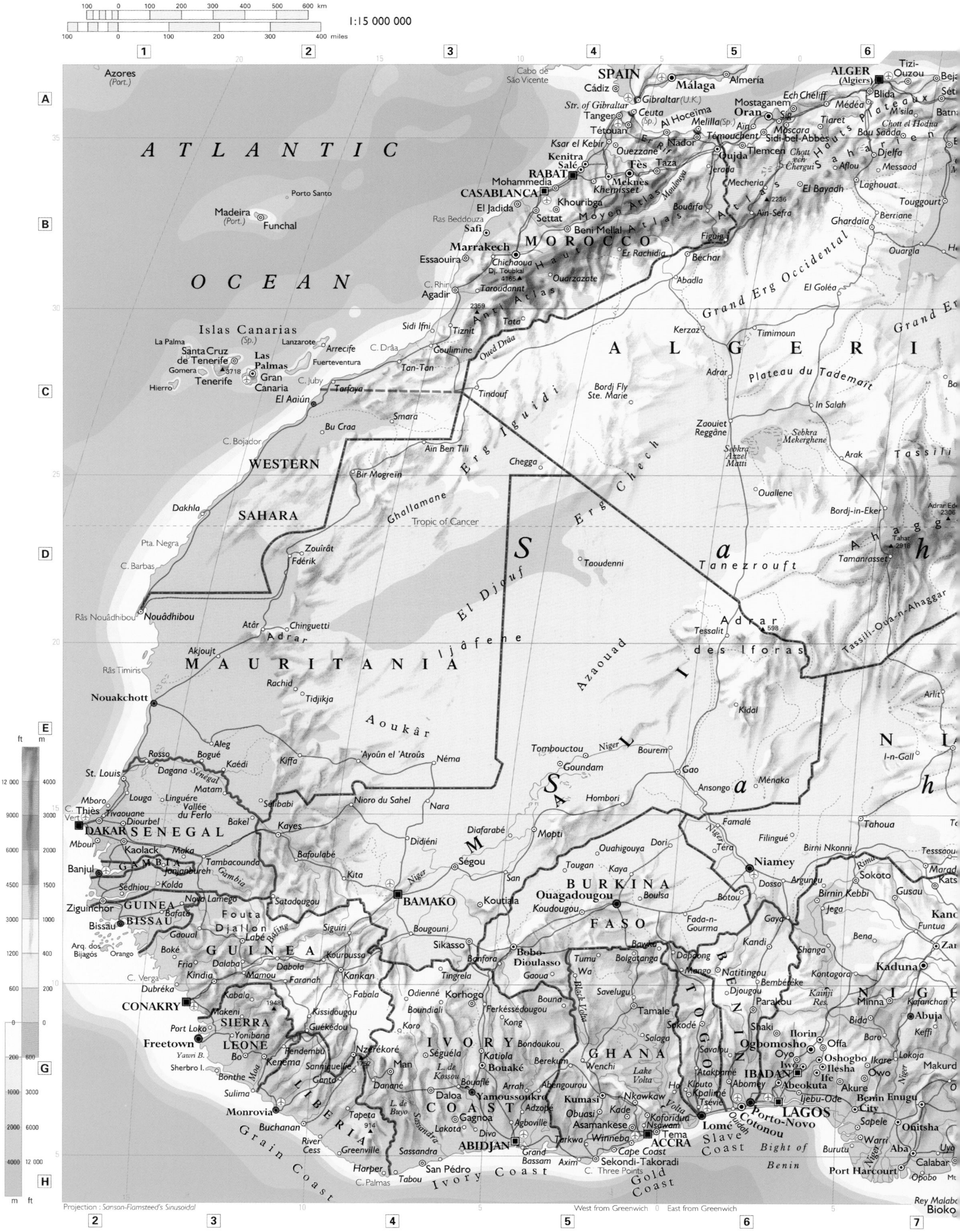

1:15 000 000

Projection : Sanson-Flamsteed's Sinusoidal

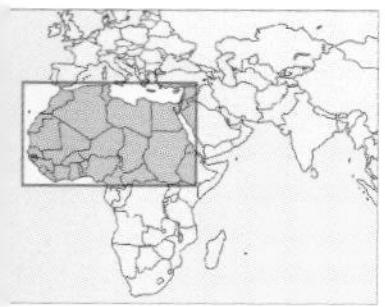

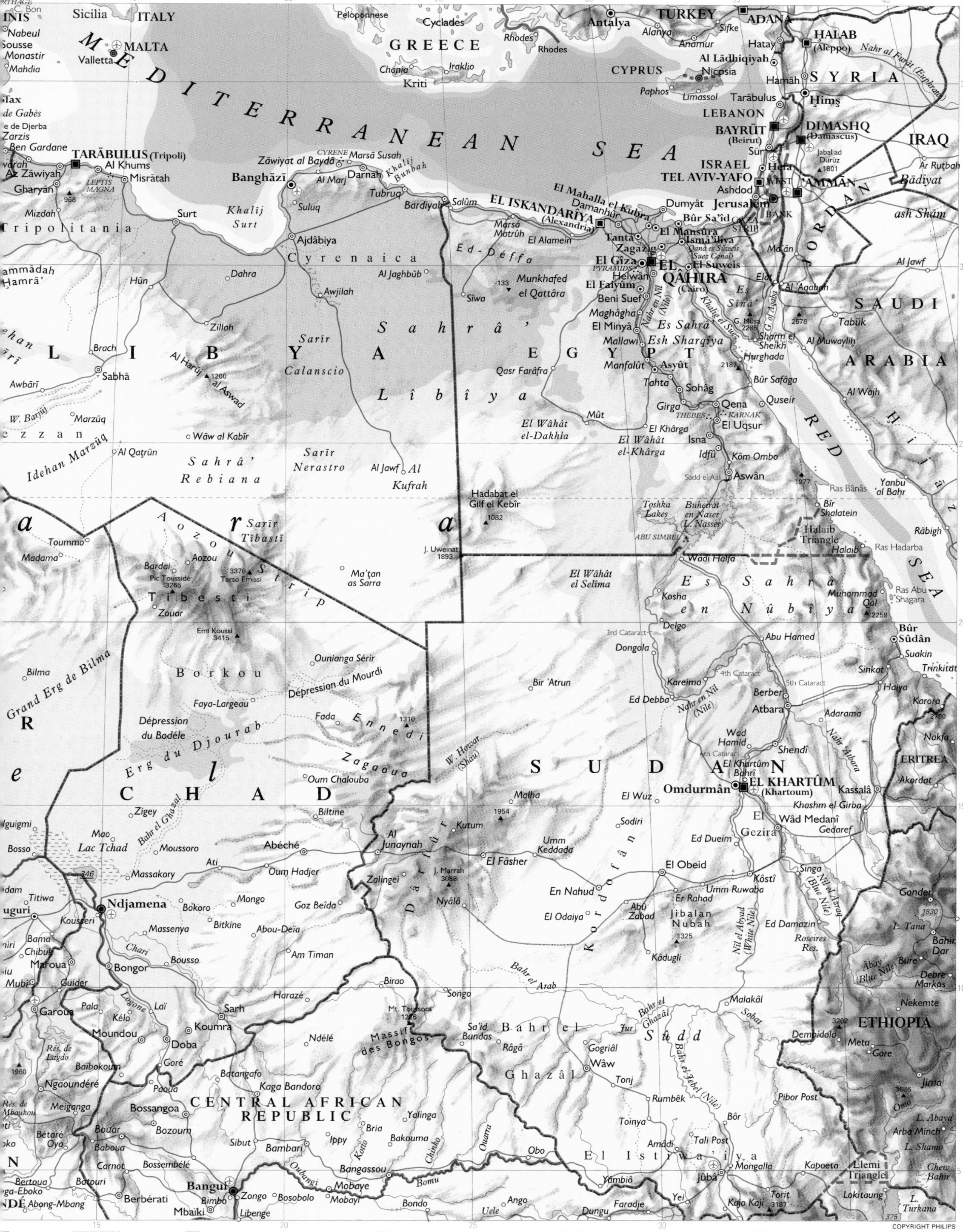
MEDITERRANEAN SEA
Sicilia
ITALY
MALTA
Valletta
GREECE
Peloponnese
Cyclades
Kriti
Chania
Iraklio
Rhodes
TURKEY
Antalya
Alanya
Anamur
ADANA
CYPRUS
Nicosia
Paphos
Limassol
HALAB (Aleppo)
SYRIA
Hamāh
Hims
Al Lādhiqiyah
Tarābulus
LEBANON
BAYRŪT (Beirut)
DIMASHQ (Damascus)
IRAQ
ISRAEL
TEL AVIV-YAFO
Ashdod
Jerusalem
WEST BANK
GAZA STRIP
'AMMĀN
JORDAN
Bādiyat ash Shām
Ar Rutbah
Al Jawf
Ma'ān
Al 'Aqabah
Elat
SAUDI ARABIA
Tabūk
Al Muwaylih
Al Wajh
Hijaz
Yanbu 'al Bahr
Rābigh
Ras Hadarba
TARĀBULUS (Tripoli)
Al Khums
LEPTIS MAGNA
Misrātah
Az Zāwiyah
Gharyān
Mizdah
Tripolitania
Nabeul
Sousse
Monastir
Mahdia
Sfax
Zarzis
Ben Gardane
Surt
Khalīj Surt
Banghāzī
Zāwiyat al Baydā
CYRENE
Marsā Susah
Al Marj
Darnah
Khalīj Bumbah
Tubruq
Bardīyah
Suluq
Ajdābiya
Cyrenaica
Dahra
Hūn
Awjilah
Zillah
Al Jaghbūb
LIBYA
Brach
Sabhā
Awbārī
Al Harūj al Aswad
Sarīr Calanscio
Marzūq
Idehan Marzūq
Wāw al Kabīr
Al Qatrūn
Sahrâ' Rebiana
Sarīr Nerastro
Al Jawf
Al Kufrah
Sahrâ' Lîbîya
EGYPT
Salûm
EL ISKANDARÎYA (Alexandria)
Marsâ Matrûh
El Alamein
Ed-Déffa
Siwa
Munkhafed el Qattâra
Qasr Farâfra
El Wâhât el-Dakhla
Mût
El Mahalla el Kubra
Damanhûr
Tanta
Dumyât
Bûr Sa'îd
El Mansûra
Zagazig
Ismâ'iliya
Qanâ es Suweis (Suez Canal)
El Suweis
El Gîza
EL QÂHIRA (Cairo)
PYRAMIDS
Helwân
El Faiyûm
Beni Suef
Maghâgha
El Minyâ
Mallawi
Manfalût
Asyût
Tahta
Sohâg
Girga
Qena
THEBES
KARNAK
El Uqsur
El Khârga
El Wâhât el-Khârga
Isna
Idfû
Kôm Ombo
Sadd el Aali
Aswân
Es Sahrâ Esh Sharqîya
Es Sînâ'
G. Mûsa 2285
Sharm el Sheikh
Hurghada
Bûr Safâga
Quseir
RED SEA
Ras Bânâs
Bîr Shalatein
Halaib Triangle
Halaib
Toshka Lakes
Buheirat en Naser (L. Nasser)
ABU SIMBEL
Hadabat el Gilf el Kebîr
J. Uweinat 1893
Wadi Halfa
El Wâhât el Selima
Ma'tan as Sarra
Aozou Strip
Sarīr Tibastī
Tibesti
Tousmo
Madama
Bardai
Aozou
Pic Toussidé 3265
Tarso Emissi 3376
Zouar
Emi Koussi 3415
Bilma
Grand Erg de Bilma
Borkou
Ounianga Sérir
Dépression du Mourdi
Faya-Largeau
Dépression du Bodélé
Erg du Djourab
Fada
Ennedi
Zagaoua
Oum Chalouba
CHAD
Biltine
Zigey
Bahr el Ghazal
Mao
Lac Tchad
Moussoro
Abéché
Ati
Massakory
Oum Hadjer
Ndjamena
Kousseri
Bokoro
Mongo
Goz Beïda
Massenya
Bitkine
Abou-Deïa
Bongor
Bousso
Chari
Am Timan
Sarh
Koumra
Moundou
Doba
Laï
Kélo
Pala
Garoua
Maroua
Guider
Ngaoundéré
Baïbokoum
Goré
Logone
Rés. de Lagdo
Meiganga
Bétaré Oya
Bouar
Baboua
Bossangoa
Bozoum
Batangafo
Paoua
Kaga Bandoro
CENTRAL AFRICAN REPUBLIC
Carnot
Bossembélé
Sibut
Bambari
Berbérati
Bangui
Bimbo
Zongo
Bosobolo
Mbaïki
Libenge
Batouri
Bertoua
Abong-Mbang
Mobaye
Bangassou
Bria
Ippy
Yalinga
Bakouma
Birao
Harazé
Ndélé
Massif des Bongos
Mt. Toussoro 1255
Bondo
Ubangi
Bomu
Obo
Ango
Uele
Dungu
Faradje
Kotto
Ouarra
Chinko
SUDAN
Es Sahrâ en Nûbîya
Kosha
Delgo
3rd Cataract
Dongola
Abu Hamed
Kareima
4th Cataract
5th Cataract
Berber
Atbara
Ed Debba
Nahr en Nîl (Nile)
Wad Hamid
6th Cataract
Shendî
El Khartûm Bahrî
EL KHARTÛM (Khartoum)
Omdurmân
El Wuz
Bîr 'Atrun
W. Howar (Shau)
Malha
Kutum
Al Junaynah
Dârfûr
El Fâsher
Umm Keddada
J. Marrah 3088
Zalingei
Nyâlâ
Sodiri
Kordofân
Ed Dueim
El Obeid
En Nahud
El Odaiya
Abû Zabad
Er Rahad
Umm Ruwaba
Jibalan Nubah 1325
Kâdugli
Kôstî
El Gezira
Wad Medanî
Gedaref
Khashm el Girba
Kassalâ
Singa
Nîl el Azraq (Blue Nile)
Nîl el Abyad (White Nile)
Ed Damazin
Roseires Res.
Muhammad Qol
Ras Abu Shagara
Bûr Sûdân
Suakin
Sinkat
Haiya
Trinkitat
Karora
Nakfa
ERITREA
Akordat
Adarama
Nahr Atbara
Bahr el Arab
Songo
Sa'id Bundas
Râgâ
Bahr el Ghazâl
Jur
Sudd
Bahr el Ghazâl
Gogriâl
Wâw
Tonj
Rumbêk
Bahr el Jebel (Nile)
Toinya
Bôr
Amâdi
Tali Post
El Istiwa'iya
Mongalla
Jûba
Yambiô
Yei
Kajo Kaji
Torit
Kapoeta
Elemi Triangle
Lokitaung
L. Turkana
Pibor Post
Malakâl
Sobat
ETHIOPIA
Dembidolo
Metu
Gore
Jima
Omo
Nekemte
Gonder
L. Tana
Bahir Dar
Abay (Blue Nile)
Bure
Debre Markos
L. Abaya
Arba Minch
L. Shamo
Chew Bahir
COPYRIGHT PHILIPS

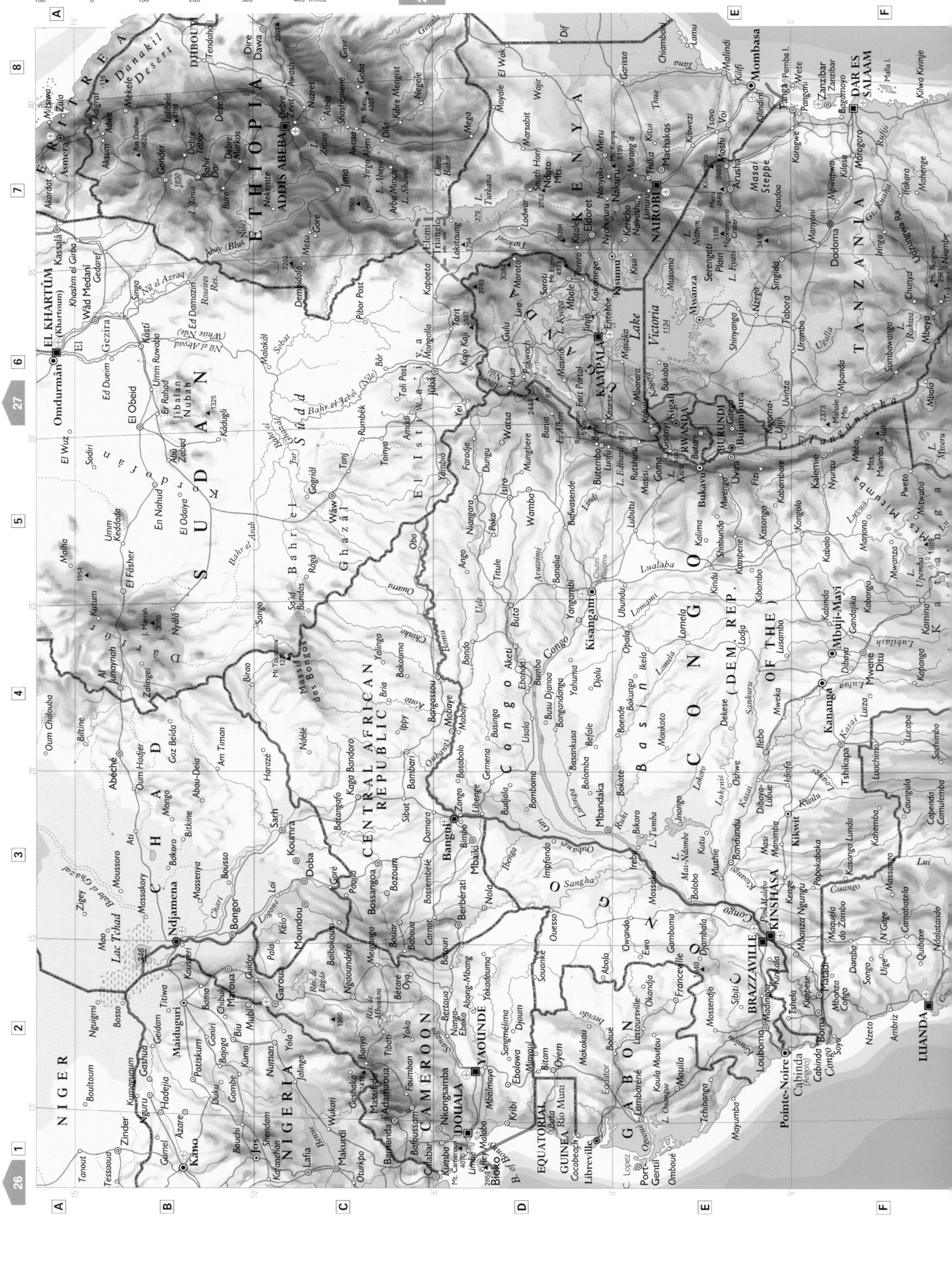

1:15 000 000

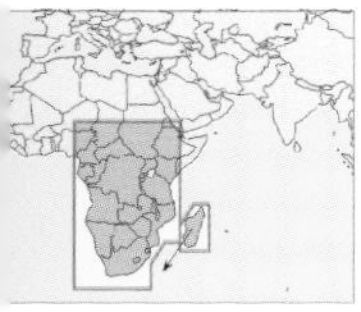

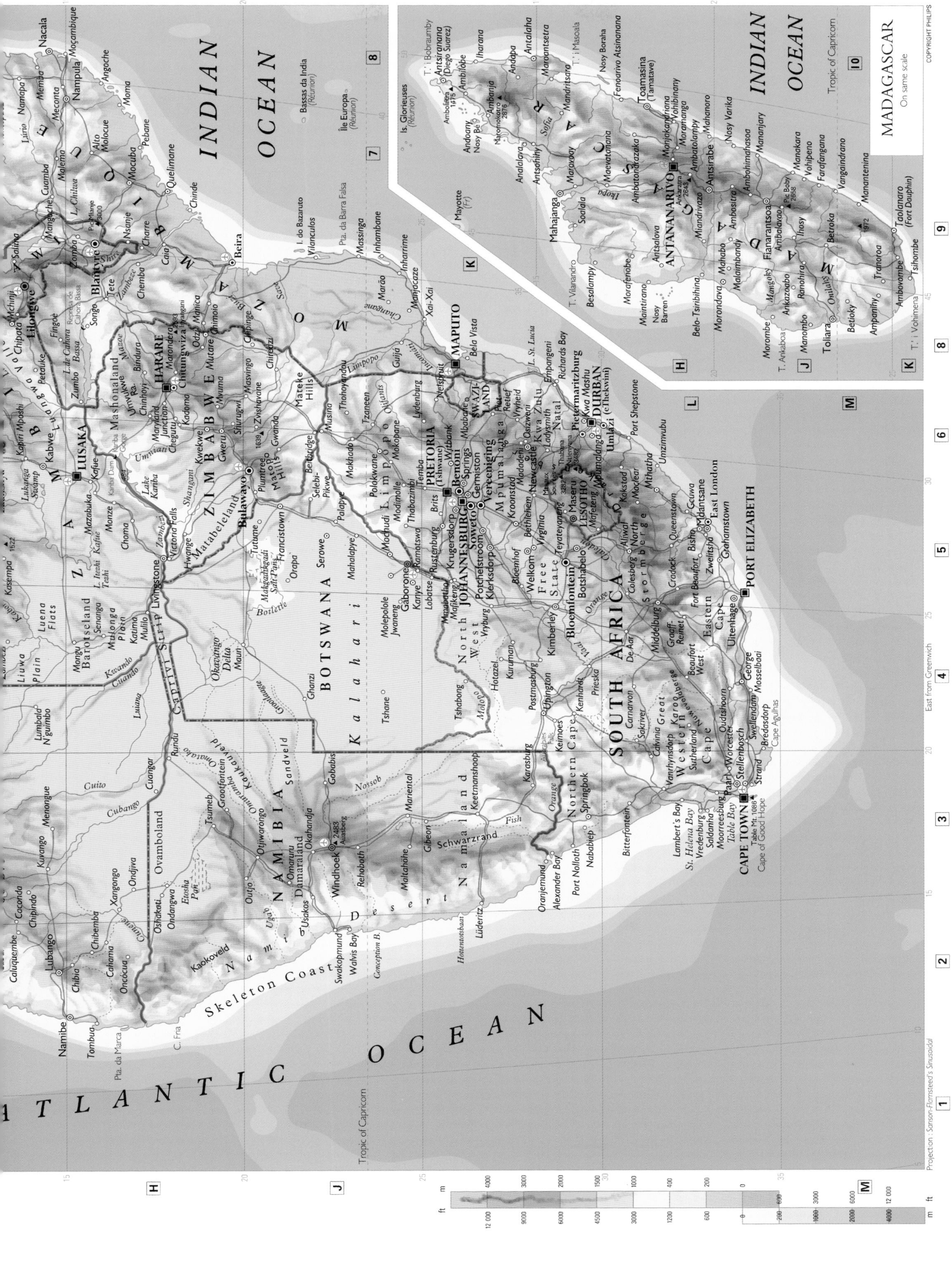

MADAGASCAR
On same scale

COPYRIGHT PHILIPS

Projection: Sanson-Flamsteed's Sinusoidal

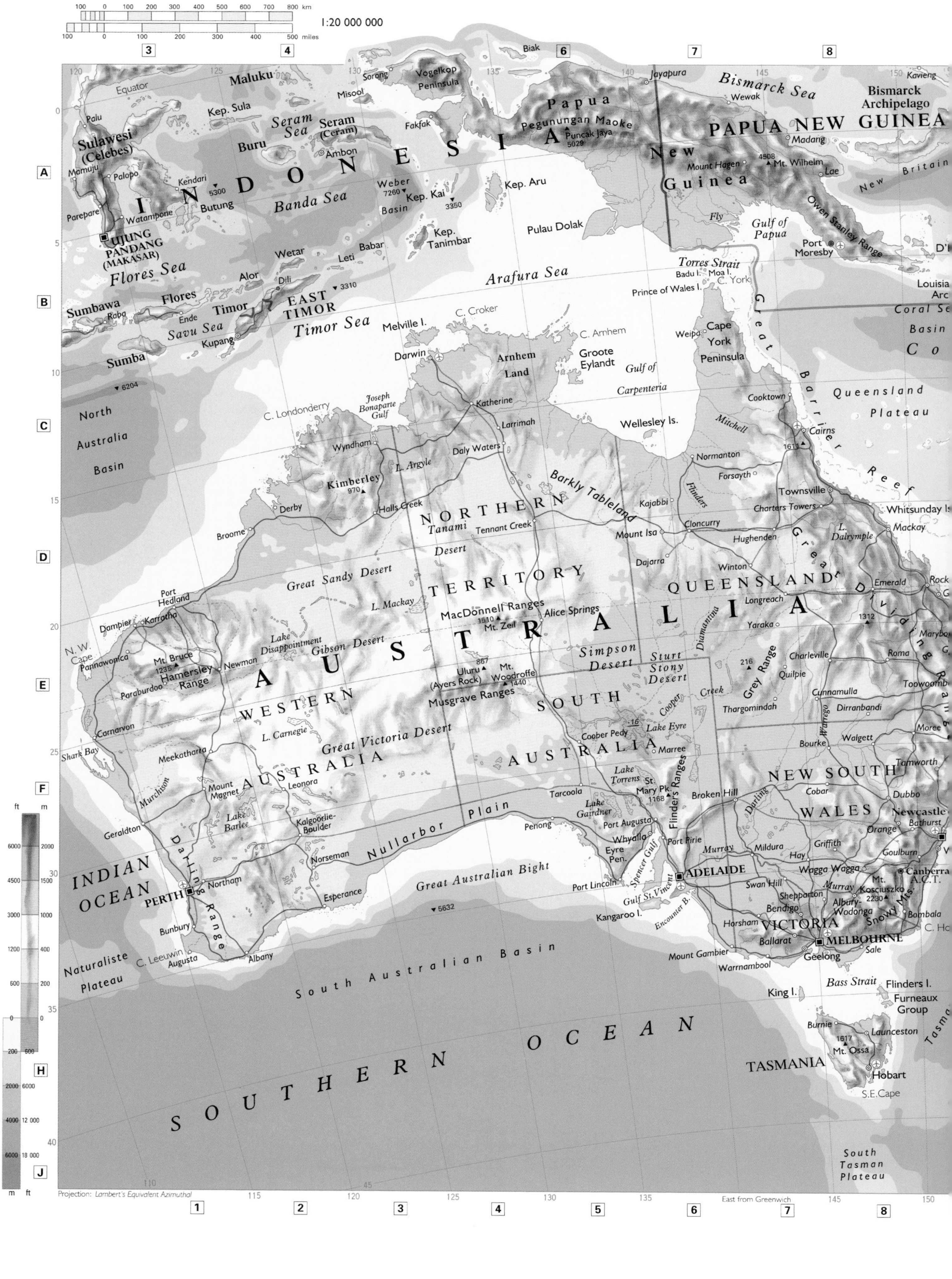

1:20 000 000

Projection: Lambert's Equivalent Azimuthal

East from Greenwich

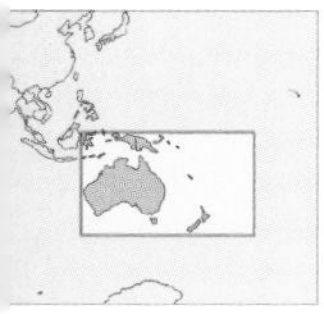

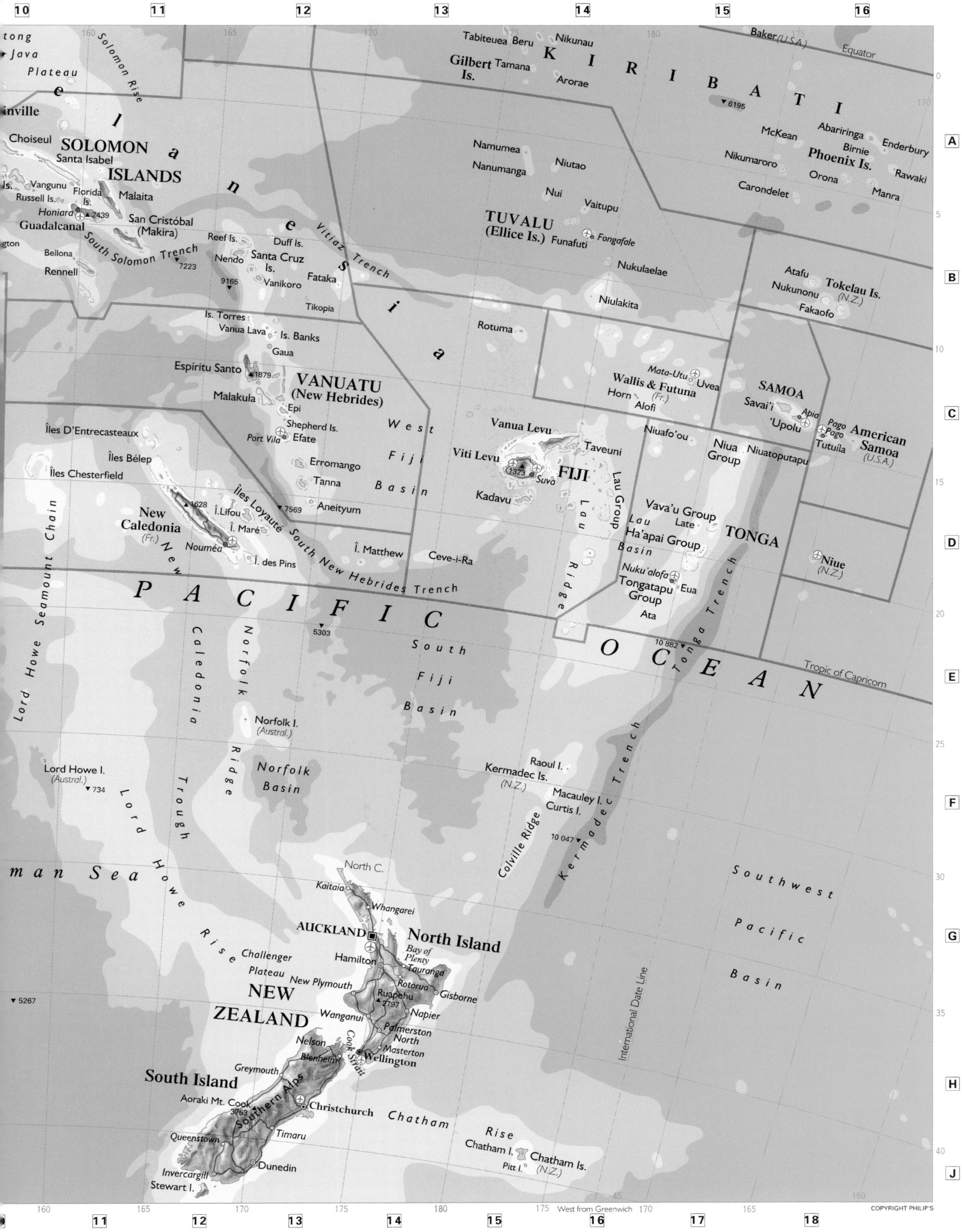

10   11   12   13   14   15   16

K I R I B A T I

Baker (U.S.A.)   Equator

Tabiteuea Beru   Nikunau

Gilbert Tamana
Is.

Aborao
Arorae

▼ 6195

Namumea

Nanumanga   Niutao

McKean   Abariringa   Enderbury
Birnie
Nikumaroro   **Phoenix Is.**   Rawaki
Nui   Vaitupu   Orona
Carondelet   Manra

TUVALU
(Ellice Is.) Funafuti   ● Fongafale

Nukulaelae

Atafu   **Tokelau Is.**
Nukunonu   (N.Z.)
Fakaofo

Niulakita

Rotuma

Mata-Utu ⊙ Uvea
Wallis & Futuna   **SAMOA**
Horn   (Fr.)   Savai'i
Alofi   'Upolu   Apia
● Pago
Niuafo'ou   Pago   **American**
Niua   Niuatoputapu   Tutuila   **Samoa**
Group   (U.S.A.)

Vanua Levu   Taveuni

Viti Levu
☉1323   **FIJI**   Vava'u Group
Suva   Late   **Niue**
Kadavu   Lau   Ha'apai Group   (N.Z.)
Group   Lau   **TONGA**
Basin

Nuku'alofa   Eua
Tongatapu
Group
Ata

SOLOMON
Santa Isabel
ISLANDS
Choiseul
Vangunu Florida   Malaita
Russell Is. Is.
Honiara ⊙ ▲2439 San Cristóbal
Guadalcanal   (Makira)
Bellona   Reef Is.   Duff Is.
Rennell   9165   Santa Cruz   Fataka
Is.   7223   Nendo   Vanikoro
Tikopia
Is. Torres
Vanua Lava ● Is. Banks
● Gaua
Espíritu Santo ▲1879
VANUATU
Malakula   **(New Hebrides)**
Epi
Îles D'Entrecasteaux   Shepherd Is.
Port Vila Efate
Îles Bélep   Erromango
Îles Chesterfield   Tanna
Aneityum
4628 Î. Lifou
New   7569
Caledonia   Î. Maré
(Fr.)   Nouméa ⊙
Î. des Pins   Î. Matthew   Ceve-i-Ra

P A C I F I C   **O C E A N**

Tropic of Capricorn
10 882

5303

West
Fiji
Basin

South
Fiji
Basin

Raoul I.
Kermadec Is.
(N.Z.)
Macauley I.
Curtis I.
10 047

Southwest

Pacific

Basin

North C.
Kaitaia
Whangarei
AUCKLAND   ☐   **North Island**
Hamilton   Bay of
Challenger   Plenty
Plateau New Plymouth   Tauranga
Rotorua   Gisborne
Ruapehu
NEW   Wanganui   ▲2797 Napier
ZEALAND   Palmerston
Nelson   North
Greymouth   Blenheim   Masterton
South Island   Cook Wellington
Strait
Aoraki Mt. Cook   Chatham
3753   Christchurch   Rise
Queenstown   Timaru   Chatham I. ● ● **Chatham Is.**
Invercargill   Dunedin   Pitt I. ● (N.Z.)
Stewart I.

▼ 5267

Lord Howe Seamount Chain

Caledonia Trough

Norfolk Ridge

Norfolk I.
(Austral.)

Norfolk
Basin

Lord Howe I.
(Austral.)   ▼ 734

Lord Howe Rise

man Sea

Colville Ridge

Kermadec Trench

Tonga Trench

Lau Ridge

Lau Group

South New Hebrides Trench

South Solomon Trench

Solomon Rise

Vitiaz Trench

International Date Line

Challenger
Plateau

160 165 170 175 180 175 West from Greenwich 170 165 160

10   11   12   13   14   15   16   17   18

A
B
C
D
E
F
G
H
J

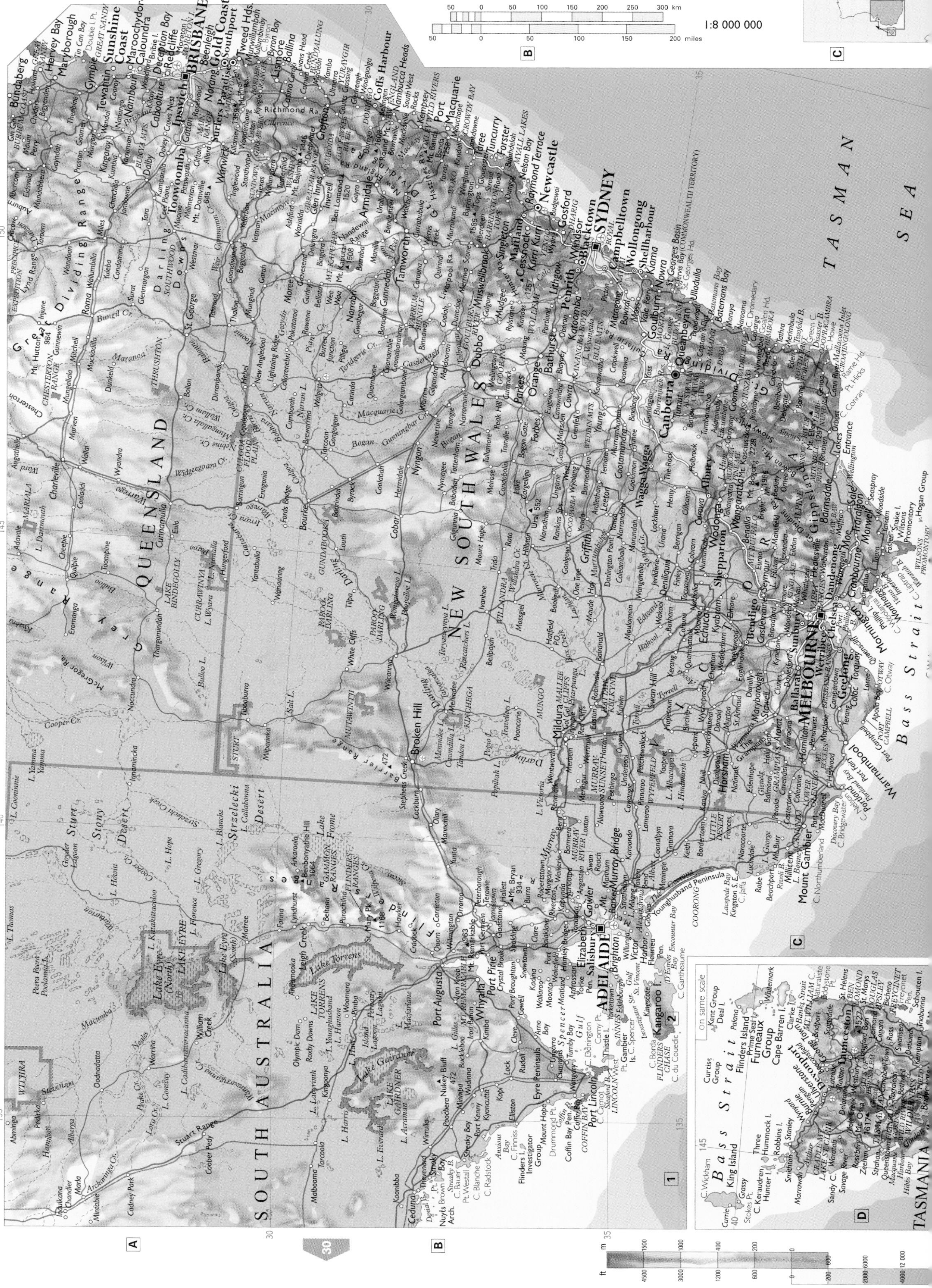
1:8 000 000
0 50 100 150 200 250 300 km
0 50 100 150 200 miles
QUEENSLAND
NEW SOUTH WALES
SOUTH AUSTRALIA
TASMANIA
TASMAN SEA
Bass Strait
BRISBANE
SYDNEY
MELBOURNE
ADELAIDE
Canberra
Newcastle
Wollongong
Geelong
Gold Coast
Toowoomba
Broken Hill
Mildura
Bendigo
Ballarat
Albury
Wagga Wagga
Dubbo
Tamworth
Armidale
Port Augusta
Whyalla
Port Lincoln
Mount Gambier
Kangaroo I.
Lake Eyre (North)
Lake Torrens
Lake Gairdner
Great Dividing Range
Launceston
Devonport
Flinders Island
King Island
on same scale
m ft
1500 4500
1000 3000
400 1200
200 600
0 0
200 600
2000 6000
4000 12 000

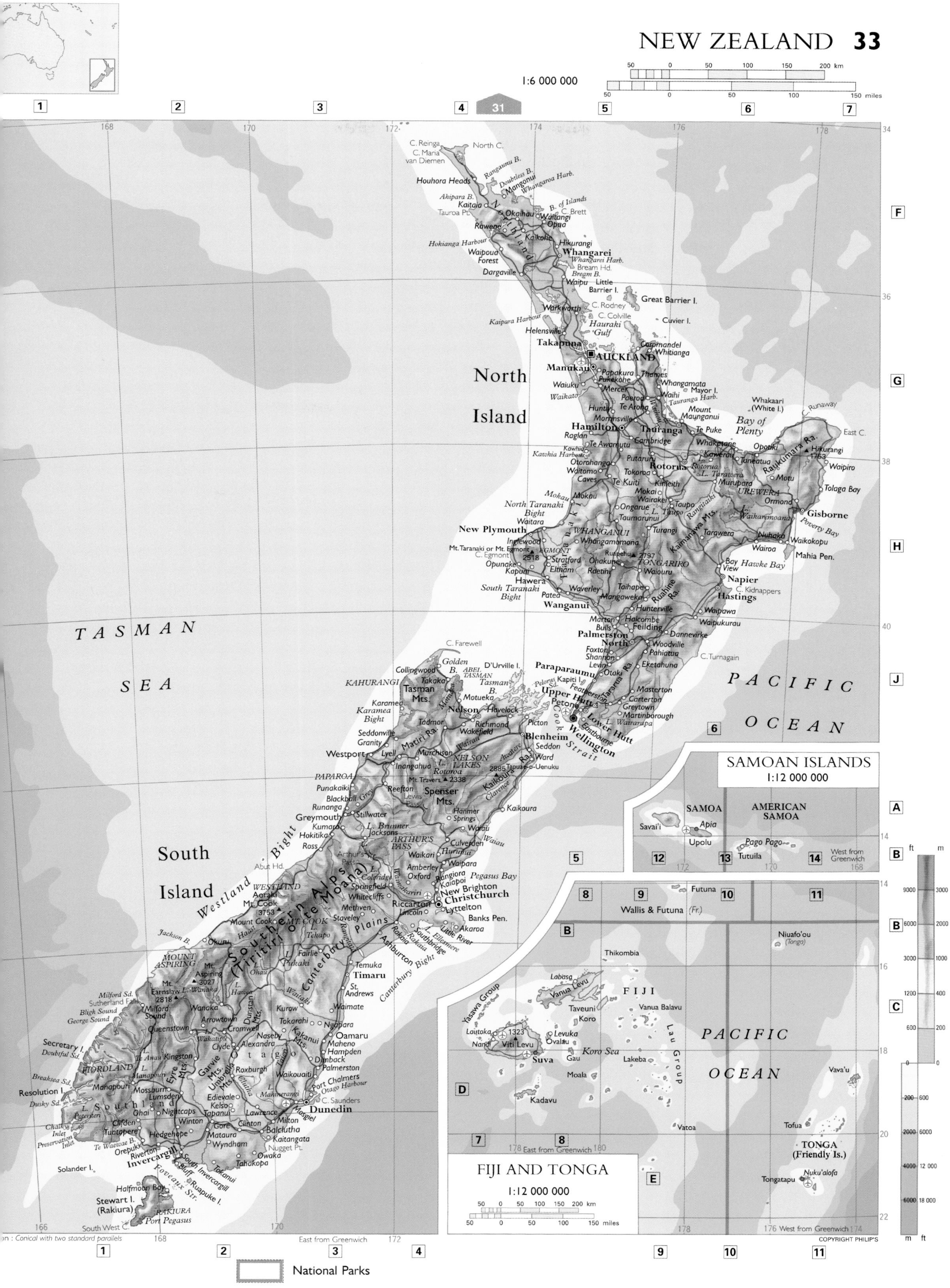

1:6 000 000

50 0 50 100 150 200 km
50 0 50 100 150 miles

North Island

South Island

TASMAN SEA

PACIFIC OCEAN

C. Reinga
C. Maria van Diemen
North C.
Houhora Heads
Rangaunu B.
Doubtless B.
Mangonui
Whangaroa Harb.
Ahipara B.
Kaitaia
Tauroa Pt.
Okaihau
Rawene
Waitangi
Opua
B. of Islands
C. Brett
Hokianga Harbour
Kaikohe
Hikurangi
Whangarei
Whangarei Harb.
Bream Hd.
Bream B.
Waipoua Forest
Waipu
Little Barrier I.
Dargaville
Great Barrier I.
Warkworth
C. Rodney
C. Colville
Cuvier I.
Helensville
Kaipara Harbour
Hauraki Gulf
Coromandel
Whitianga
Takapuna
AUCKLAND
Manukau
Papakura
Pukekohe
Themes
Whangamata
Mayor I.
Waiuku
Mercer
Waihi
Tauranga Harb.
Waikato
Huntly
Te Aroha
Mount Maunganui
Whakaari (White I.)
C. Runaway
Morrinsville
Tauranga
Bay of Plenty
East C.
Hamilton
Cambridge
Whakatane
Raglan
Te Awamutu
Te Puke
Opotiki
Kawhia
Putaruru
Kawerau
Raukumara Ra.
Hikurangi 1753
Kawhia Harbour
Otorohanga
Rotorua
Taneatua
Waitomo Caves
Te Kuiti
L. Tarawera
Murupara
Motu
Waipiro
Mokau
Kihikihi
UREWERA
Mokau
Wairakei
Taupo
Ongarue
L. Taupo
Rangitaiki
Waikaremoana
Tolaga Bay
North Taranaki Bight
Taumarunui
Turangi
Kaimanawa Mts.
Gisborne
Waitara
WHANGANUI
Tarawera
Poverty Bay
New Plymouth
Whangamomona
Ormond
Inglewood
EGMONT
Ruapehu 2797
TONGARIRO
Nuhaka
Waikokopu
Mt. Taranaki or Mt. Egmont
C. Egmont 2518
Stratford
Ohakune
Waiouru
Bay View
Wairoa
Mahia Pen.
Opunake
Kapuni
Eltham
Raetihi
Taihape
Napier
Hawke Bay
Hawera
Mangaweka
Ruahine Ra.
Hastings
C. Kidnappers
South Taranaki Bight
Waverley
Patea
Hunterville
Waipawa
Wanganui
Marton
Halcombe
Waipukurau
Bulls
Feilding
Dannevirke
Foxton
Palmerston North
Woodville
Shannon
Pahiatua
C. Turnagain
Levin
Eketahuna
C. Farewell
Paraparaumu
Otaki
Collingwood
Golden B.
D'Urville I.
Masterton
Takaka
ABEL TASMAN
Tasman B.
Kapiti I.
Carterton
KAHURANGI
Tasman Mts.
Pelorus
Featherston
Greytown
Karamea
Motueka
Upper Hutt
Martinborough
Karamea Bight
Nelson
Havelock
Petone
Wairarapa
Seddonville
Richmond
Picton
Lower Hutt
Granity
Wakefield
Wellington
Eastbourne
Westport
Lyell
Matiri Ra.
NELSON LAKES
Cook Strait
Blenheim
Munchison
Rotoroa
Seddon
Inangahua
2885 Tapuae-o-Uenuku
Ward
PAPAROA
Gre
Mt. Travers 2338
Punakaiki
Reefton
Spenser Mts.
Kaikoura Ra.
Blackball
Clarence
Runanga
Lewis
Hanmer Springs
Greymouth
Stillwater
Kaikoura
Kumara
L. Brunner
Waiau
Hokitika
Jacksons
Wairau
Ross
ARTHUR'S PASS
Waikari
Hurunui
Arthur's
Culverden
Amberley
Abut Hd.
WESTLAND
Oxford
Pegasus Bay
WESTLAND
Rangiora
Kaiapoi
Mt. Cook
MT. COOK
New Brighton
Aoraki 3753
Springfield
Christchurch
Whitecliffs
Darfield
Lyttelton
Mount Cook
Methven
Riccarton
Banks Pen.
Southern Alps (Tiritiri o te Moana)
Staveley
Lincoln
Akaroa
Jackson B.
Okuru
L. Pukaki
L. Ellesmere
Little River
MOUNT ASPIRING
Fairlie
Canterbury Plains
Southbridge
Mt. Aspiring 3027
Ohau
Rakaia
Milford Sd.
Earnslaw 2818
L. Tekapo
Temuka
Canterbury Bight
Sutherland Falls
Wanaka
Ashburton
Bligh Sound
Milford Sound
Timaru
George Sound
Arrowtown
St. Andrews
Secretary I.
Cromwell
Waimate
Doubtful Sd.
Queenstown
Waitaki
FIORDLAND
Wakatipu
Kurow
Ngapara
Breaksea Sd.
Manapouri
Eyre Mts.
Naseby
Oamaru
Resolution I.
Mossburn
Grevie
Umbrella Mts.
Clyde
Maheno
Dusky Sd.
Lumsden
Alexandra
Hampden
Te Waewae B.
Ohai
Roxburgh
Danback
Chalky Inlet
Nightcaps
Otago
Palmerston
Preservation Inlet
Tuntupere
Winton
Kelso
Waikouaiti
Port Chalmers
Solander I.
Orepuki
Gore
Mataura
Lawrence
Otago Harbour
Riverton
Edievale
Milton
Dunedin
Invercargill
Wyndham
Kaitangata
C. Saunders
Halfmoon Bay
Tahakopa
Owaka
Nugget Pt.
Stewart I. (Rakiura)
South West C.
RAKIURA
Port Pegasus

National Parks

SAMOAN ISLANDS
1:12 000 000

SAMOA
AMERICAN SAMOA
Savai'i
Apia
Upolu
Pago Pago
Tutuila
West from Greenwich

FIJI AND TONGA
1:12 000 000

50 0 50 100 150 200 km
50 0 50 100 150 miles

Wallis & Futuna (Fr.)
Futuna
Niuafo'ou (Tonga)
Thikombia
Labasa
Vanua Levu
Taveuni
Vanua Balavu
Yasawa Group
FIJI
Koro
Lautoka
1323
Levuka
Nandi
Viti Levu
Ovalau
Koro Sea
Lau Group
Suva
Gau
Lakeba
PACIFIC OCEAN
Moala
Vava'u
Kadavu
Vatoa
Tofua
TONGA (Friendly Is.)
East from Greenwich
West from Greenwich
Nuku'alofa
Tongatapu

ft m
9000 3000
6000 2000
3000 1000
1200 400
600 200
0 0
200 600
2000 6000
4000 12 000
6000 18 000
m ft

Projection : Conical with two standard parallels
East from Greenwich

COPYRIGHT PHILIP'S

Equatorial Scale 1:54 000 000

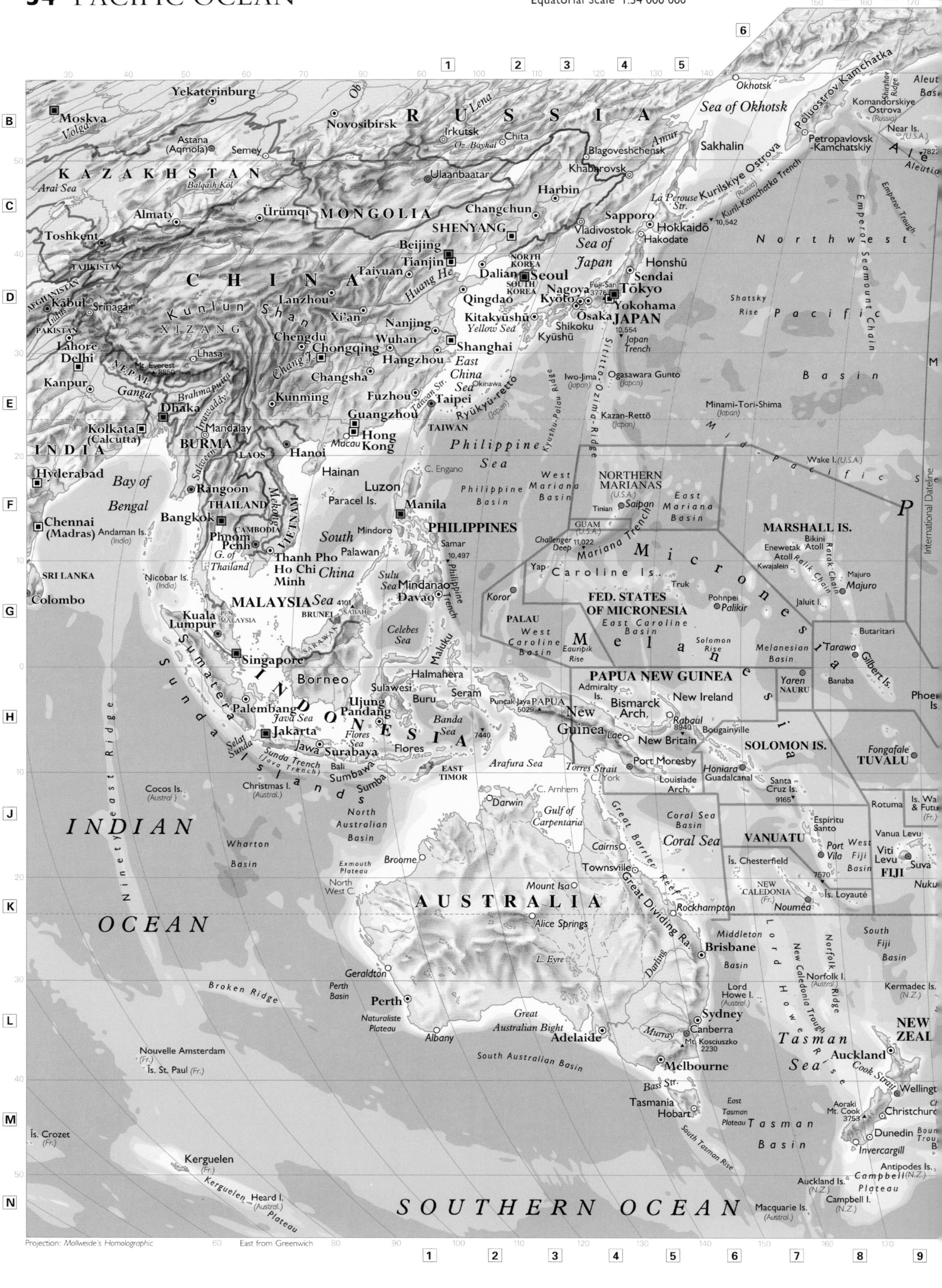

Projection: Mollweide's Homographic   East from Greenwich

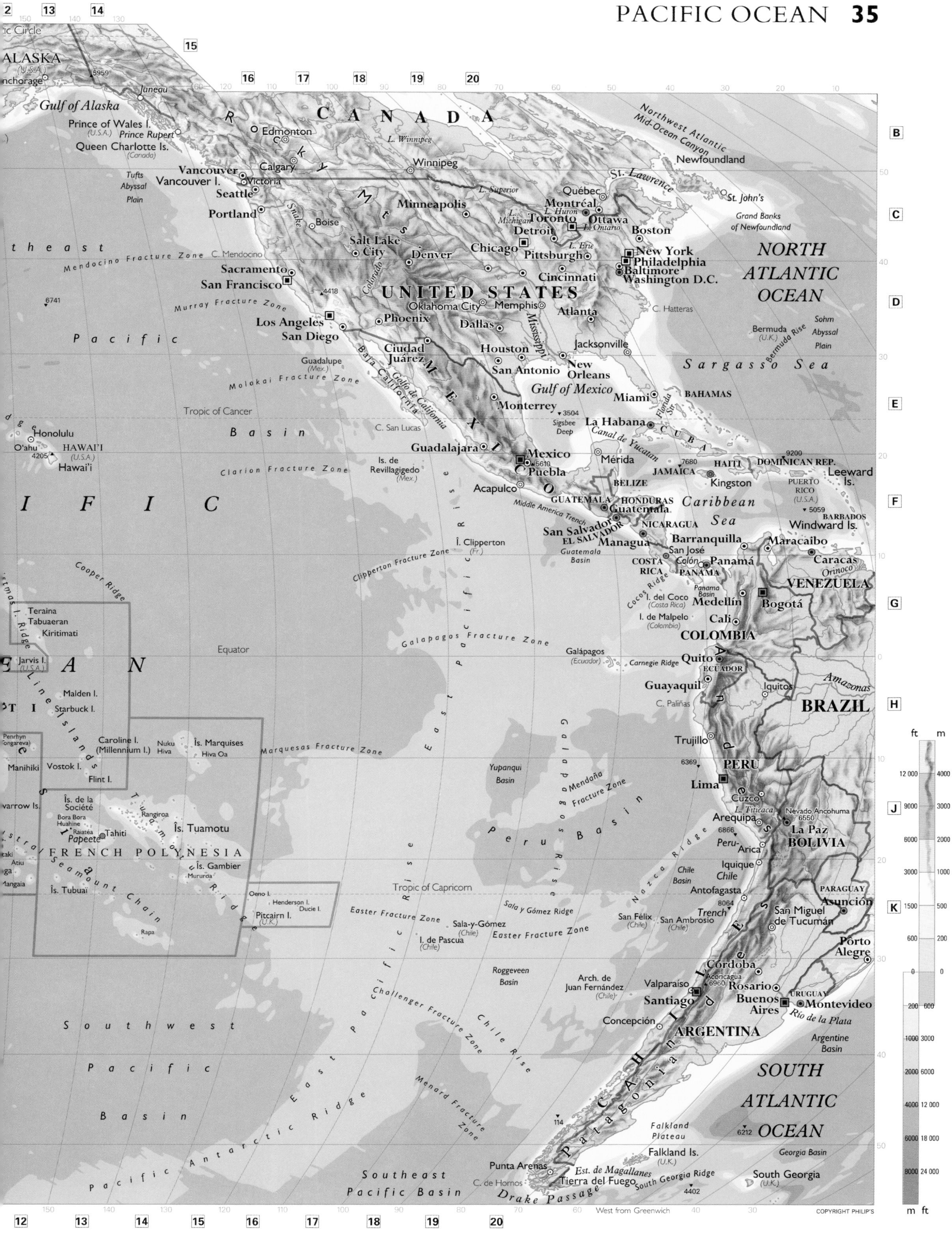

ic Circle

2 | 13 | 14
150 140 130

ALASKA
(USA)
Anchorage
8959
Juneau

15

160

16 | 17 | 18 | 19 | 20
120 110 100 90 80

Gulf of Alaska
Prince of Wales I.
(USA) *Prince Rupert*
Queen Charlotte Is.
(Canada)

Edmonton

C A N A D A

R

O

C

K

Y

M

t

s

L. Winnipeg

Calgary

Winnipeg

*Northwest Atlantic
Mid-Ocean Canyon*

Newfoundland

B

*Tufts
Abyssal
Plain*

Vancouver
Vancouver I.
Seattle
Portland

Victoria

Snake

Boise

L. Superior

Minneapolis

St. Lawrence

Québec
Montréal

L. Huron

Toronto
Detroit

L. Michigan

L. Ontario

Ottawa
Boston

St. John's

*Grand Banks
of Newfoundland*

50

C

the ast

Mendocino Fracture Zone C. Mendocino

6741

Sacramento
San Francisco

Murray Fracture Zone

4418

Salt Lake
City

U N I T E D   S T A T E S

Denver

Colorado

Chicago

Cincinnati

Pittsburgh

L. Erie

New York
Philadelphia
Baltimore
Washington D.C.

*NORTH
ATLANTIC
OCEAN*

40

D

P a c i f i c

Los Angeles
San Diego

Molokai Fracture Zone

Baja California

Phoenix

Oklahoma City

Mississippi

Memphis

Dallas

Houston

Atlanta

San Antonio

New
Orleans

Jacksonville

C. Hatteras

Sargasso Sea

*Bermuda
(U.K.)*
Bermuda Rise

*Sohm
Abyssal
Plain*

30

E

Basin

Guadalupe
(Mex.)

Tropic of Cancer

Golfo de California

C. San Lucas

Ciudad
Juárez

M
E
X
I
C
O

Monterrey

Gulf of Mexico

Miami

3504
*Sigsbee
Deep*

La Habana

Canal de Yucatan

7680

9200

BAHAMAS

Florida Str.

C U B A

HAITI

DOMINICAN REP.

20

F

Honolulu
O'ahu
4205
HAWAI'I
(U.S.A.)
Hawai'i

Clarion Fracture Zone

Is. de
Revillagigedo
(Mex.)

Guadalajara

Mexico
5610
Puebla

Acapulco

Mérida

Middle America Trench

GUATEMALA **HONDURAS**
Guatemala

BELIZE

*Caribbean
Sea*

JAMAICA
Kingston

5059

**PUERTO
RICO**
(U.S.A.)

Leeward
Is.

BARBADOS
Windward Is.

I F I C

Î. Clipperton
(Fr.)

Clipperton Fracture Zone

San Salvador
EL SALVADOR **NICARAGUA**
Managua

*Guatemala
Basin*

Barranquilla
San José

Maracaibo

Caracas
Orinoco

VENEZUELA

G

Cooper Ridge

Teraina
Tabuaeran
Kiritimati

*L
i
n
e
I
s
l
a
n
d
s*

Jarvis I.
(U.S.A.)

Galapagos Fracture Zone

Galápagos
(Ecuador)

Carnegie Ridge

**COSTA
RICA**

Colón
Panamá
PANAMA

*Panama
Basin*

Cocos Ridge
I. del Coco
(Costa Rica)

I. de Malpelo
(Colombia)

Medellín

Quito

Cali

Bogotá

COLOMBIA

ECUADOR

Equator

N
A

Malden I.
Starbuck I.

Caroline I.
(Millennium I.)

Nuku
Hiva

Îs. Marquises

Hiva Oa

Marquesas Fracture Zone

Guayaquil

C. Paliñas

Amazonas

Iquitos

BRAZIL

H

Penrhyn
(Tongareva)

Manihiki

Vostok I.

Flint I.

Galapagos

*Yupanqui
Basin*

Mendaña

Fracture Zone

Trujillo

6369

PERU

Lima

Cuzco

10

J

arrow Is.

Îs. de la
Société
Bora Bora
Huahine
Raiatéa
Papeete
Tahiti

Rangiroa

Îs. Tuamotu

*P
e
r
u
B
a
s
i
n*

*N
a
z
c
a
R
i
d
g
e*

Arequipa
6866
Peru-
Arica

L. Titicaca
Nevado Ancohuma
6550
La Paz

BOLIVIA

Atiu

Mangaia

FRENCH POLYNESIA

Îs. Gambier

Mururoa

Tropic of Capricorn

Iquique
Chile

*Chile
Basin*

Antofagasta

PARAGUAY

Asunción

K

Îs. Tubuai

*S
e
a
m
o
u
n
t
C
h
a
i
n*

Oeno I.
Henderson I.
Ducie I.
Pitcairn I.
(U.K.)

Easter Fracture Zone

Sala-y-Gómez
(Chile)

Sala y Gómez Ridge

Easter Fracture Zone

8064

San Félix
(Chile)

San Ambrosio
(Chile)

Trench

San Miguel
de Tucumán

Porto
Alegre

Rapa

I. de Pascua
(Chile)

Córdoba

Valparaíso

Aconcagua
6960

Rosario

Buenos
Aires

URUGUAY

Montevideo

30

Southwest

*Roggeveen
Basin*

Arch. de
Juan Fernández
(Chile)

*C
h
i
l
e
R
i
s
e*

Santiago

Concepción

ARGENTINA

Rio de la Plata

*Argentine
Basin*

SOUTH

Pacific

Challenger Fracture Zone

Menard Fracture Zone

ATLANTIC

40

Basin

*P
a
c
i
f
i
c
A
n
t
a
r
c
t
i
c
R
i
d
g
e*

*E
a
s
t
P
a
c
i
f
i
c
R
i
s
e*

114

*P
a
t
a
g
o
n
i
a*

OCEAN

6212

Falkland
Plateau

Falkland Is.
(U.K.)

Georgia Basin

*Southeast
Pacific Basin*

Punta Arenas
C. de Hornos

Est. de Magallanes
Tierra del Fuego

Drake Passage

4402

South Georgia Ridge

South Georgia
(U.K.)

50

West from Greenwich

COPYRIGHT PHILIP'S

m ft

Elevation scale (right margin):

ft m
12 000 4000
9000 3000
6000 2000
3000 1000
1500 500
600 200
0 0
200 600
1000 3000
2000 6000
4000 12 000
6000 18 000
8000 24 000
m ft

1:15 000 000

37

Projection : Bonne

ALASKA
1:30 000 000

West from Greenwich

40

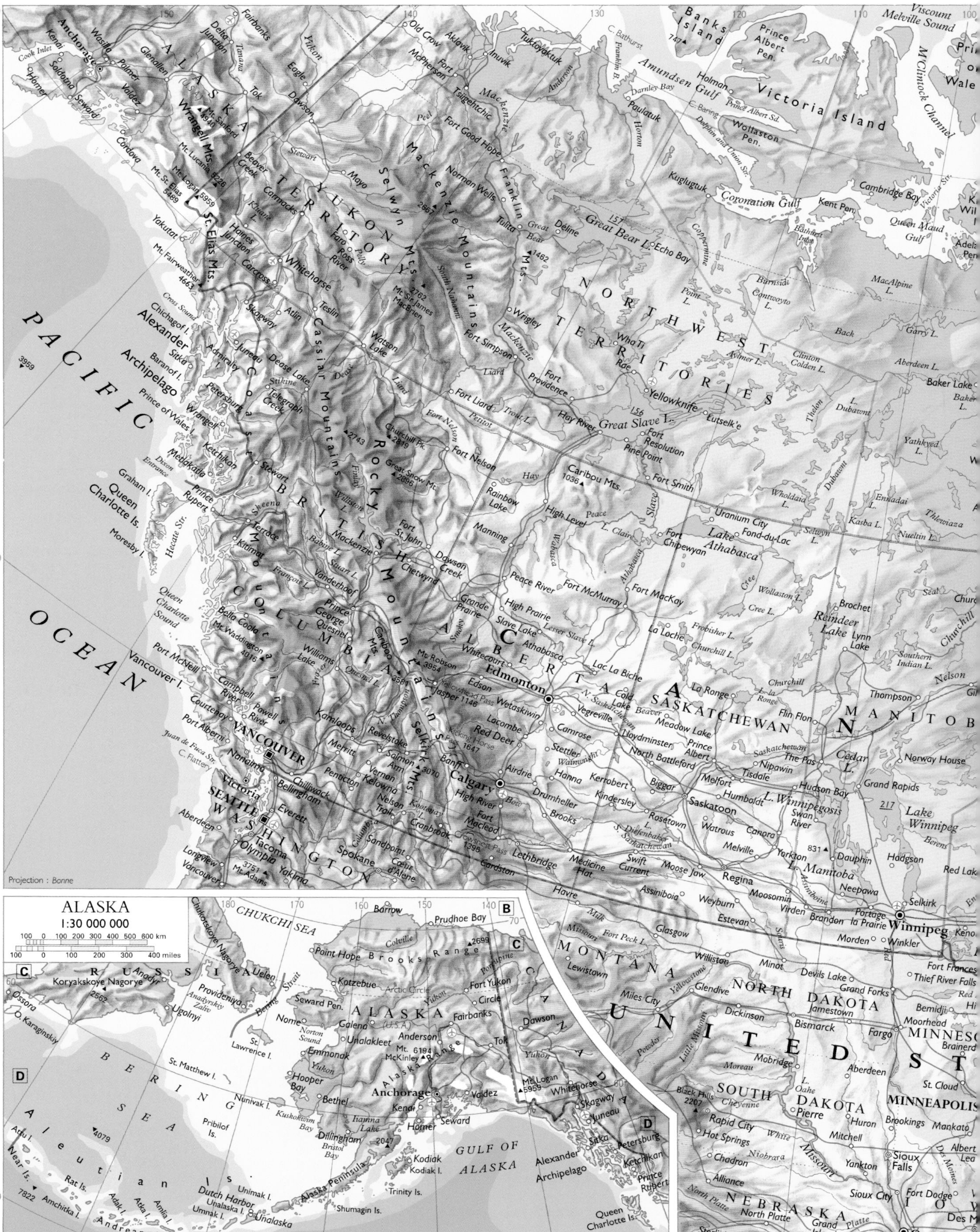

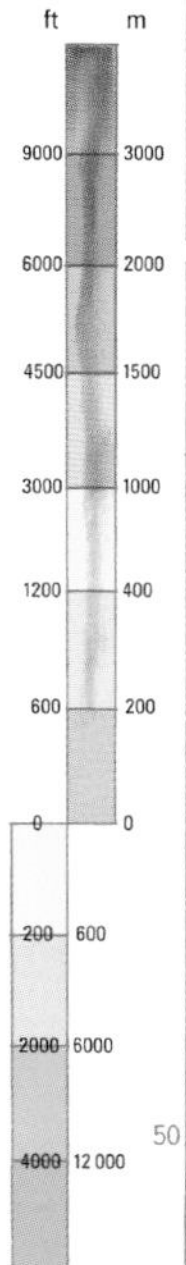

NORTHERN CANADA
Continuation northwards on same scale as main map

ARCTIC OCEAN

Baffin Bay

Greenland (Denmark)

Sverdrup Islands

Queen Elizabeth Is.

Ellesmere Island

Devon Island

Baffin Island

NUNAVUT

NORTHWEST TERRITORIES

Victoria Island

Banks Island

Labrador Sea

ATLANTIC OCEAN

Hudson Strait

Foxe Basin

James Bay

Hudson Bay

QUÉBEC

NEWFOUNDLAND & LABRADOR

Newfoundland

Gulf of St. Lawrence

NEW BRUNSWICK

NOVA SCOTIA

PR. EDWARD I.

MAINE

ONTARIO

Lake Superior

Lake Michigan

Lake Huron

TORONTO

MONTRÉAL

OTTAWA

Québec

NEW YORK

VERMONT

NEW HAMPSHIRE

MASS.

BOSTON

NEW YORK

PENNSYLVANIA

OHIO

INDIANA

DETROIT

CLEVELAND

West from Greenwich

COPYRIGHT PHILIP'S

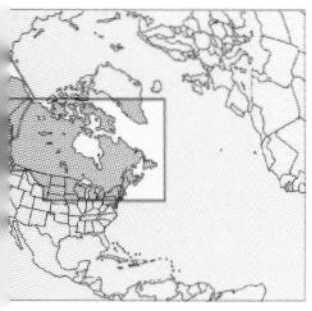

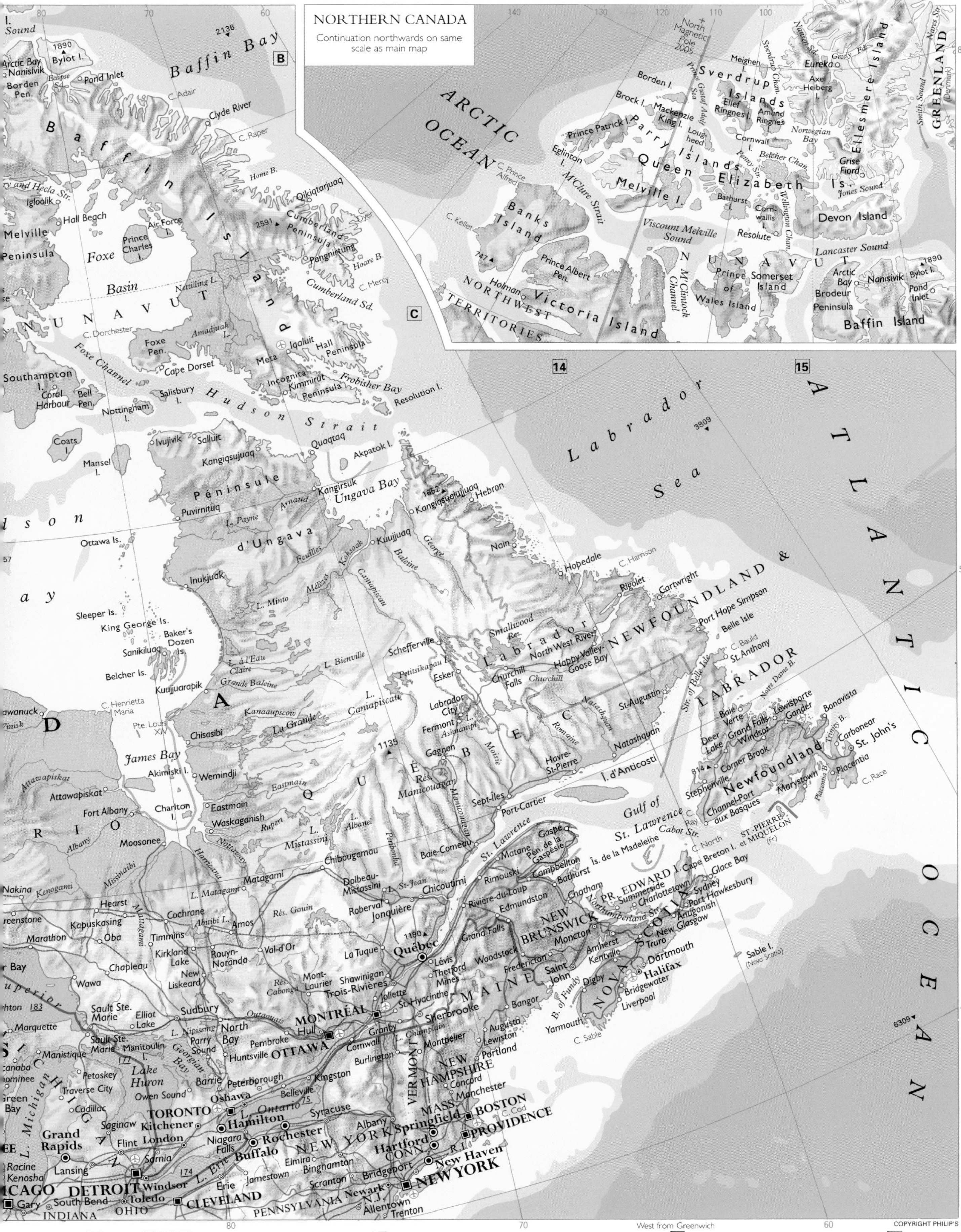

50 0 50 100 150 200 km

1:6 000 000

50 0 50 100 150 miles

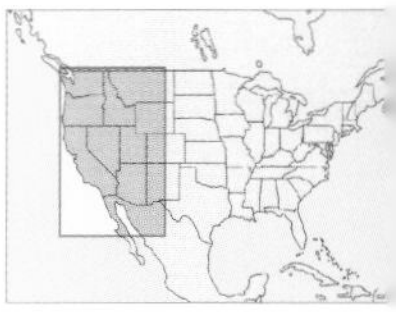

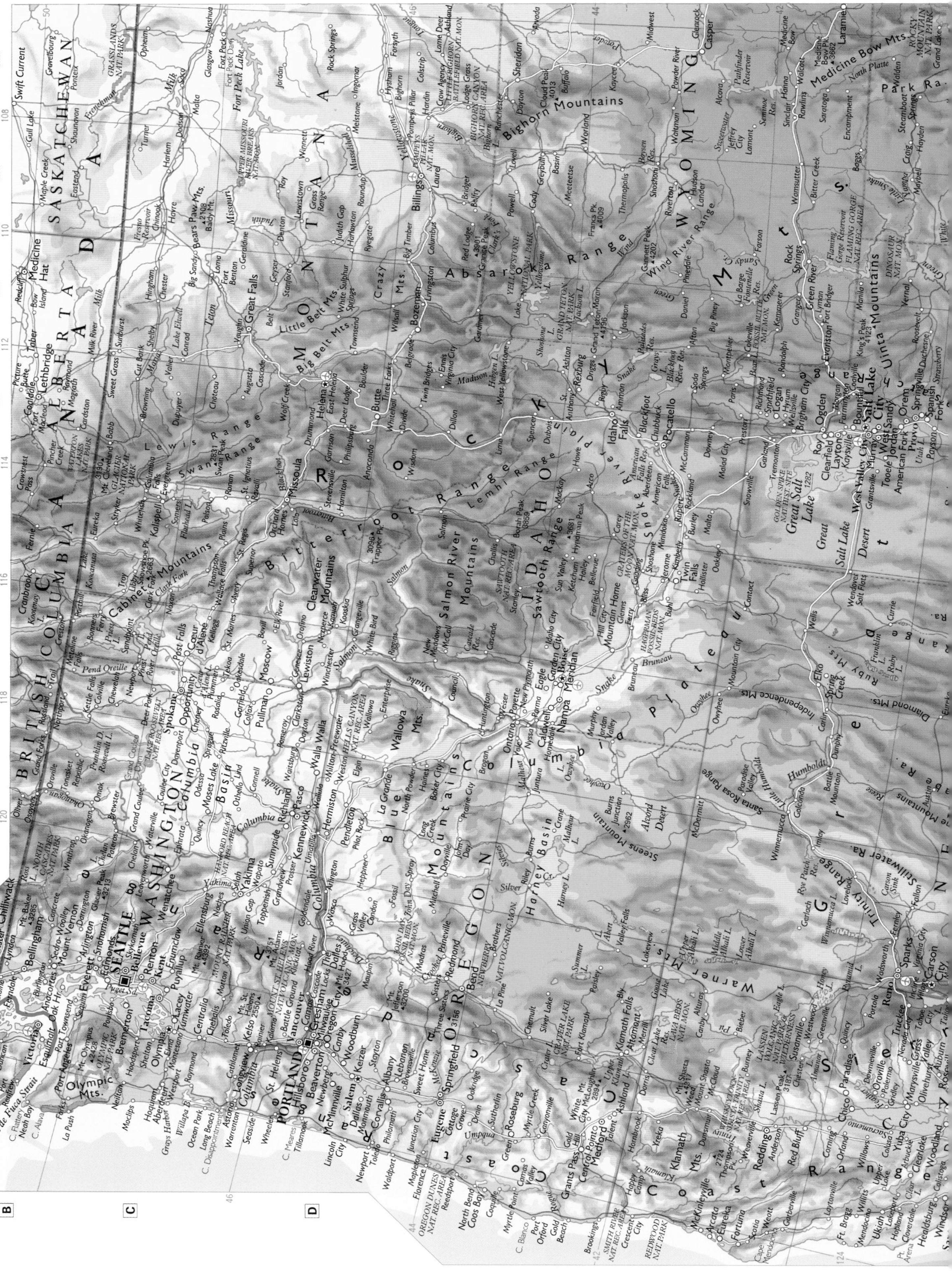

WASHINGTON
OREGON
IDAHO
MONTANA
WYOMING
BRITISH COLUMBIA
ALBERTA
SASKATCHEWAN
SEATTLE
PORTLAND
VANCOUVER
Great Salt Lake
Salt Lake City
Boise
Helena
Bighorn Mountains
Wind River Range
Salmon River Mountains
Blue Mountains
Columbia Basin

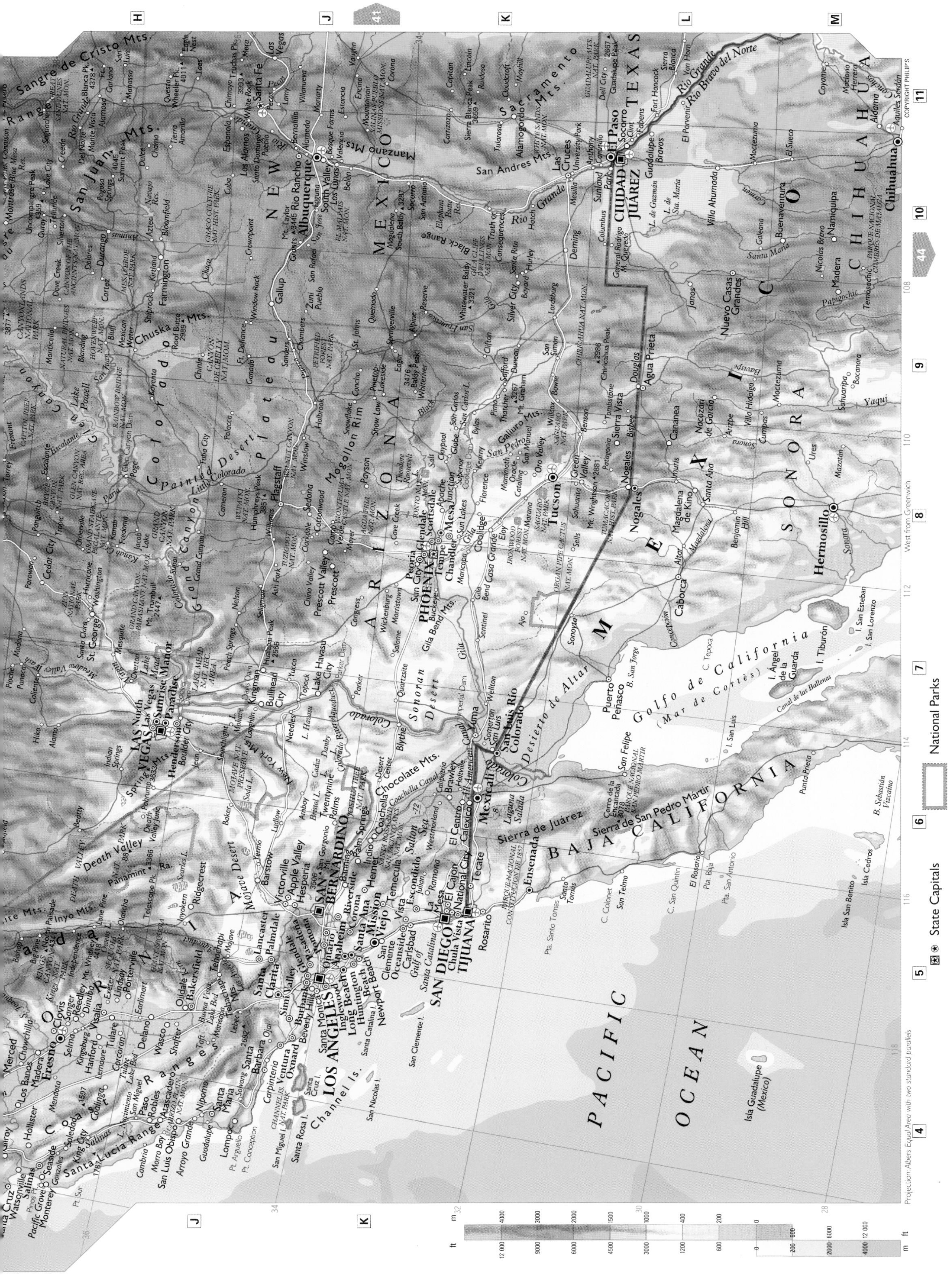

National Parks

State Capitals

Projection: Albers Equal Area with two standard parallels

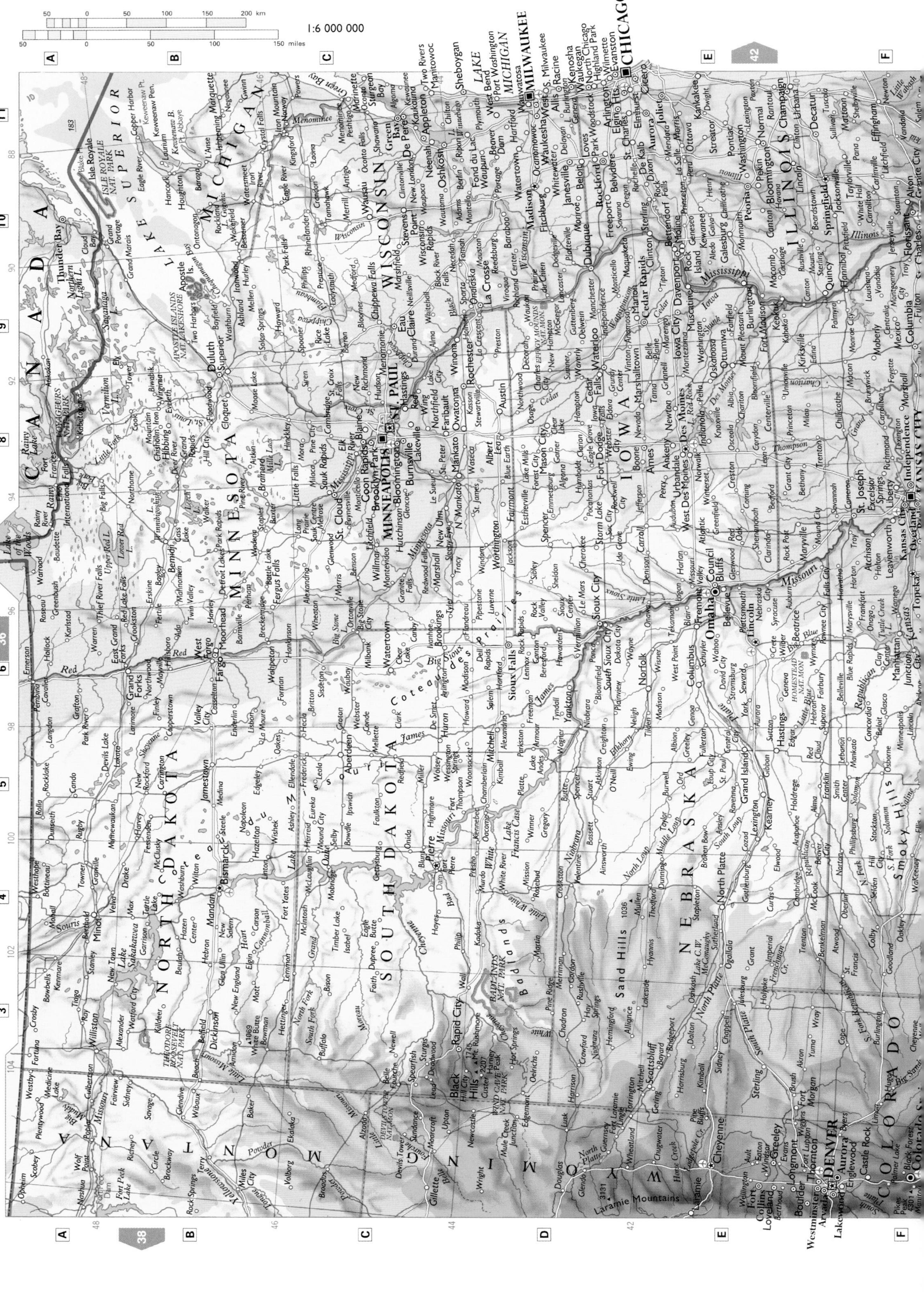
50 0 50 100 150 200 km
1:6 000 000
50 0 50 100 150 miles
CANADA
NORTH DAKOTA
SOUTH DAKOTA
NEBRASKA
MINNESOTA
IOWA
WISCONSIN
MICHIGAN
ILLINOIS
MONTANA
WYOMING
COLORADO
LAKE SUPERIOR
LAKE MICHIGAN
MILWAUKEE
CHICAGO
MINNEAPOLIS
ST. PAUL
DENVER
KANSAS CITY

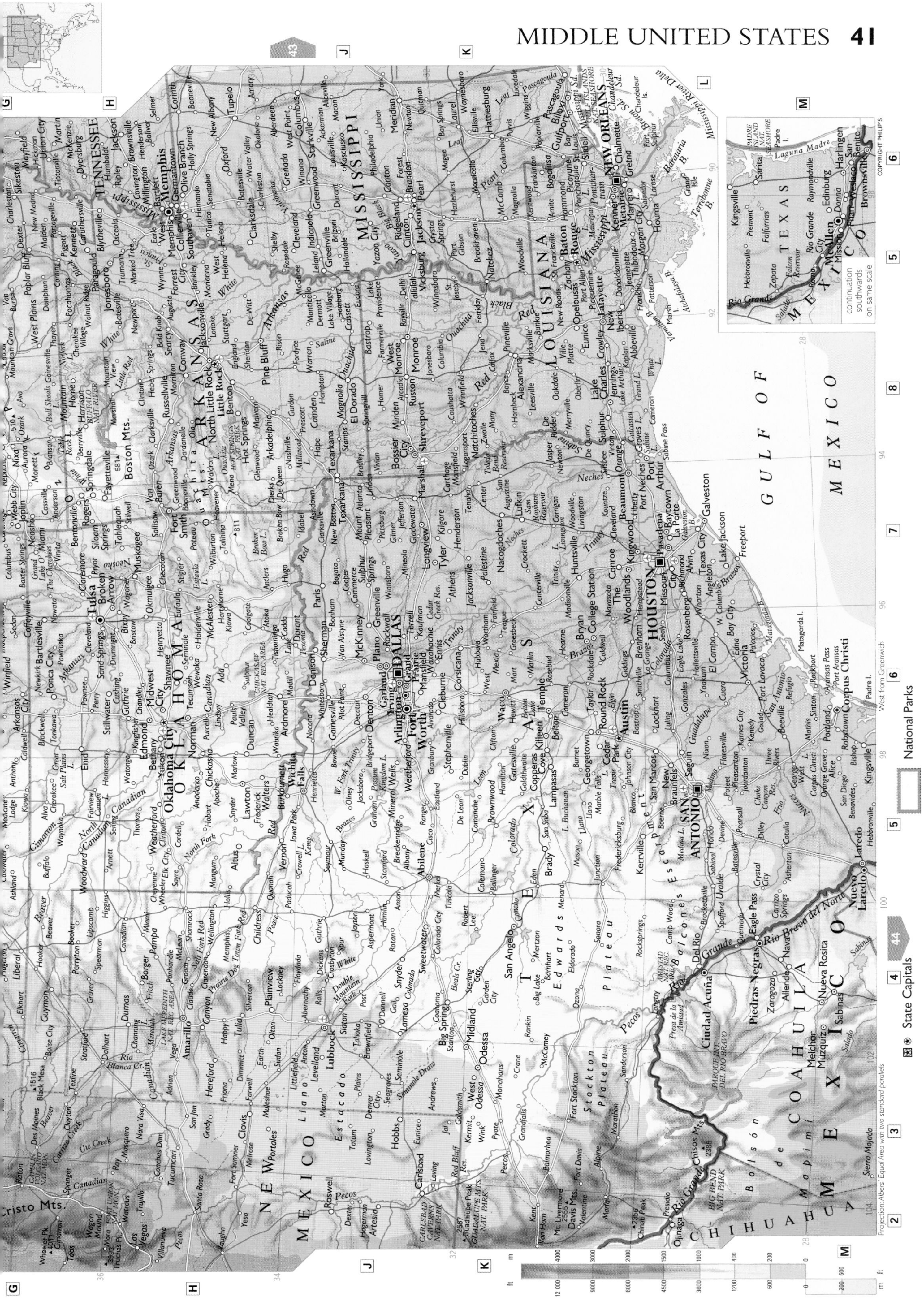

MISSISSIPPI

TENNESSEE

ARKANSAS

LOUISIANA

OKLAHOMA

TEXAS

NEW MEXICO

MEXICO

COAHUILA

CHIHUAHUA

GULF OF MEXICO

NEW ORLEANS

Memphis

Tulsa

DALLAS

Fort Worth

Arlington

Garland

HOUSTON

SAN ANTONIO

Austin

Corpus Christi

Oklahoma City

Wichita Falls

Lubbock

Amarillo

Little Rock

Baton Rouge

Nuevo Laredo

Laredo

Del Rio

Ciudad Acuña

Piedras Negras

National Parks

⊛ State Capitals

COPYRIGHT PHILIP'S

Projection: Albers Equal Area with two standard parallels

West from Greenwich

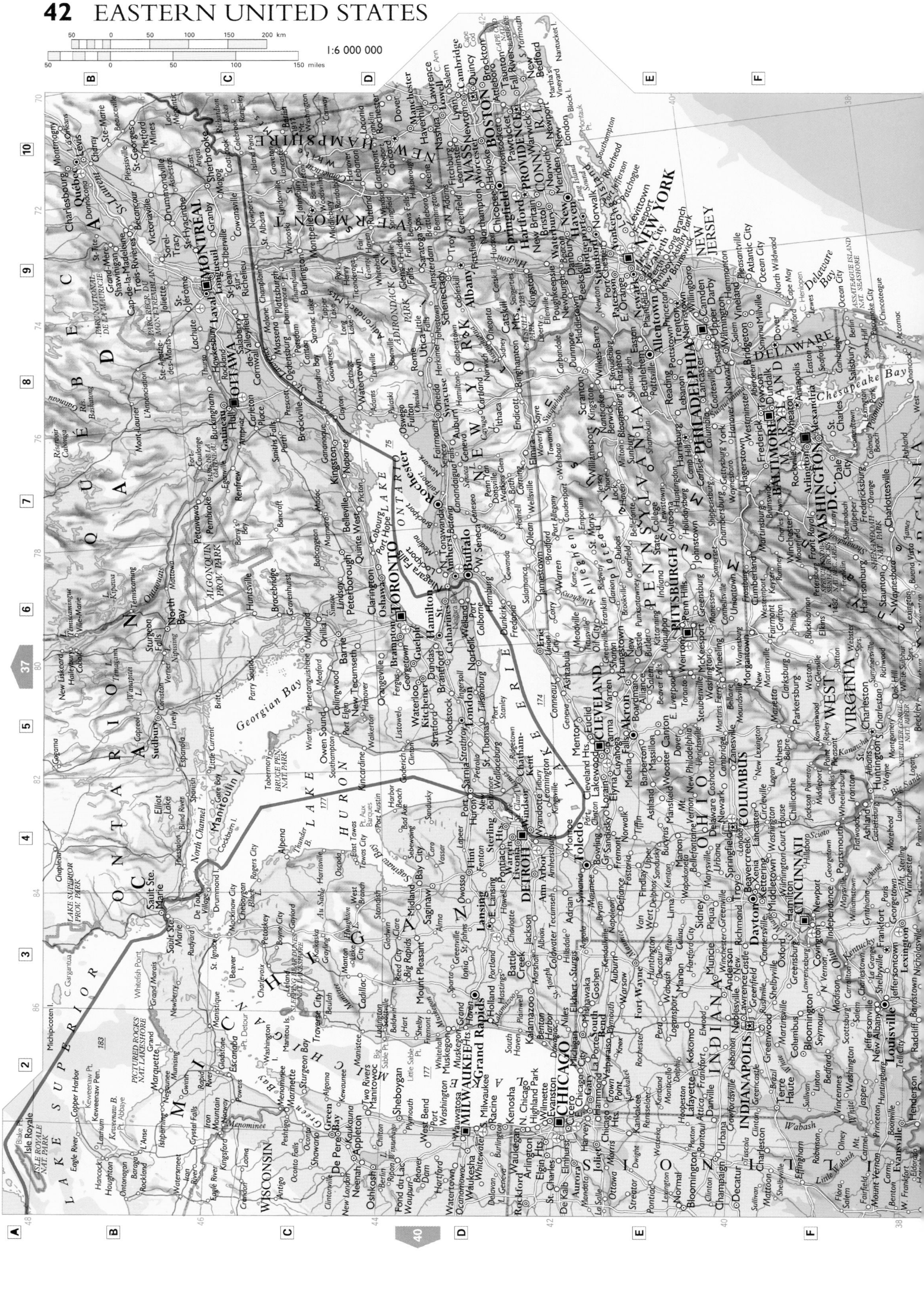

50 km 0 50 100 150 200 km

1:6 000 000

50 0 50 100 150 miles

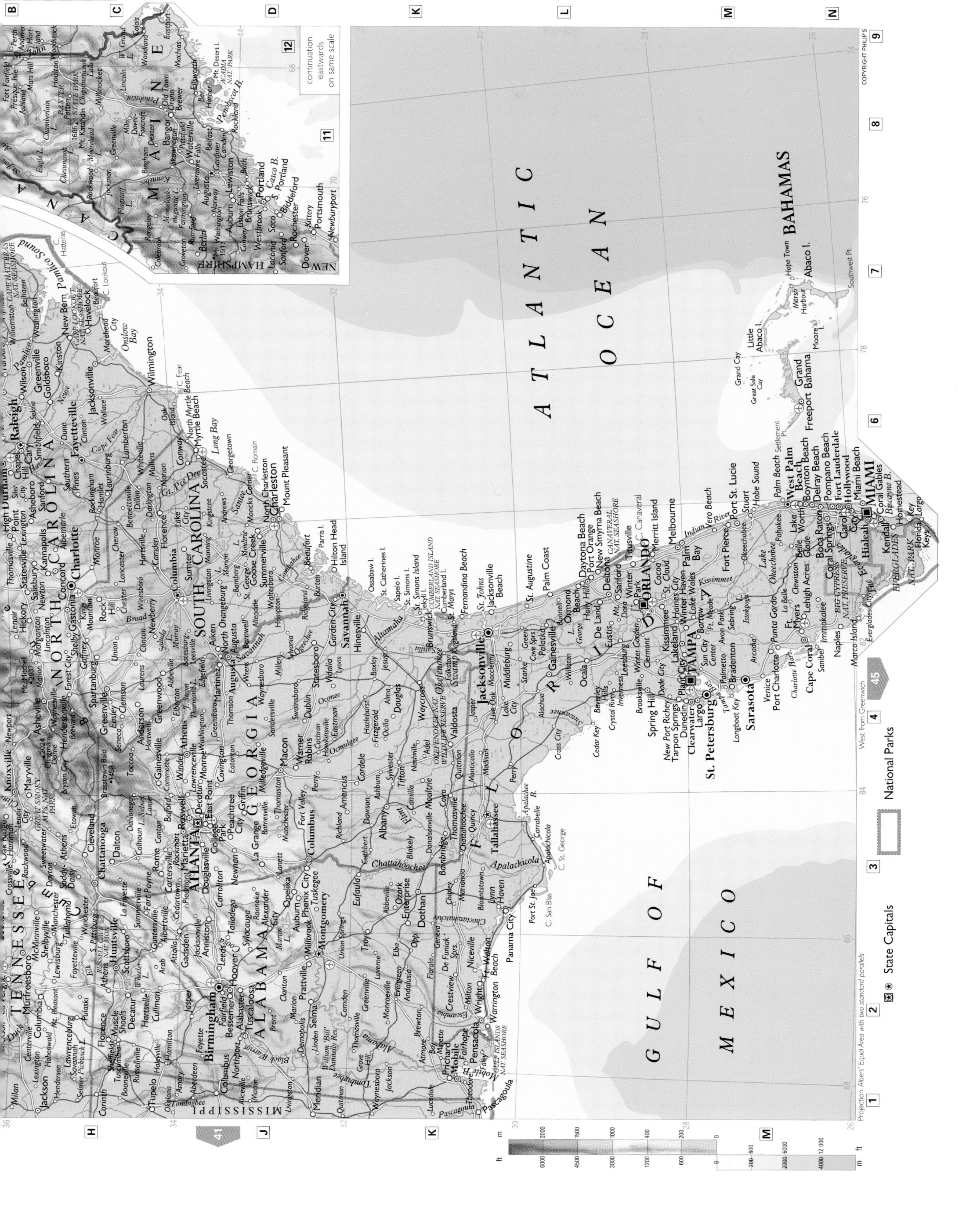
ATLANTIC OCEAN
GULF OF MEXICO
BAHAMAS
TENNESSEE
NORTH CAROLINA
SOUTH CAROLINA
GEORGIA
ALABAMA
FLORIDA
MISSISSIPPI
MAINE
NEW HAMPSHIRE
Raleigh
Charlotte
Wilmington
Columbia
Charleston
Savannah
Atlanta
Macon
Augusta
Columbus
Montgomery
Birmingham
Mobile
Pensacola
Tallahassee
Jacksonville
Orlando
Tampa
St. Petersburg
Miami
Knoxville
Chattanooga
Huntsville
Portland
Augusta
State Capitals
National Parks
Projection: Albers' Equal Area with two standard parallels
West from Greenwich
continuation eastwards on same scale
41
45
COPYRIGHT PHILIP'S

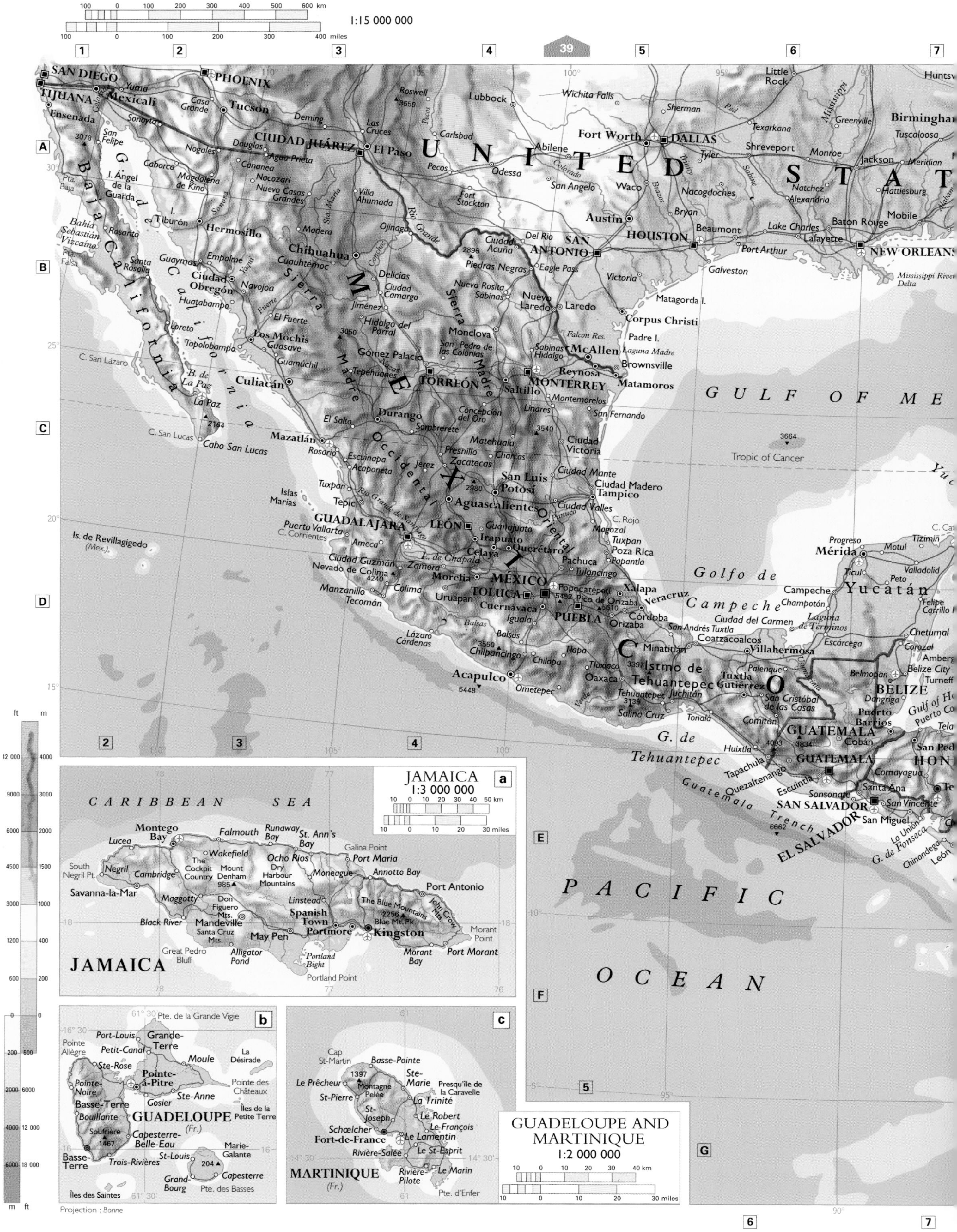

1:15 000 000

UNITED STATES

SAN DIEGO · PHOENIX · Yuma · Tucson · Roswell · Lubbock · Wichita Falls · Little Rock

TIJUANA · Mexicali · Casa Grande · Deming · Las Cruces · Carlsbad · Sherman · Red

Ensenada · Nogales · Douglas · El Paso · Odessa · San Angelo · Abilene · FORT WORTH · DALLAS · Tyler · Texarkana · Shreveport · Monroe · Greenville · Birmingham

Caborca · Agua Prieta · Cananea · Nacozari · Villa Ahumada · Fort Stockton · Pecos · Waco · Bryan · HOUSTON · Beaumont · Lake Charles · Baton Rouge · Mobile · Tuscaloosa

Hermosillo · Madera · Ciudad Camargo · Del Rio · SAN ANTONIO · Austin · Port Arthur · Lafayette · Alexandria · Jackson · Meridian · Hattiesburg

CHIHUAHUA · Cuauhtémoc · Delicias · Eagle Pass · Victoria · Galveston · NEW ORLEANS · Natchez

Ciudad Obregón · Navojoa · Jiménez · Hidalgo del Parral · Piedras Negras · Nueva Rosita · Sabinas · Nuevo Laredo · Laredo · Corpus Christi · Matagorda I. · Mississippi River Delta

Los Mochis · Guasave · Gómez Palacio · San Pedro de las Colonias · Monclova · Sabinas Hidalgo · McAllen · Reynosa · Brownsville · Padre I. · Laguna Madre · GULF OF ME

Culiacán · TORREÓN · Saltillo · MONTERREY · Matamoros · Falcon Res. · San Fernando

La Paz · El Salto · Durango · Concepción del Oro · Sombrerete · Montemorelos · Linares · Ciudad Victoria · Ciudad Mante · 3664 · Tropic of Cancer

Mazatlán · Rosario · Jerez · Zacatecas · Charcas · Matehuala · Ciudad Madero · Tampico · Yuca

Tuxpan · Escuinapa · Acaponeta · Río Grande de Santiago · Fresnillo · SAN LUIS POTOSÍ · Ciudad Valles · Ciudad Madero · Progreso · Mérida · Motul · Ca

Islas Marías · Tepic · AGUASCALIENTES · Guanajuato · Panuco · C. Rojo · Tuxpan · Mogozal · Poza Rica · Tizimín · Valladolid · Peto

GUADALAJARA · LEÓN · Irapuato · Querétaro · Pachuca · Papantla · Tulancingo · Campeche · Yucatán · Ticul · Felipe Carrillo

Puerto Vallarta · C. Corrientes · Ameca · Celaya · MÉXICO · Xalapa · Veracruz · Champotón · Laguna de Términos

Ciudad Guzmán · Zamora · L. de Chapala · Morelia · TOLUCA · Popocatépetl · Pico de Orizaba · Córdoba · Orizaba · Ciudad del Carmen · Escárcega · Chetumal

Nevado de Colima · Colima · Uruapan · Cuernavaca · Iguala · PUEBLA · San Andrés Tuxtla · Coatzacoalcos · Villahermosa · Corozal · Amber

Manzanillo · Tecomán · Balsas · Chilpancingo · Chilapa · Tlapa · Oaxaca · Minatitlán · Istmo de Tehuantepec · Palenque · Belmopan · BELIZE · Belize City · Turneff

Lázaro Cárdenas · Balsas · Tlaxiaco · Tuxtla Gutiérrez · San Cristóbal de las Casas · Comitán · Puerto Barrios · Gulf of Ho

Acapulco · Ometepec · Juchitán · Salina Cruz · Tonalá · GUATEMALA · Cobán · San Ped

G. de Tehuantepec · Huixtla · Tapachula · Quezaltenango · Escuintla · GUATEMALA · HON

Guatemala Trench · SAN SALVADOR · Santa Ana · San Vicente · Comayagua

EL SALVADOR · San Miguel · La Unión · G. de Fonseca · Chinandega · Leó

GULF OF ME

PACIFIC OCEAN

JAMAICA · a

1:3 000 000

CARIBBEAN SEA

Montego Bay · Falmouth · Runaway Bay · St. Ann's Bay · Galina Point

Lucea · Wakefield · Ocho Rios · Port Maria

Negril · Cambridge · The Cockpit Country · Mount Denham 985 · Dry Harbour Mountains · Moneague · Annotto Bay · Port Antonio

South Negril Pt. · Maggotty · Don Figuero Mts. · Linstead · The Blue Mountains · John Crow Mts.

Savanna-la-Mar · Black River · Mandeville · Santa Cruz Mts. · Spanish Town · Blue Mt. Pk. 2256 · Port Antonio

Great Pedro Bluff · May Pen · Portmore · Kingston · Morant Point

JAMAICA · Alligator Pond · Portland Bight · Morant Bay · Port Morant

Portland Point

GUADELOUPE AND MARTINIQUE

1:2 000 000

b

Pte. de la Grande Vigie

Port-Louis · Grande-Terre

Pointe Allègre · Petit-Canal · Moule · La Désirade

Ste-Rose · Pointe-à-Pitre · Gosier · Ste-Anne · Pointe des Châteaux

Pointe-Noire · Basse-Terre · Îles de la Petite Terre

Bouillante · GUADELOUPE (Fr.)

Soufrière 1467 · Capesterre-Belle-Eau · Marie-Galante

Basse-Terre · St-Louis

Trois-Rivières · Grand Bourg · 204 · Capesterre

Îles des Saintes · Pte. des Basses

c

Cap St-Martin · Basse-Pointe

Le Prêcheur · Montagne Pelée 1397 · Ste-Marie · Presqu'île de la Caravelle

St-Pierre · La Trinité

Schœlcher · St-Joseph · Le Robert · Le François

Fort-de-France · Le Lamentin · Le St-Esprit

Rivière-Salée · Le Marin

MARTINIQUE (Fr.) · Rivière Pilote

Pte. d'Enfer

Projection : Bonne

ft m · 12 000 · 4000 · 9000 · 3000 · 6000 · 2000 · 4500 · 1500 · 3000 · 1000 · 1200 · 400 · 600 · 200 · 0 · 200 · 600 · 2000 · 6000 · 4000 · 12 000 · 6000 · 18 000 · m ft

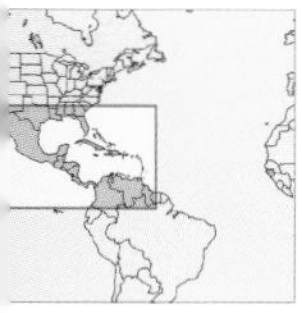

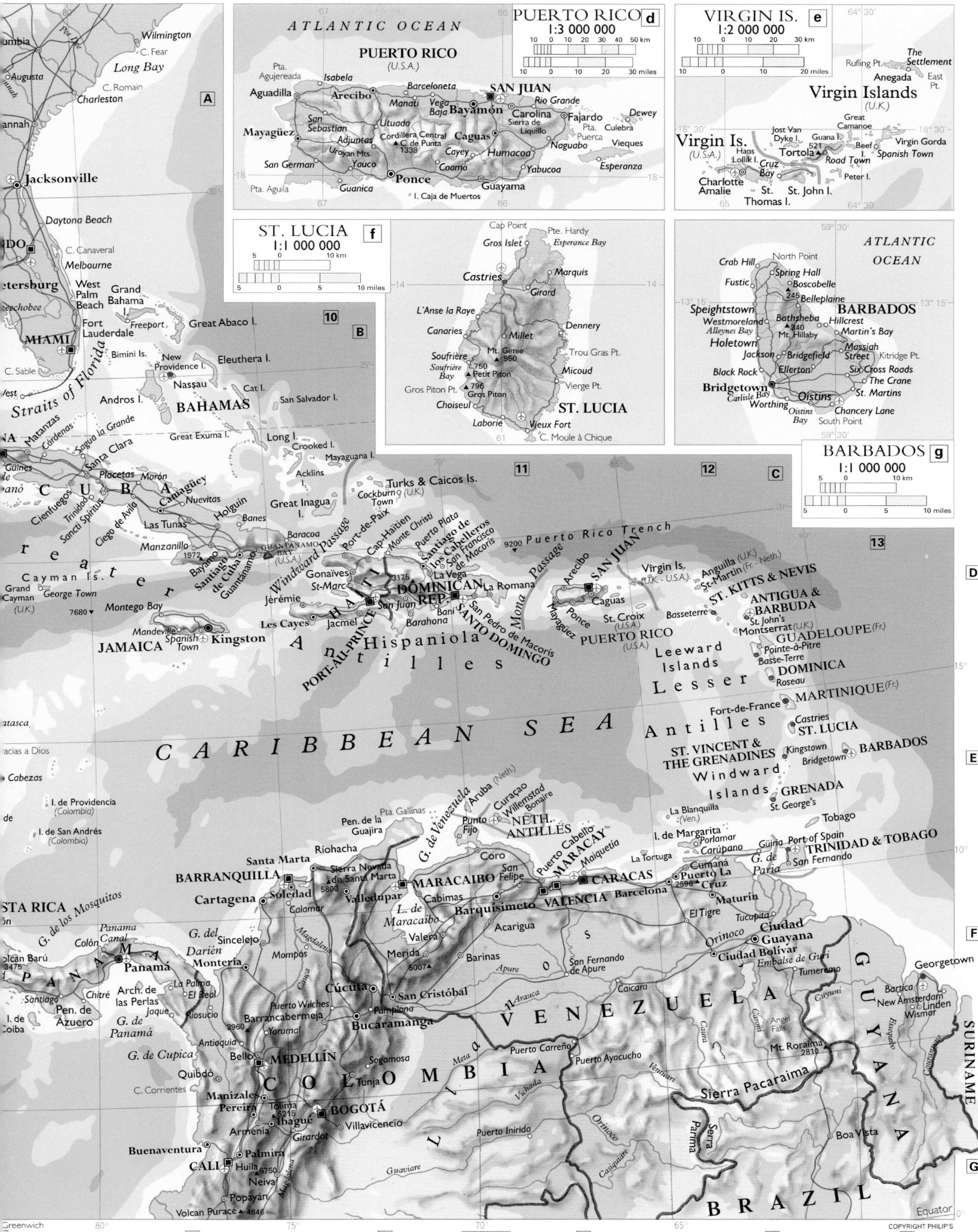

PUERTO RICO **d**
1:3 000 000

VIRGIN IS. **e**
1:2 000 000

ST. LUCIA **f**
1:1 000 000

BARBADOS **g**
1:1 000 000

PUERTO RICO
(U.S.A.)

ATLANTIC OCEAN

Pta. Agujereada · Isabela · Barceloneta
Aguadilla · Arecibo · Manati · Vega · **SAN JUAN**
Vega Baja · **Bayamón** · Carolina · Rio Grande
Mayagüez · San Sebastián · Utuado · Caguas · Sierra de Loquillo · Fajardo · Dewey
Adjuntas · Cordillera Central · Cayey · Humacao · Pta. Puerca · Culebra
San German · Uroyan Mts. · ▲ C. de Punta 1338 · Coamo · Yabucoa · Vieques
Yauco · Guanica · Ponce · Guayama · Esperanza
Pta. Aguila · I. Caja de Muertos

Virgin Islands (U.K.)
Rufling Pt. · The Settlement
Anegada · East Pt.
Virgin Is. (U.S.A.) · Jost Van Dyke I. · Guana I. · Great Camanoe
Hans Lollik I. · Cruz Bay · Tortola · Road Town · Beef I. · Virgin Gorda · Spanish Town
Charlotte Amalie · St. Thomas I. · St. John I. · Peter I.

ATLANTIC OCEAN
Cap Point
Gros Islet · Pte. Hardy · Esperance Bay
Castries · Marquis
Girard
L'Anse la Raye · Dennery
Canaries · Millet
Soufrière · Mt. Gimie 960 · Trou Gras Pt.
Soufrière Bay · ▲ 750 · Micoud
▲ Petit Piton · Vierge Pt.
Gros Piton Pt. · ▲ 796 · Gros Piton
Choiseul · **ST. LUCIA**
Laborie · Vieux Fort · C. Moule à Chique

BARBADOS
Crab Hill · North Point
Fustic · Spring Hall · Boscobelle
Speightstown · ▲ 245 · Belleplaine
Westmoreland · Bathsheba · Hillcrest
Alleynes Bay · ▲ 340 · Martin's Bay
Holetown · Mt. Hillaby
Jackson · Massiah Street · Kitridge Pt.
Black Rock · Bridgefield · Six Cross Roads
Ellerton · The Crane
Bridgetown · Oistins · St. Martins
Carlisle Bay · Worthing · Chancery Lane
Oistins Bay · South Point

ATLANTIC OCEAN

Wilmington · C. Fear · Long Bay
Augusta · C. Romain
Charleston
Jacksonville
Daytona Beach
Melbourne · C. Canaveral
West Palm Beach
Grand Bahama I. · Great Abaco I.
MIAMI · Freeport
Fort Lauderdale · Bimini Is. · New Providence I. · Eleuthera I.
C. Sable · Nassau · Cat I. · San Salvador I.
Straits of Florida · Andros I. · **BAHAMAS**
Matanzas · Sagua la Grande · Great Exuma I. · Long I.
Cárdenas · Santa Clara · Crooked I.
Güines · Placetas · Morón · Acklins · Mayaguana I.
Cienfuegos · Sancti Spíritus · Ciego de Ávila · Camagüey · **Turks & Caicos Is.**
Trinidad · Las Tunas · Cockburn Town (U.K.)
C U B A · Holguín · Banes · Great Inagua I.
Manzanillo · Nuevitas · Baracoa · Port-de-Paix · Cap-Haïtien · Monte Cristi · Puerto Plata
1972 · Bayamo · **GUANTÁNAMO** (U.S.A.) · Gonaïves · St-Marc · 3175 · **DOMINICAN**
Santiago de Cuba · Guantánamo · Windward Passage · **HAITI** · La Vega · San Cabelleros · **REP.** · La Romana
Cayman Is. · Jérémie · **PORT-AU-PRINCE** · Jacmel · San Juan · Bani · San Pedro de Macorís
Grand Cayman · George Town (U.K.) · Les Cayes · Barahona · **SANTO DOMINGO**
7680 · Montego Bay · Mandeville · Spanish Town · Kingston · **Hispaniola** · Antilles
JAMAICA · Greater · Antilles · Lesser

San Juan · Arecibo · **SAN JUAN** · Virgin Is. (U.K. - U.S.A.) · Anguilla (U.K.)
Puerto Rico Trench · 9200 · Mona Passage · St-Martin (Fr. - Neth.)
Mayagüez · Ponce · St. Croix (U.S.A.) · Basseterre · **ST. KITTS & NEVIS**
Caguas · **PUERTO RICO** (U.S.A.) · Leeward Islands · Montserrat (U.K.) · **ANTIGUA & BARBUDA** · St. John's
GUADELOUPE (Fr.)
Pointe-à-Pitre · Basse-Terre
DOMINICA · Roseau
Fort-de-France · **MARTINIQUE** (Fr.)
Castries · **ST. LUCIA**
ST. VINCENT & THE GRENADINES · Kingstown · **BARBADOS**
Windward · Bridgetown
Islands · **GRENADA** · St. George's · Tobago
La Blanquilla (Ven.)

CARIBBEAN SEA · Lesser Antilles

Gracias a Dios · I. de Providencia (Colombia)
Cabezas · I. de San Andrés (Colombia)
Pen. de la Guajira · Pta. Gallinas · Aruba (Neth.) · Curaçao · Willemstad · Bonaire
Punto Fijo · **NETH. ANTILLES**
Santa Marta · Ríohacha · I. de Margarita · Porlamar
BARRANQUILLA · Sierra Nevada de Santa Marta 5800 · Coro · Puerto Cabello · La Tortuga · Cumaná · Carúpano · Güiria · Port of Spain
Cartagena · Soledad · Valledupar · San Felipe · **MARACAY** · Maiquetía · **TRINIDAD & TOBAGO**
Calamar · Cabimas · Barquisimeto · **VALENCIA** · Barcelona · Puerto La Cruz · San Fernando
MARACAIBO · **CARACAS** · G. de Paria
L. de Maracaibo · Valera · Acarigua · Maturín
Sincelejo · Mompós · Mérida · Barinas · El Tigre
Montería · Cúcuta · 5007 · **Ciudad Guayana**
G. del Darién · San Cristóbal · Apure · San Fernando de Apure · Ciudad Bolívar · Embalse de Guri · Tumereno
Panamá Canal · Colón · **PANAMÁ** · Barrancabermeja · Yarumal · Arauca · Caicara · **G U Y A N A** · Georgetown
Volcán Barú 3475 · Santiago · Chitré · Arch. de las Perlas · La Palma · El Real · Puerto Wilches · Bucaramanga · Caroní · Bartica · New Amsterdam
Pen. de Azuero · G. de Panamá · Riosucio · Pamplona · **VENEZUELA** · Angel Falls · Linden · Wismar
I. de Coiba · Antioquia · Meta · Puerto Carreño · Mt. Roraima 2810 · **SURINAME**
Bello · Sogamoso · Puerto Ayacucho · Sierra Pacaraima · Boa Vista
Quibdó · **MEDELLÍN** · Tunja · Vichada · Ventuari · Serra Parima
C. Corrientes · Manizales · Tolima 5215 · Villavicencio · Orinoco · Casiquiare
Pereira · Ibagué · **BOGOTÁ** · Puerto Inírida
Armenia · Girardot · Guaviare
Buenaventura · Palmira · **C O L O M B I A**
CALI · Huila 5750 · Neiva
Popayán · Guaviare · **B R A Z I L** · Equator
Volcán Puracé 4646

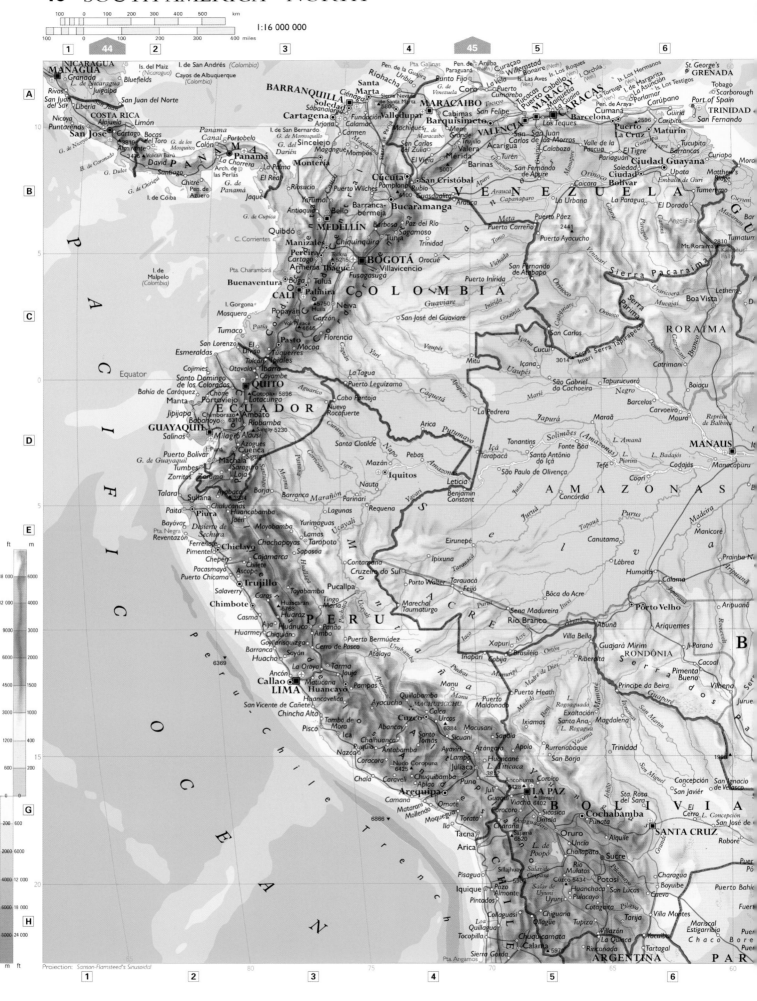

1:16 000 000

Projection: Sanson-Flamsteed's Sinusoidal

8 9 10 14 15 16

TRINIDAD AND TOBAGO
1:2 500 000

10 0 10 20 30 40 50 km
10 0 10 20 30 miles

J

North Pt.
Charlotteville
Tobago Castara 565 Little
Plymouth Main Ridge Tobago
Buccoo Reef Roxborough
Crown Pt. **Scarborough**
Rockly Bay

K

ATLANTIC

OCEAN

Blanchisseuse
La Vache Pt.
Maracas Bay Sans Souci
Chupara Pt. Matelot Toco Galera Pt.
Corozal *Northern Range* Redhead
Pt. Maraval 936 Salybia
VENEZUELA Monos 940 Mt. Aripo
Pen. de Macuro **Tunapuna** Valencia *Matura
Paria* **Port** San Arima *Bay*
Güiria **of** Juan Caroní Sangre Grande Upper Manzanilla
Spain Chaguanas Talparo Nariva *Cocos
Couva Swamp Bay* **Trinidad**
Golfo de Paria Point Lisas Guatuaro Pt.
Otaheite Bay Gasparillo **Rio Claro**
San Fernando Pierreville
Brighton La Brea Penal Mayaro Bay
Point Fortin Guapo Bay Pitch Princes Town Guayaguayare
Lake Basse Terre Galeota Pt.
Cedros Bay Palo Seco 304
Bonasse Siparia Trinity
Icacos Pt. Erin Pt. La Lune Moruga Hills
Serpent's Mouth Pta. Bombedor
VENEZUELA 62 61 West from Greenwich

L

A T L A N T I C

O C E A N

Equator

São Paulo
(Braz.)

D

E

F

G

H

(The main map area contains numerous place names in Brazil, French Guiana, and surrounding regions including:)

**FRENCH
GUIANA**
Paramaribo Nieuw Amsterdam Moengo Albina
St-Laurent Sinnamary Kourou Cayenne
Kaw C. Orange St-Georges Oiapoque
Camopi

AMAPÁ Amapá I. de Maracá
Meriruma Serra do Navio Macapá
Mazagão Afuá I. de Soure Salinópolis
I. Caviana Chaves Curuçá
I. Mexiana C. Maguarinho Vigia Bragança
I. Grande Marajó **BELÉM** Castanhal Viseu
de Gurupá Breves Curralinho Abaetetuba Turiaçu
Almeirim Pôrto de Móz Cametá Baião Cururupu
Monte Prainha Gurupá São Luís
Alegre Santarém Altamira Tucuruí
Óbidos Alcântara Barreirinhas
PARÁ Represa de Pinheiro Rosário Tutóia
Tucuruí Itapecuru- Parnaíba
Santa Inés Mirim Luís Correia
Viana Brejo Camocim
Maraba Bacabal Piracuruca Itapipoca
Carajás Acailândia Codó Piripiri **FORTALEZA**
Serra dos São João do Campo Caxias Ipu Quixadá Cascavel
Carajás Araguaia **MARANHÃO** Maior Oiticica Baturité Aracati
Conceição do Imperatriz Pedreiras Sobral Russas
Araguaia Barra Maranguape Areia Branca
Grajaú do Corda Teresina *CEARÁ* Mossoró Macau
Araguaína Pôrto Franco Colinas Crateús Ceará Mirim
Estreito Senador Pompeu **RIO GRANDE** C. de São Roque
Carolina Amarante Valença Caraúbas **DO NORTE** **Natal**
Riachão Loreto do Piauí Iguatu Currais Canguaretama
PIAUÍ Floriano Picos Cajazeiras Novos Mamanguape
Conceição do Uruçuí Oeiras Crato Souza Alagoa Cabedelo
Araguaia Juàzeiro Patos Grande
Araguacema São João do Norte **PARAÍBA** **João Pessoa**
do Piauí Ouricuri Chapada do Campina **Olinda**
Paulistana Araripe Grande **RECIFE**
Palmas São João Salgueiro Caruaru **Jaboatão**
do Piauí Pesqueira Vitória de Santo Antão
Pôrto Nacional Petrolina *PERNAMBUCO* Garanhuns
Santa Nova Palmares
Filomena Caracol Casa Palmeira
Nova Juàzeiro Garanhuns dos
TOCANTINS Remanso São Indios Arapiraca
Senhor do Francisco Propriá **Maceió**
Bonfim *ALAGOAS* Penedo
Pedro Afonso Represa de **SERGIPE** Capela
Sobradinho Xique-Xique Serrinha **Aracaju**
Jacobina Mundo São Cristóvão
Taguatinga Barreiras Queimadas Estância
BAHIA Feira de Alagoinhas
Ibotirama Santa Santo Amaro
Barra Itaberaba Cachoeira **SALVADOR**
Campos Belos Bom Jesus Castro Valença
da Lapa Alves Nazaré
Paraná Serra do Sincorá
São Domingos Santa Maria Caetité Jequié
da Vitória Contas
Barragem de Posse Carinhanha Brumado Ubaitaba
Serra da Mesa Condeúba Vitória da Itabuna
Niquelândia Conquista Ilhéus
Aruanã Uruaçu 1678 Januária Monte Azul Canavieiras
DIST. Formosa São Francisco Belmonte
FED. Taguatinga **BRASÍLIA** Janaúba Pedra Azul Pôrto Seguro
Anápolis Luziânia Montes Salinas Itamaraju
GOIÂNIA Claros Araçuaí Prado Caravelas
GOIÁS Vianópolis Paracatu Teófilo Otoni Nanuque Mucuri
Morrinhos Ibiraí Diamantina Governador
Rio Verde Itumbiara Catalão Patos de Valadares Conceição da Barra
Minas São Mateus
Ituiutaba Araguari Corinto Ipatinga Nova
MINAS GERAIS Curvelo Itabira Venécia Linhares
Uberlândia Patrocínio Ibiá Sete Lagoas Colatina
Prata Araxá Caratinga **Cariacica**
Uberaba Frutal **BELO HORIZONTE** Sabará Ponte Nova **Vitória**
Igarapava Ouro Cachoeiro de Itapemirim **Vila Velha**
São José do Prêto Divinópolis Nova Preto
Rio Prêto Franca Conselheiro Lima Campos
Andradina Conselheiro Lafaiete São
Panorama Araçatuba Penápolis Guaxupé São João Barbacena Lourenço **Campos**
Presidente Epitácio Catanduva del Rei Caldas Nova Friburgo
SÃO PAULO Lins Três Rios
Presidente Marília São Carlos Juiz de Fora **RIO DE JANEIRO**
Prudente Bauru Araraquara Poços de Volta Petrópolis
Assis Piracicaba Caldas Redonda Niterói
Jaú São Cabo Frio
Botucatu **CAMPINAS** Lourenço **RIO DE JANEIRO**

Rocas

Fernando de Noronha
(Braz.)

6059 ▾

Trindade
(Braz.)

COPYRIGHT PHILIP'S

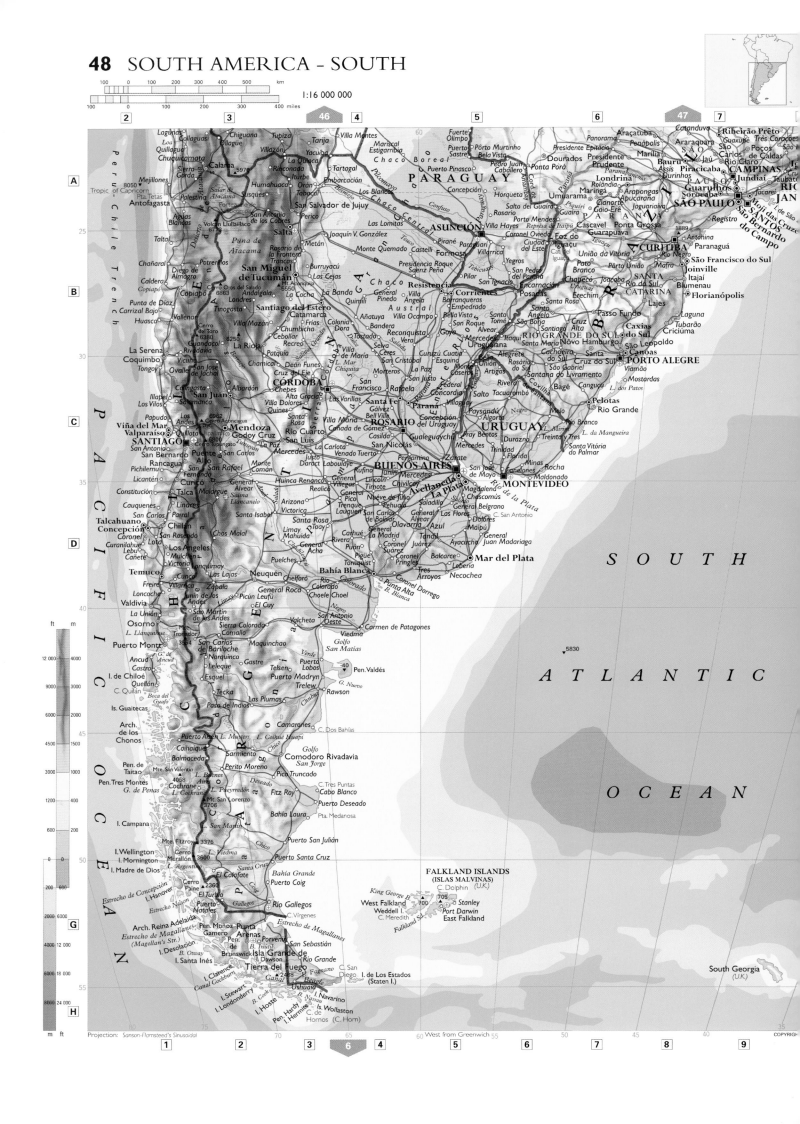

INDEX

ex contains the names of all the principal places and s shown on the maps. The alphabetical order of names sed of two or more words is governed primarily by the rd and then by the second. This is an example of the

New South Wales □ **32 B4**
New York □ **42 D8**
New Zealand ■ **33 J6**
Newark, *Del., U.S.A.* **42 F8**
Newark, *N.J., U.S.A.* **42 E8**

l features composed of a proper name (Erie) and a tion (Lake) are positioned alphabetically by the proper name. The description is positioned after the proper name and is usually abbreviated:

Erie, L. **42 D5**
Everest, Mt. **25 C7**

Where a description forms part of a settlement name or administrative name, however, it is always written in full and put in its true alphabetical position:

Lake Charles **41 K8**
Mount Isa **30 E6**

The number in bold type which follows each name in the index refers to the number of the map page where that place or feature will be found. This is usually the largest scale at which the place or feature appears.

The letter and figure which are immediately after the page number give the grid square on the map page, within which the feature is situated. The letter represents the latitude and the figure the longitude. In some cases the feature itself may fall within the specified square, while the name is outside.

Rivers are indexed to their mouths or confluences and carry the symbol → after their names. The following symbols are also used in the index: ■ country, ⧄ overseas territory or dependency, □ first order administrative area, △ national park or reserve.

13 A1
16 C3
7 F5
12 C8
12 C8
26 G7
45 B9
24 B3
19 D10
31 A16
42 B1
ance 12 A4
a.,
43 K3
.,
41 L8
C.,
43 H4
11 D2
n △ 33 J4
26 G6
9 E3
10 D6
32 A5
9 F4
32 B5
hina 21 G11
.K. 10 D6
a.,
43 J1
daho,
38 E7
d.,
42 F7
Dak.,
40 C5
Vash.,
38 C2
re □ 10 D6
9 E3
10 E5
10 E4
9 F4
8 D4
41 J4
38 E3
9 E3
24 D3
26 G5
s.,
40 F6
,
41 J5
.K. 9 F6
.S.A. 43 G5
37 E12
32 A1
10 D6
ange 38 D9
Abū
24 C4
24 C4
26 G7
33 K3
43 C11
44 C3
44 D5
46 B5
42 G8
26 G5
8 D5
23 C1
11 C1
11 C1
19 D10
41 J10
45 C10
Cerro 48 C3
os 26 A1
32 B2
46 E4
24 C4
24 C4
h 24 B3
U.S.A. 40 B6
U.S.A. 41 H6
37 B12
36 D2
Massif
27 G8
32 C4
42 D7
40 D10
38 C3
17 C5
6 E15
32 A3
28 C7
43 K4
32 B2
6 D3
n. 36 C10
6 D14
dan 24 D3
24 D3
△ 42 D8
Mts. 42 D8
=
eba 28 C7
45 d
34 H6
25 D6
12 E3
26 C6
.,
42 E3
41 H3
14 C6
24 D2
15 E11
20 B4
■ 24 B5
3 D11
38 E8
26 B4
5 E13
12 D4
25 C6
17 C6
14 F5
39 J7
44 A3
45 d
tes 44 C4
a 45 d
Pta. 45 d
29 L4
26 D7
33 F4
25 C6
r 25 D6
43 G7

Ahvāz 24 B3
Ahvenanmaa = Åland 7 E8
Aihui 21 A7
Aiken 43 J5
Ailsa Craig 10 F3
Ainsworth 40 D5
Aïr 26 E7
Air Force I. 37 C12
Airdrie, *Canada* 36 D8
Airdrie, *U.K.* 10 F5
Aire → 8 D7
Aisne → 12 B5
Aitkin 40 B8
Aitutaki 35 J12
Aix-en-Provence 12 E6
Aix-les-Bains 12 D6
Aizuwakamatsu 22 E6
Ajaccio 12 F8
Ajmer 25 C6
Ajo 39 K7
Akaroa 33 K4
Akimiski I. 37 D11
Akita 22 D7
'Akko 17 D5
Aklavik 36 C6
Akola 25 C6
Akpatok I. 37 C13
Akron, *Colo., U.S.A.* 40 E3
Akron, *Ohio, U.S.A.* 42 E5
Aksai Chin 25 B6
Aksu 20 B3
Aksum 24 D2
Akure 26 G7
Al 'Adan 24 D3
Al 'Amārah 24 B3
Al 'Aqabah 24 C2
Al 'Ayn 24 C4
Al Başrah 24 B3
Al Ḥajar al Gharbī 24 C4
Al Ḥillah 24 B3
Al Ḥudaydah 24 D3
Al Hufūf 24 C3
Al Jawf 24 C2
Al Jazirah 24 B3
Al Jubayl 24 C3
Al Khamāsīn 24 C3
Al Kūt 24 B3
Al Kuwayt 24 C3
Al Lādhiqīyah 24 B2
Al Madīnah 24 C2
Al Manāmah 24 C4
Al Mawşil 24 B3
Al Mubarraz 24 C3
Al Mukallā 24 D3
Al Mukhā 24 D3
Al Qā'im 24 B3
Al Qaţīf 24 C4
Al Qunfudhah 24 D3
Al Wajh 24 C2
Alabama □ 43 J2
Alabama → 43 K2
Alabaster 43 J2
Alachua 43 L4
Alameda 39 J10
Alamo 39 H6
Alamogordo 39 K11
Alamosa 39 H11
Åland 7 E8
Alaska □ 36 C4
Alaska, G. of 36 D5
Alaska Peninsula 36 D4
Alaska Range 36 C4
Alava, C. 38 B1
Alawoona 32 B3
Alba-Iulia 15 A10
Albacete 13 C5
Albacutya, L. 32 C3
Albanel, L. 37 D12
Albania ■ 15 D9
Albany, *Australia* 30 H2
Albany, *Ga., U.S.A.* 43 K3
Albany, *N.Y., U.S.A.* 42 D9
Albany, *Oreg., U.S.A.* 38 D2
Albany, *Tex., U.S.A.* 41 J5
Albany → 37 D11
Albemarle 43 H5
Albemarle Sd. 43 H7
Alberga → 32 A2
Albert, L., *Africa* 28 D6
Albert, L., *Australia* 32 C2
Albert Lea 40 D8
Alberta □ 36 D8
Albertville, *France* 12 D7
Albertville, *U.S.A.* 43 H2
Albi 12 E5
Albia 40 E8
Albion, *Mich., U.S.A.* 42 D3
Albion, *Nebr., U.S.A.* 40 E6
Alborz, Reshteh-ye Kūhhā-ye 24 B4
Albuquerque 39 J10
Albury 32 C4
Alcalá de Henares 13 B4
Alchevsk 17 A5
Alcova 38 E10
Aldabra Is. 5 E13
Aldan → 19 C13
Aldeburgh 9 E9
Alderney 9 H5
Aldershot 9 F7
Aledo 40 E9
Aleksandrovsk-Sakhalinskiy 19 D15
Alençon 12 B4
Alert 37 A13
Alès 12 D6
Alessándria 12 D8
Ålesund 7 E5
Aleutian Basin 34 B9
Aleutian Is. 36 D2
Aleutian Trench 34 C10
Alexander 40 B3
Alexander Arch. 36 D6
Alexander City 43 J3
Alexander I. 6 D3
Alexandra, *Australia* 32 C4
Alexandra, *N.Z.* 33 L2
Alexandria = El Iskandarîya 27 B11
Alexandria, *U.K.* 10 F4
Alexandria, *La., U.S.A.* 41 K8
Alexandria, *Minn., U.S.A.* 40 C7
Alexandria, *S. Dak., U.S.A.* 40 D6
Alexandria, *Va., U.S.A.* 42 F7
Alexandria Bay 42 C8
Alexandrina, L. 32 C2
Alford, *Aberds., U.K.* 10 D6
Alford, *Lincs., U.K.* 8 D8
Alfreton 8 D6
Algarve 13 D1
Algeciras 13 D3
Alger 26 A6
Algeria ■ 26 C6
Algiers = Alger 26 A6
Algoma 42 C2
Algona 40 D7
Alicante 13 C5
Alice 41 M5
Alice Springs 30 E5
Aliceville 43 J1
Aligarh 25 C6
Aliquippa 42 E5
Aliwal North 29 L5
Alkmaar 16 B2
All American Canal 39 K6
Allagash → 43 B11
Allahabad 25 C7
Allegheny → 42 E6
Allegheny Mts. 42 G6
Allegheny Plateau 42 E6
Allègre, Pte. 44 b
Allen, Bog of 11 C5
Allen, L. 11 B3
Allendale 43 J5
Allentown 42 E8
Alleppey 25 E6
Alleynes B. 45 g
Alliance, *Nebr., U.S.A.* 40 D3
Alliance, *Ohio, U.S.A.* 42 E5
Allier → 12 C5
Alligator Pond 44 a
Alloa 10 E5
Allora 32 A5
Alma, *Ga., U.S.A.* 43 K4
Alma, *Kans., U.S.A.* 40 F6
Alma, *Mich., U.S.A.* 42 D3
Alma, *Nebr., U.S.A.* 40 E5
Alma, *Wis., U.S.A.* 40 C9
Alma Ata = Almaty 18 E8
Almanor, L. 38 F3
Almaty 18 E8
Almelo 16 B3
Almería 13 D4
Alness 10 D4
Alnmouth 8 B6
Alnwick 8 B6
Alofi, I. 31 C15
Alor 23 D4
Alor Setar 23 C2
Alpena 42 C4
Alpine, *Ariz., U.S.A.* 39 K9
Alpine, *Tex., U.S.A.* 41 K3
Alps 12 C8
Alsace □ 12 B7
Alsask 36 D9
Alston 8 C5
Altai = Aerhtai Shan 20 B4
Altamaha → 43 K5
Altanbulag 20 A5
Altavista 42 G6
Altay 20 B3
Altiplano 46 G5
Alton, *U.K.* 9 F7
Alton, *U.S.A.* 40 F9
Altoona 42 E6
Altun Shan 20 C3
Alturas 38 F3
Altus 41 H5
Alva 41 G5
Alvarado 41 J6
Alvin 41 L7
Alvord Desert 38 E4
Alxa Zuoqi 20 C5
Alyth 10 E5
Alzada 40 C2
Amadjuak L. 37 C12
Amagasaki 22 F4
Amarillo 41 H4
Amazon = Amazonas → 47 D8
Amazonas □ 46 E6
Amazonas → 47 D8
Ambala 25 B6
Ambergris Cay 44 D7
Amberley 33 K4
Amble 8 B6
Ambleside 8 C5
Ambon 23 D4
Amboy 39 J6
Amboyna Cay 23 C3
Amchitka I. 36 D1
Ameca 44 C4
American Falls 38 E7
American Falls Res. 38 E7
American Fork 38 F8
American Highland 6 E10
American Samoa ⧄ 33 B13
Americus 43 K3
Ames 40 E8
Amherst, *Canada* 37 E13
Amherst, *U.S.A.* 42 D6
Amidon 40 B3
Amiens 12 B5
Amirante Is. 5 E13
Amistad △ 41 L4
Amite 41 K9
Amlia I. 36 D2
Amlwch 8 D3
'Ammān 24 B2
Ammanford 9 F4
Ammon 38 E8
Amory 43 J1
Amos 37 E12
Amravati 25 C6
Amritsar 25 B6
Amsterdam, *Neths.* 16 B2
Amsterdam, *U.S.A.* 42 D8
Amudarya → 18 E6
Amund Ringnes I. 37 A12
Amundsen Gulf 36 B7
Amundsen Sea 6 E1
Amuntai 23 D3
Amur → 19 D15
An Nafūd 24 C3
An Najaf 24 B3
An Nāşirīyah 24 B3
An Uaimh 11 C5
Anaconda 38 C7
Anacortes 38 B2
Anadarko 41 H5
Anadolu 17 C4
Anadyr 19 C18
Anadyrskiy Zaliv 19 C19
Anaheim 39 K5
Anambas, Kepulauan 23 C2
Anamosa 40 D9
Anápolis 47 G9
Anār 24 B4
Anatolia = Anadolu 17 C4
Anchorage 36 C5
Ancohuma, Nevado 46 G5
Ancona 14 C5
Anda 21 B7
Andalucía □ 13 D3
Andalusia 43 K2
Andaman Is. 25 D8
Andaman Sea 25 D8
Andamooka 32 B2
Anderson, *Alaska, U.S.A.* 36 C5
Anderson, *Calif., U.S.A.* 38 F2
Anderson, *Ind., U.S.A.* 42 E3
Anderson, *Mo., U.S.A.* 41 G7
Anderson, *S.C., U.S.A.* 43 H4
Anderson → 36 C7
Andes, Cord. de los 46 H5
Andhra Pradesh □ 25 D6
Andijon 18 E8
Andorra ■ 12 E4
Andover 9 F6
Andreanof Is. 36 D2
Andrews, *S.C., U.S.A.* 43 J6
Andrews, *Tex., U.S.A.* 41 J3
Ándria 14 D7
Andros I. 45 C9
Anegada 45 e
Aneityum 31 E12
Angara → 19 D10
Angarsk 19 D11
Angaston 32 B2
Ånge 7 E7
Angel Falls 46 B6
Angeles 23 B4
Angels Camp 39 G3
Ångermanälven → 7 E7
Angers 12 C3
Anglesey, Isle of □ 8 D3
Angleton 41 L7
Angola 42 E3
Angola ■ 29 G3
Angoulême 12 D4
Angoumois 12 D3
Angren 18 E8
Anguilla ⧄ 45 D12
Angus □ 10 E6
Anhui □ 21 C6
Animas → 39 H9
Anjou 12 C3
Ankaboa, Tanjona 29 J8
Ankang 21 C5
Ankara 17 C4
Ankeny 40 E8
Ann, C. 42 D10
Ann Arbor 42 D4
Anna 41 G10
Annaba 26 A7
Annalee → 11 B4
Annan 10 G5
Annan → 10 G5
Annapolis 42 F7
Annapurna 25 C7
Annecy 12 D7
Anning 20 D5
Anniston 43 J3
Annotto B. 44 a
Anqing 21 C6
Anse la Raye 45 f
Anshan 21 B7
Anshun 20 D5
Ansley 40 E5
Anson 41 J5
Anstruther 10 E6
Antalya = Hatay 17 C4
Antananarivo 29 H9
Antarctic Pen. 6 D4
Antarctica 6 F7
Antero, Mt. 39 G10
Anthony, *Kans., U.S.A.* 41 G5
Anthony, *N. Mex., U.S.A.* 39 K10
Anti Atlas 26 C4
Antibes 12 E7
Anticosti, Î. d' 37 E13
Antigo 40 C10
Antigonish 37 E13
Antigua & Barbuda ■ 45 D12
Antipodes Is. 34 M9
Antlers 41 H7
Antofagasta 48 A2
Anton 41 J3
Antrim 11 B5
Antrim □ 11 B5
Antrim, Mts. of 11 A5
Antsiranana 29 G9
Antwerpen 16 C2
Anxi 20 B4
Anxious B. 32 B1
Anyang 21 C6
Anzhero-Sudzhensk 18 D9
Aomori 22 C7
Aoraki Mount Cook 33 K3
Apache 41 H5
Apache Junction 39 K8
Apalachee B. 43 L4
Apalachicola 43 L3
Apalachicola → 43 L3
Apeldoorn 16 B2
Apia 33 A13
Apostle Is. 40 B9
Apostle Islands △ 40 B9
Appalachian Mts. 42 G6
Appennini 14 B4
Appleby-in-Westmorland 8 C5
Appledore 9 F3
Appleton 42 C1
Aqtöbe 18 D6
Ar Ramādī 24 B3
Ar Riyāḍ 24 C3
Ara 25 C7
Arab 43 H2
Arab, Shatt al → 24 C3
Arabia 3 C13
Arabian Gulf = Persian Gulf 24 C4
Arabian Sea 24 D5
Aracaju 47 F11
Araçatuba 47 H8
Arad 15 A9
Arafura Sea 23 D5
Aragón □ 13 B5
Araguaia → 47 E9
Arak, *Algeria* 26 C6
Arāk, *Iran* 24 B3
Arakan Yoma 25 D8
Aral 18 E7
Aral Sea 18 E7
Aran I. 11 A3
Aran Is. 11 C2
Aransas Pass 41 M6
Arapahoe 40 E5
Arapiraca 47 E11
Ar'ar 24 B3
Araraquara 47 H9
Ararat 32 C3
Ararat, Mt. = Ağrı Dağı 17 C6
Arbīl 24 B3
Arbroath 10 E6
Arbuckle 38 G2
Arcachon 12 D3
Arcadia, *Fla., U.S.A.* 43 M5
Arcadia, *La., U.S.A.* 41 J8
Arcata 38 F1
Arches △ 39 G9
Arckaringa Cr. → 32 A2
Arco 38 E7
Arctic Bay 37 B11
Arctic Ocean 6 B17
Ardabīl 24 B3
Ardara 11 B3
Ardee 11 C5
Ardenne 16 D2
Arderin 11 C4
Ardfert 11 D2
Ardglass 11 B6
Ardivachar Pt. 10 D1
Ardlethan 32 B4
Ardmore 41 H6
Ardnamurchan, Pt. of 10 E2
Ardnave Pt. 10 F2
Ardrossan, *Australia* 32 B2
Ardrossan, *U.K.* 10 F4
Ards Pen. 11 B6
Arecibo 45 d
Arena, Pt. 38 G2
Arendal 7 F5
Arequipa 46 G4
Argentan 12 B3
Argentina ■ 48 D3
Arguello, Pt. 39 J3
Argyle, L. 30 D4
Argyll △ 10 E4
Argyll & Bute □ 10 E3
Århus 7 F6
Arica 46 G4
Arima 47 K15
Arinos → 46 F7
Aripuanã → 46 E6
Arisaig 10 E3
Arizona □ 39 J8
Arkadelphia 41 H8
Arkaig, L. 10 E3
Arkansas □ 41 H8
Arkansas → 41 J9
Arkansas City 41 G6
Arkaroola 32 B2
Arkhangelsk 18 C5
Arklow 11 D5
Arles 12 E6
Arlington, *Oreg., U.S.A.* 38 D3
Arlington, *S. Dak., U.S.A.* 40 C6
Arlington, *Tex., U.S.A.* 41 J6
Arlington, *Va., U.S.A.* 42 F7
Arlington, *Wash., U.S.A.* 38 B2
Arlington Heights 42 D2
Arlon 16 D2
Armagh 11 B5
Armagh □ 11 B5
Armavir 17 A6
Armenia 46 C3
Armidale 32 B5
Armour 40 D5
Arnaud → 37 D13
Arnett 41 G5
Arnhem 16 C2
Arnhem, C. 30 C6
Arnhem Land 30 C5
Arno Bay 32 B2
Arnold 8 D6
Arorae 31 A14
Arran 10 F3
Arras 12 A5
Arrow, L. 11 B3
Arrowtown 33 L2
Arroyo Grande 39 J3
Artesia 41 J2
Arthur → 32 D3
Arthur's Pass 33 K3
Arthur's Pass △ 33 K3
Artois 12 A5
Aru, Kepulauan 23 D5
Aruba ⧄ 45 E11
Arun → 9 G7
Arunachal Pradesh □ 25 C8
Arusha 28 E7
Arvada, *Colo., U.S.A.* 40 F2
Arvada, *Wyo., U.S.A.* 38 D10
Arviat 36 C10
Arxan 21 B6
As Sulaymānīyah, *Iraq* 24 B3
As Sulaymānīyah, *Si. Arabia* 24 C3
As Sulayyil 24 C3
As Suwayq 24 C4
Asahigawa 22 B8
Asansol 25 C7
Asbury Park 42 E8
Ascension I. 4 E9
Aseb 24 D3
Ash Fork 39 J7
Ash Grove 41 G8
Ash Shāriqah 24 C4
Ash Shurayf 24 C2
Ashbourne 8 D6
Ashburn 43 K4
Ashburton 33 K3
Ashdown 41 J7
Asheboro 43 H6
Asherton 41 L5
Asheville 43 H4
Ashford, *Australia* 32 A5
Ashford, *U.K.* 9 F8
Ashgabat 18 F6
Ashington 8 B6
Ashland, *Kans., U.S.A.* 41 G5
Ashland, *Ky., U.S.A.* 42 F4
Ashland, *Maine, U.S.A.* 43 B11
Ashland, *Mont., U.S.A.* 38 D10
Ashland, *Ohio, U.S.A.* 42 E4
Ashland, *Oreg., U.S.A.* 38 E2
Ashland, *Va., U.S.A.* 42 G7
Ashland, *Wis., U.S.A.* 40 B9
Ashley 40 B5
Ashtabula 42 E5
Ashton 38 D8
Ashuanipi, L. 37 D13
Asia 3 B14
'Asīr 24 D3
Asir, Ras 24 D4
Asmera 24 D2
Aspatria 8 C4
Aspen 39 G10
Aspermont 41 J4
Aspiring, Mt. 33 L2
Assam □ 25 C8
Assateague Island △ 42 F8
Assen 16 B3
Assiniboia 36 E9
Assiniboine → 36 E10
Assisi 14 C5
Assynt, L. 10 C3
Astana 18 D8
Asti 12 D8
Astoria 38 C2
Astrakhan 17 A7
Asturias □ 13 A3
Asunción 48 B5
Aswân 27 D12
Asyût 27 C12
Aţ Tā'if 24 C3
Atacama, Desierto de 48 A3
Atafu 31 B16
Atascadero 39 J3
'Atbara 27 E12
'Atbara, Nahr → 27 E12
Atchafalaya B. 41 L9
Atchison 40 F7
Athabasca 36 D8
Athabasca → 36 D8
Athabasca, L. 36 D9
Athboy 11 C5
Athenry 11 C3
Athens = Athina 15 F10
Athens, *Ala., U.S.A.* 43 H2
Athens, *Ga., U.S.A.* 43 J4
Athens, *Ohio, U.S.A.* 42 F4
Athens, *Tenn., U.S.A.* 43 H3
Athens, *Tex., U.S.A.* 41 J7
Athina 15 F10
Athlone 11 C4
Atholl, Forest of 10 E5
Athy 11 C5
Atiu 35 J12
Atka I. 36 D2
Atkinson 40 D5
Atlanta, *Ga., U.S.A.* 43 J3
Atlanta, *Tex., U.S.A.* 41 J7
Atlantic 40 E7
Atlantic City 42 F8
Atlantic Ocean 2 D8
Atlas Mts. = Haut Atlas 26 B4
Atlin 36 D6
Atmore 43 K2
Atoka 41 H6
Attalla 43 H2
Attawapiskat 37 D11
Attawapiskat → 37 D11
Attica 42 E2
Attleboro 42 E10
Attu I. 36 D1
Atwater 39 H3
Atwood 40 F4
Atyraū 18 E6
Au Sable → 42 C4
Aube → 12 B5
Auburn, *Ala., U.S.A.* 43 J3
Auburn, *Calif., U.S.A.* 38 G3
Auburn, *Ind., U.S.A.* 42 E3
Auburn, *Maine, U.S.A.* 43 C10
Auburn, *N.Y., U.S.A.* 42 D7
Auburn, *Nebr., U.S.A.* 40 E7
Auburn Ra. 32 A5
Auburndale 43 L5
Aubusson 12 D5
Auch 12 E4
Auchterarder 10 E5
Auchtermuchty 10 E5
Auckland 33 G5
Auckland Is. 34 N8
Aude → 12 E5
Audubon 40 E7
Augathella 32 A4
Aughnacloy 11 B5
Aughrim 11 C3
Augrabies Falls 29 K4
Augsburg 16 D5
Augusta, *Australia* 30 G2
Augusta, *Ark., U.S.A.* 41 H9
Augusta, *Ga., U.S.A.* 43 J5
Augusta, *Kans., U.S.A.* 41 G6
Augusta, *Maine, U.S.A.* 43 C11
Augusta, *Mont., U.S.A.* 38 C7
Ault 40 E2
Aunis 12 C3
Aurangabad 25 C7
Aurillac 12 D5
Aurora, *Colo., U.S.A.* 40 F2
Aurora, *Ill., U.S.A.* 42 E1
Aurora, *Mo., U.S.A.* 41 G8
Aurora, *Nebr., U.S.A.* 40 E6
Austin, *Minn., U.S.A.* 40 D8
Austin, *Nev., U.S.A.* 38 G5
Austin, *Tex., U.S.A.* 41 K6
Austral Seamount Chain 35 K13
Australia ■ 30 E3
Australian Capital Territory □ 32 C4
Austria ■ 16 E7
Autun 12 C6
Auvergne □ 12 D5
Auxerre 12 C5
Ava 41 G8
Avallon 12 C5
Avellino 14 D6
Avery 38 C6
Aviemore 10 D5
Avignon 12 E6
Ávila 13 B3
Avoca →, *Australia* 32 C3
Avoca →, *Ireland* 11 D5
Avon →, *Bristol, U.K.* 9 F5
Avon →, *Dorset, U.K.* 9 G6
Avon →, *Warks., U.K.* 9 E5
Avon Park 43 M5
Avonmouth 9 F5
Avranches 12 B3
Awash 24 E3
Awatere → 33 J5
Awe, L. 10 E3
Axe → 9 F5
Axel Heiberg I. 37 B11
Axios → 15 D10
Axminster 9 G4
Ayers Rock = Uluru 30 F5
Aylesbury 9 F7
Aylmer, L. 36 C9
Ayr 10 F4
Ayr → 10 F4
Ayre, Pt. of 8 C3
Az Ẓahrān 24 C4
Azores = Açores, Is. dos 26 A1
Azov, Sea of 17 A5
Aztec 39 H10
Azuero, Pen. de 46 B2

B

Bab el Mandeb 24 D3
Babb 38 B7
Babine L. 36 D7
Bābol 24 B4
Babruysk 18 D3
Babuyan Chan. 23 B4
Babuyan Is. 23 B4
Bac Lieu 23 C2
Bacabal 47 D10
Bacău 17 A3
Back → 36 C9
Bacolod 23 B4
Bad → 40 C4
Bad Axe 42 D4
Badajoz 13 C2
Badalona 13 B7
Baden-Württemberg □ 16 D4
Badin 24 C5
Badlands 40 D3
Badlands △ 40 D3
Badu I. 30 C7
Baffin B. 37 B13
Baffin I. 37 C12
Baggs 38 F10
Baghdād 24 B3
Baghlān 25 B5
Bagley 40 B7
Baguio 23 B4
Bahamas ■ 45 C10
Bahawalpur 25 C6
Bahía = Salvador 47 F11
Bahía □ 47 F10
Bahía Blanca 48 D4
Bahrain ■ 24 C4
Baia Mare 17 A2
Baidoa 24 E3
Baie-Comeau 37 E13
Baie Verte 37 E14
Baikal, L. = Baykal, Oz. 19 D11
Bainbridge 43 K3
Baing 23 E4
Bairnsdale 32 C4
Baiyin 20 C5
Baja, Pta. 44 B1
Baja California 44 A1
Bajimba, Mt. 32 A5
Baker, *Calif., U.S.A.* 39 J5
Baker, *Mont., U.S.A.* 40 B2
Baker, L. 36 C10
Baker, Mt. 38 B3
Baker City 38 D5
Baker I. 31 A15
Baker Lake 36 C10
Bakers Dozen Is. 37 D12
Bakersfield 39 J4
Bākhtarān = Kermānshāh 24 B3
Bakı 17 B7
Bakony 16 E8
Baku = Bakı 17 B7
Bala 8 E4
Bala, L. 8 E4
Balabac I. 23 C3
Balabac Str. 23 C3
Balakovo 18 D5
Balaton 16 E8
Balbi, Mt. 31 B10
Balbriggan 11 C5
Balclutha 33 M2
Balcones Escarpment 41 L5
Bald Knob 41 H9
Baldwin 42 D3
Baldy Peak 39 K9
Baleares, Is. 13 C7
Baleshare 10 D1
Bali 23 D3
Balikeşir 15 E12
Balikpapan 23 D3
Balkan Mts. = Stara Planina 15 C10
Ballachulish 10 E3
Ballaghaderreen 11 C3
Ballarat 32 C3
Ballater 10 D5
Ballenas, B. de 44 B2
Ballina, *Australia* 32 A5
Ballina, *Ireland* 11 B2
Ballinasloe 11 C3
Ballinger 41 K5
Ballinrobe 11 C2
Ballinskelligs B. 11 E1
Ballyboghil 11 C5
Ballybunion 11 D2
Ballycanew 11 D5
Ballycastle 11 A5
Ballyclare 11 B5
Ballydehob 11 E2
Ballygawley 11 B4
Ballyhaunis 11 C3
Ballyheige 11 D2
Ballymena 11 B5
Ballymoney 11 A5
Ballymote 11 B3
Ballynahinch 11 B6
Ballyquintin Pt. 11 B6
Ballyshannon 11 B3
Balmoral 32 C3
Balmorhea 41 K3
Balonne → 32 A4
Balqash 18 E8
Balqash Köl 18 E8
Balranald 32 B3
Balsas → 44 D4
Bălţi 17 A3
Baltic Sea 7 F7
Baltimore, *Ireland* 11 E2
Baltimore, *U.S.A.* 42 F7
Baltinglass 11 D5
Baluchistan □ 24 C5
Bam 24 C4
Bamako 26 F4
Bamberg, *Germany* 16 D5
Bamberg, *U.S.A.* 43 J5
Bamburgh 8 B6
Bamenda 28 C2
Banaba 34 H8
Banbridge 11 B5
Banbury 9 E6
Banchory 10 D6
Banda, Kepulauan 23 D4
Banda Aceh 23 C1
Banda Banda, Mt. 32 B5
Banda Sea 23 D5
Bandar-e Abbās 24 C4
Bandar-e Emām Khomeynı 24 B3
Bandar Seri Begawan 23 C3
Bandon 11 E3
Bandon → 11 E3
Bandundu 28 E3
Bandung 23 D2
Banes 45 C9
Banff, *Canada* 36 D8
Banff, *U.K.* 10 D6
Bangalore 25 D6
Banggai, Kepulauan 23 D4
Banggi, Pulau 23 C3
Banghāzī 27 B10
Bangka 23 D2
Bangka, Selat 23 D2
Bangkok 23 B2
Bangladesh ■ 25 C8
Bangor, *Down, U.K.* 11 B6
Bangor, *Gwynedd, U.K.* 8 D3
Bangor, *U.S.A.* 43 C11
Bangui 28 D3
Bangweulu, L. 28 G6
Baní 45 D10
Banja Luka 14 B7
Banjarmasin 23 D3
Banjul 26 F2
Banks I. 36 B7
Banks Is. 31 C12
Banks Pen. 33 K4
Banks Str. 32 D4
Bann →, *Armagh, U.K.* 11 B5
Bann →, *L'derry., U.K.* 11 A5
Banning 39 K5
Bannockburn 10 E5
Banská Bystrica 16 D9
Bantry 11 E2
Bantry B. 11 E2
Banyak, Kepulauan 23 C1
Banyuwangi 23 D3
Baoding 21 C6
Baoji 20 C5
Baoshan 20 D4
Baotou 21 B6
Bar Harbor 43 C11
Bar-le-Duc 12 B6
Baraboo 40 D10
Baracoa 45 C10
Baraga 40 B10
Barahona 45 D10
Barakaldo 13 A4
Baranavichy 18 D3
Baranof I. 36 D6
Barataria B. 41 L10
Barbados ■ 45 g
Barberton 42 E5
Barbourville 43 G4
Barcelona 13 B7
Barceloneta 45 d
Bardera 24 E3
Bardsey I. 8 E3
Bardstown 42 G3
Bareilly 25 C6
Barents Sea 6 B8
Bari 14 D7
Baring, C. 36 C8
Barisal 25 C8
Barisan, Bukit 23 D2
Barito → 23 D3
Barkley, L. 43 G2
Barkly Tableland 30 D6
Barkol Kazak Zizhixian 20 B4
Barlee, L. 30 F2
Barletta 14 D7
Barmedman 32 B4
Barmera 32 B3
Barmouth 8 E3
Barnard Castle 8 C6
Barnaul 18 D9
Barnesville, *Ga., U.S.A.* 43 J3
Barnesville, *Minn., U.S.A.* 40 B6
Barnet □ 9 F7
Barnhart 41 K4
Barnsley 8 D6
Barnstaple 9 F3
Barnwell 43 J5
Barques, Pt. Aux 42 C4
Barquísimeto 46 A5
Barra 10 E1
Barra, Sd. of 10 D1
Barra Hd. 10 E1
Barraba 32 B5
Barrancabermeja 46 B4
Barranquilla 46 A4
Barre 42 C9
Barrie 37 E12
Barrier Ra. 32 B3
Barrington Tops 32 B5
Barringun 32 A4
Barron 40 C9
Barrow 36 B4
Barrow → 11 D5
Barrow-in-Furness 8 C4
Barry 9 F4
Barstow 39 J5
Bartlesville 41 G7
Bartlett 41 H10
Barton upon Humber 8 D7
Bartow 43 M5
Barysaw 7 C9
Basel 12 C7
Bashi Channel 23 A4
Basilan I. 23 C4
Basildon 9 F8
Basin 38 D9
Basingstoke 9 F6
Basle = Basel 12 C7
Basque Provinces = País Vasco □ 13 A4
Basra = Al Başrah 24 B3
Bass Str. 32 C4
Basse-Pointe 44 c
Basse-Terre 44 b
Bassein 25 D8
Basses, Pte. des 44 b
Basseterre 45 D12
Bassett 40 D5
Bastia 12 E8
Bastrop, *La., U.S.A.* 41 J9
Bastrop, *Tex., U.S.A.* 41 K6
Bata 28 D1
Batabanó, G. de 45 C8
Batan I. 23 A4
Batangas 23 B4
Batavia 42 D6
Batdambang 23 B2
Batemans B. 32 C5
Batemans Bay 32 C5
Batesburg-Leesville 43 J5
Batesville, *Ark., U.S.A.* 41 H9
Batesville, *Miss., U.S.A.* 41 H10
Batesville, *Tex., U.S.A.* 41 L5
Bath, *U.K.* 9 F5
Bath, *Maine, U.S.A.* 43 D11
Bath, *N.Y., U.S.A.* 42 D7
Bathsheba 45 g
Bathurst, *Australia* 32 B4
Bathurst, *Canada* 37 E13
Bathurst, C. 36 B7
Bathurst Harb. 32 D4
Bathurst I. 37 B11
Bathurst Inlet 36 C9
Batlow 32 C4
Batna 26 A7
Baton Rouge 41 K9
Batticaloa 25 E7
Battle 9 G8
Battle → 36 D9
Battle Creek 42 D3
Battle Ground 38 D2
Battle Lake 40 B7
Battle Mountain 38 F5
Batu, Kepulauan 23 D1
Batu Pahat 23 C2
Batumi 17 B6
Baudette 40 A7
Bauer, C. 32 B1
Bauld, C. 37 D14
Bauru 47 H9
Bavaria = Bayern □ 16 D6
Bawean 23 D3
Baxley 43 K4
Baxter 40 B7
Baxter Springs 41 G7
Baxter State △ 43 B11
Bay City, *Mich., U.S.A.* 42 D4
Bay City, *Tex., U.S.A.* 41 L7
Bay Minette 43 K2
Bay St. Louis 41 K10
Bay Springs 41 K10
Bay View 33 H6
Bayamo 45 C9
Bayamón 45 d
Bayan Har Shan 20 C4
Bayanhongor 20 B5
Bayard, *N. Mex., U.S.A.* 39 K9
Bayard, *Nebr., U.S.A.* 40 E3
Bayern □ 16 D6
Bayeux 12 B3
Bayfield 40 B9
Baykal, Oz. 19 D11
Bayonne 12 E3
Baýramaly 24 B5
Bayrūt 17 D5
Baytown 41 L7
Beach 40 B3
Beachport 32 C3
Beachy Hd. 9 G8
Beacon 42 E9
Beaconsfield 32 D4
Beagle, Canal 48 H3
Beals Cr. → 41 J4
Bear I. 11 E2
Bear L. 38 F8
Beardmore Glacier 6 F15
Beardstown 40 F9
Béarn 12 E3
Bearpaw Mts. 38 B9
Beatrice 40 E6
Beatty 39 H5
Beauce, Plaine de la 12 B4
Beaudesert 32 A5
Beaufort, *N.C., U.S.A.* 43 H7
Beaufort, *S.C., U.S.A.* 43 J5
Beaufort Sea 6 B18
Beaufort West 29 L4
Beauly 10 D4
Beauly → 10 D4
Beaumaris 8 D3
Beaumont 41 K7
Beaune 12 C6
Beauvais 12 B5
Beaver, *Okla., U.S.A.* 41 G4
Beaver, *Utah, U.S.A.* 39 G7
Beaver →, *Canada* 36 D9
Beaver →, *U.S.A.* 41 G5
Beaver City 40 E5
Beaver Creek 36 C5
Beaver Dam 40 D10
Beaver Falls 42 E5
Beaver I. 42 C3
Beavercreek 42 F3
Beaverton 38 D2
Beawar 25 C6
Bécancour 42 B9
Beccles 9 E9
Béchar 26 B5
Beckley 42 G5
Bedford, *U.K.* 9 E7
Bedford, *Ind., U.S.A.* 42 F2
Bedford, *Iowa, U.S.A.* 40 E7
Bedford, *Va., U.S.A.* 42 G6
Bedfordshire □ 9 E7
Beef I. 45 e
Beenleigh 32 A5
Beeston 8 E6
Beeville 41 L6
Bega 32 C4
Bei Jiang → 21 D6
Bei'an 21 B7
Beihai 21 D5
Beijing 21 C6
Beilpajah 32 B3
Beira 29 H6
Beirut = Bayrūt 17 D5
Bejaïa 26 A7
Bela 24 C5
Belarus ■ 18 D3
Belau = Palau ■ 23 C5
Belawan 23 C1
Belcher Chan. 37 B11
Belcher Is. 37 D12
Belém 47 D9
Belen 39 J10
Belep, Îs. 31 D11
Belet Uen 24 E3
Belfast, *U.K.* 11 B6
Belfast, *U.S.A.* 43 C11
Belfast L. 11 B6
Belfield 40 B3
Belfort 12 C7
Belfry 38 D9
Belgaum 25 D6
Belgium ■ 16 C2
Belgorod 18 D4
Belgrade = Beograd 15 B9
Belgrade 38 D8
Belhaven 43 H7
Belitung 23 D2
Belize ■ 44 D7
Belize City 44 D7
Bell Peninsula 37 C11
Bella Coola 36 D7
Bellaire 42 E5
Bellary 25 D6
Bellata 32 A4
Belle Fourche 40 C3
Belle Fourche → 40 C3
Belle Glade 43 M5
Belle-Île 12 C2
Belle Isle 37 D14
Belle Isle, Str. of 37 D14
Belle Plaine 40 E8
Bellefontaine 42 E4
Bellefonte 42 E7
Belleplaine 45 g
Belleville, *Canada* 37 E12
Belleville, *Ill., U.S.A.* 40 F10
Belleville, *Kans., U.S.A.* 40 F6
Bellevue, *Idaho, U.S.A.* 38 E6
Bellevue, *Nebr., U.S.A.* 40 E7
Bellevue, *Wash., U.S.A.* 38 C2
Bellingen 32 B5
Bellingham 38 B2
Bellingshausen Sea 6 D3
Bellinzona 12 C8
Bello 46 B3
Bellona 31 C10
Bellows Falls 42 D9
Belmopan 44 D7
Belmullet 11 B2
Belo Horizonte 47 G10
Beloit, *Kans., U.S.A.* 40 F5
Beloit, *Wis., U.S.A.* 40 D10
Belorussia = Belarus ■ 18 D3
Belovo 18 D9
Beloye More 7 D11
Belpre 42 F5
Belt 38 C8
Beltana 32 B2
Belton 41 K6
Belton L. 41 K6
Belturbet 11 B4
Belukha 18 E9
Belvidere 40 D10
Belzoni 41 J9
Bemidji 40 B7
Ben Cruachan 10 E3
Ben Dearg 10 D4
Ben Hope 10 C4
Ben Lawers 10 E4
Ben Lomond, *N.S.W., Australia* 32 B5
Ben Lomond, *Tas., Australia* 32 D4
Ben Lomond, *U.K.* 10 E4
Ben Lomond △ 32 D4
Ben Macdhui 10 D5
Ben Mhor 10 D1
Ben More, *Argyll & Bute, U.K.* 10 E2
Ben More, *Stirling, U.K.* 10 E4
Ben More Assynt 10 C4
Ben Nevis 10 E3
Ben Vorlich 10 E4
Ben Wyvis 10 D4
Benalla 32 C4
Benares = Varanasi 25 C7
Benavides 41 M5
Benbecula 10 D1
Benbonyathe Hill 32 B2
Bend 38 D3
Bender Beila 24 E4
Bendigo 32 C3
Benevento 14 D6
Bengal, Bay of 25 D7
Bengbu 21 C6
Benghazi = Banghāzī 27 B10
Bengkulu 23 D2
Beni Mellal 26 B4
Beni Suef 27 C12
Benidorm 13 C5
Benin ■ 26 G6
Benin, Bight of 26 H6
Benin City 26 G7
Benkelman 40 E4
Bennettsville 43 H6
Bennington 42 D9
Benoni 29 K5
Benson, *Ariz., U.S.A.* 39 L8
Benson, *Minn., U.S.A.* 40 C7
Benton, *Ark., U.S.A.* 41 H8
Benton, *Ill., U.S.A.* 40 G10
Benton Harbor 42 D2
Bentonville 41 G7
Benue → 26 G7
Benxi 21 B7
Beograd 15 B9
Beppu 22 G2
Berau, Teluk 23 D5
Berbera 24 D3
Berbérati 28 D3
Berdyansk 17 A5
Berea 42 G3
Bereda 24 D4
Berens → 36 D10
Beresford 40 D6
Berezniki 18 D6
Bérgamo 12 D8
Bergen 7 E5
Bergerac 12 D4
Berhala, Selat 23 D2
Bering Sea 36 D2
Bering Strait 36 C3
Berkeley 38 H2
Berkner I. 6 E4
Berkshire Downs 9 F6
Berlin, *Germany* 16 B6
Berlin, *Md., U.S.A.* 42 F8
Berlin, *N.H., U.S.A.* 42 C10
Berlin, *Wis., U.S.A.* 42 D1
Bermuda ⧄ 4 C6
Bern 12 C7
Bernalillo 39 J10
Berneray 10 D1
Berri 32 B3
Berry, *Australia* 32 B5
Berry, *France* 12 C5
Berryville 41 G8
Berthold 40 A4
Berthoud 40 E2
Bertraghboy B. 11 C2
Beru 31 A14
Berwick 42 E7
Berwick-upon-Tweed 8 B6
Berwyn Mts. 8 E4
Besançon 12 C7
Besar 23 D3
Bessemer, *Ala., U.S.A.* 43 J2
Bessemer, *Mich., U.S.A.* 40 B9
Bethany, *Mo., U.S.A.* 40 E7
Bethany, *Okla., U.S.A.* 41 H6
Bethel 36 C3
Bethlehem, *S. Africa* 29 K5
Bethlehem, *U.S.A.* 42 E8
Béthune 12 A5
Bettendorf 40 E9
Betws-y-Coed 8 D4
Beulah, *Mich., U.S.A.* 42 C2
Beulah, *N. Dak., U.S.A.* 40 B4
Beverley 8 D7
Beverly Hills, *Calif., U.S.A.* 39 J4
Beverly Hills, *Fla., U.S.A.* 43 L4
Bexhill 9 G8
Béziers 12 E5
Bhagalpur 25 C7
Bharuch 25 C6
Bhavnagar 25 C6
Bhilainagar-Durg 25 C7
Bhima → 25 D6
Bhopal 25 C6
Bhubaneshwar 25 C7
Bhuj 25 C5
Bhutan ■ 25 C8
Biak 23 D5
Białystok 7 G8
Biarritz 12 E3
Bicester 9 F6
Bicheno 32 D4
Biddeford 43 D10
Bideford 9 F3
Bideford Bay 9 F3
Bié, Planalto de 29 G3
Bieber 38 F3
Biel 12 C7
Bielefeld 16 B4
Bielsko-Biała 16 D9
Bien Hoa 23 B2
Bienville, L. 37 D12
Big Belt Mts. 38 C8
Big Bend △ 41 L3
Big Black → 41 K9
Big Blue → 40 F6
Big Cypress △ 43 M5
Big Falls 40 A8
Big Fork → 40 A8
Big Lake 41 K4
Big Muddy Cr. → 40 A2
Big Pine 39 H4
Big Piney 38 E8
Big Rapids 42 D3
Big Sable Pt. 42 C2
Big Sandy 38 B8
Big Sandy → 42 F4
Big Sandy Cr. → 40 F3
Big Sioux → 40 D6
Big South Fork △ 43 G3
Big Spring 41 J4
Big Stone City 40 C6
Big Stone Gap 43 G4
Big Stone L. 40 C6
Big Timber 38 D9
Big Trout L. 37 D11
Biggar, *Canada* 36 D9
Biggar, *U.K.* 10 F5
Biggenden 32 A5
Biggleswade 9 E7
Bighorn 38 C10
Bighorn → 38 C10
Bighorn Canyon △ 38 D9
Bighorn L. 38 D9
Bighorn Mts. 38 D10
Bihar □ 25 C7
Bijapur 25 D6
Bikaner 25 C6
Bikini Atoll 34 F8
Bilaspur 25 C7
Bilauk Taungdan 25 D8
Bilbao 13 A4
Billings 38 D9
Bilma 27 E8
Biloxi 41 K10
Bimini Is. 45 B9
Binalong 32 B4
Bingara 32 A5

Bingham

Crete 40 E6
Creuse → 12 C4
Crewe 8 D5
Crewkerne 9 G5
Crianlarich 10 E4
Crieff 10 E5
Crimean Pen. = Krymskyy Pivostriv 17 B4
Croagh Patrick 11 C2
Croatia ■ 14 B7
Crockett 41 K7
Crohy Hd. 11 B3
Croker, C. 30 C5
Cromarty 10 D4
Cromer 8 E9
Cromwell 33 L2
Crook 8 C6
Crooked → 38 D3
Crooked I. 45 C10
Crookston, *Minn., U.S.A.* 40 B6
Crookston, *Nebr., U.S.A.* 40 D4
Crookwell 32 B4
Crosby, *U.K.* 8 D4
Crosby, *U.S.A.* 40 A3
Crosbyton 41 J4
Cross City 43 L4
Cross Fell 8 C5
Cross Sound 36 D6
Crossett 41 J9
Crosshaven 11 E3
Crossmaglen 11 B5
Crossmolina 11 B2
Crossville 43 G3
Crow Agency 38 D10
Crow Hd. 11 E1
Crowell 41 J5
Crowley 41 K8
Crown Point 42 E2
Crownpoint 39 J9
Crows Nest 32 A5
Crowsnest Pass 36 E8
Croydon □ 9 F7
Crozet, Is. 5 G13
Crusheen 11 D3
Cruz Bay 45 e
Cruzeiro do Sul 46 E4
Crystal Brook 32 B2
Crystal City 41 L5
Crystal Falls 42 B1
Crystal River 43 L4
Crystal Springs 41 K9
Cuando → 29 H4
Cuanza → 28 F2
Cuauhtémoc 44 B3
Cuba 39 J10
Cuba ■ 45 C9
Cubango → 29 H4
Cuckfield 9 F7
Cúcuta 46 B4
Cuenca, *Ecuador* 46 D3
Cuenca, *Spain* 13 B4
Cuernavaca 44 D5
Cuero 41 L6
Cuiabá 47 G7
Cuihangcun 21 G10
Cuillin Hills 10 D2
Cuillin Sd. 10 D2
Culbertson 40 A2
Culcairn 32 C4
Culebra 45 d
Culgoa → 32 A4
Culgoa Flood Plain △ 32 A4
Culiacán 44 C3
Cullarin Ra. 32 B4
Cullen 10 D6
Cullman 43 H2
Cullompton 9 G4
Culpeper 42 F7
Culverden 33 K4
Cumaná 46 A6
Cumberland 42 F6
Cumberland → 43 G2
Cumberland, L. 43 G3
Cumberland Gap △ 43 G4
Cumberland I. 43 K5
Cumberland Island △ 43 K5
Cumberland Pen. 37 C13
Cumberland Plateau 43 H3
Cumberland Sd. 37 C13
Cumbernauld 10 F5
Cumborah 32 A4
Cumbria □ 8 C5
Cumbrian Mts. 8 C5
Cummins 32 B2
Cumnock, *Australia* 32 B4
Cumnock, *U.K.* 10 F4
Cunene → 29 H2
Cúneo 12 D7
Cunnamulla 32 A4
Cupar 10 E5
Curaçao 45 E11
Curitiba 48 B7
Currabubula 32 B5
Currane, L. 11 E1
Currant 38 G6
Currawinya △ 32 A3
Current → 41 G9
Currie, *Australia* 32 C3
Currie, *U.S.A.* 38 F6
Curtis 40 E4
Curtis Group 32 C4
Curtis I. 31 G15
Cushendall 11 A5
Cushing 41 H6
Custer 40 D3
Cut Bank 38 B7
Cuthbert 43 K3
Cuttaburra → 32 A3
Cuttack 25 C7
Cuvier I. 33 G5
Cuxhaven 16 B4
Cuyahoga Falls 42 E5
Cuzco 46 F4
Cwmbran 9 F4
Cyclades 15 F11
Cygnet 32 D4
Cynthiana 42 F3
Cyprus ■ 17 D4
Cyrenaica 27 C10
Czech Rep. ■ 16 D7
Częstochowa 16 C9

D

Da Hinggan Ling 21 B7
Da Lat 23 B2
Da Nang 23 B2
Da Qaidam 20 C4
Daba Shan 21 C5
Dacca = Dhaka 25 C8
Dade City 43 L4
Daegu 21 C7
Daejeon 21 C7
Dagupan 23 B4
Dahlak Kebir 24 D3
Dahlonega 43 H4
Daingean 11 C4
Dajarra 30 E6
Dakar 26 F2
Dakhla 26 D2
Dakota City 40 D6
Dalandzadgad 20 B5
Dalap-Uliga-Darrit 34 G9
Dalbeattie 10 G5
Dalby 32 A5
Dale City 42 F7
Dale Hollow L. 43 G3
Dalhart 41 G3
Dali 20 D5
Dalian 21 C7
Daliang Shan 20 D5
Dalkeith 10 F5
Dallas, *Oreg., U.S.A.* 38 D2
Dallas, *Tex., U.S.A.* 41 J6
Dalles, The 38 D3
Dalmacija 14 C7
Dalmatia = Dalmacija 14 C7
Dalmellington 10 F4
Daloa 26 G4
Dalry 10 F4
Dalrymple, L. 30 E8
Dalton, *Ga., U.S.A.* 43 H3
Dalton, *Nebr., U.S.A.* 40 E3
Dalton-in-Furness 8 C4
Daly Waters 30 D5
Damanhûr 27 B12
Damaraland 29 H2
Damascus = Dimashq 24 B2
Damāvand, Qolleh-ye 24 B4
Dampier 30 E2
Danbury 42 E9
Danby L. 39 J6
Dandenong 32 C4
Dandong 21 B7
Daniel 38 E8
Dannemora 42 C9
Dannevirke 33 J6
Dansville 42 D7
Danube = Dunărea → 15 B13
Danville, *Ill., U.S.A.* 42 E2
Danville, *Ky., U.S.A.* 42 G3
Danville, *Va., U.S.A.* 43 G6
Danzig = Gdańsk 16 A9
Dar es Salaam 28 F7
Darbhanga 25 C7
Dardanelle 41 H8
Dardanelles = Çanakkale Boğazı 15 D12
Dargaville 33 F4
Darhan 20 B5
Darién, G. del 46 B3
Darjiling 25 C7
Darling → 32 B3
Darling Downs 32 A5
Darling Ra. 30 G2
Darlington, *U.K.* 8 C6
Darlington, *U.S.A.* 43 H6
Darmstadt 16 D4
Darnley, C. 6 D10
Darnley B. 36 C7
Darrington 38 B3
Dart → 9 G4
Dartford 9 F8
Dartmoor 9 G4
Dartmoor △ 9 G4
Dartmouth, *Canada* 37 E13
Dartmouth, *U.K.* 9 G4
Dartmouth Res. 32 A4
Darwen 8 D5
Darwin 30 C5
Dashen, Ras 28 B7
Dashoguz 24 A4
Dasht → 24 C5
Dasht-i-Tahlab 24 C5
Datong 21 B6
Daugavpils 18 D3
Dauphin 36 D9
Dauphiné 12 D6
Davangere 25 D6
Davao 23 C4
Davao G. 23 C4
Davenport, *Iowa, U.S.A.* 40 E9
Davenport, *Wash., U.S.A.* 38 C4
Daventry 9 E6
David 46 B2
David City 40 E6
Davis 38 G3
Davis Dam 39 J6
Davis Mts. 41 K2
Davis Str. 6 C4
Dawlish 9 G4
Dawros Hd. 11 B3
Dawson, *Canada* 36 C6
Dawson, *U.S.A.* 43 K3
Dawson Creek 36 D7
Dax 12 E3
Daxian 20 C5
Daxue Shan 20 C5
Daylesford 32 C3
Dayr az Zawr 24 B3
Dayton, *Ohio, U.S.A.* 42 F3
Dayton, *Tenn., U.S.A.* 43 H3
Dayton, *Wash., U.S.A.* 38 C4
Dayton, *Wyo., U.S.A.* 38 D10
Daytona Beach 43 L5
Dayville 38 D4
De Aar 29 L4
De Funiak Springs 43 K2
De Land 43 L5
De Leon 41 J5
De Pere 42 C1
De Queen 41 H7
De Quincy 41 K8
De Smet 40 C6
De Soto 40 F9
De Tour Village 42 C4
De Witt 41 H9
Dead Sea 17 D5
Deadwood 40 C3
Deal 9 F9
Deal I. 32 C4
Dean, Forest of 9 F5
Dease → 36 D7
Dease Lake 36 D6
Death Valley 39 H5
Death Valley △ 39 H5
Death Valley Junction 39 H5
Debrecen 17 A2
Decatur, *Ala., U.S.A.* 43 H2
Decatur, *Ga., U.S.A.* 43 J3
Decatur, *Ill., U.S.A.* 40 F10
Decatur, *Ind., U.S.A.* 42 E3
Decatur, *Tex., U.S.A.* 41 J6
Deccan 25 D6
Deception Bay 32 A5
Decorah 40 D9
Dee →, *Aberds., U.K.* 10 D6
Dee →, *Dumf. & Gall., U.K.* 10 G4
Dee →, *Wales, U.K.* 8 D4
Deepwater 32 A5
Deer Lake 37 E14
Deer Lodge 38 C7
Deer Park 38 C5
Deer River 40 B8
Defiance 42 E3
Dehiwala 25 E6
Dehra Dun 25 B6
DeKalb 40 E10
Del Norte 39 H10
Del Rio 41 L4
Delano 39 J4
Delano Peak 39 G7
Delavan 40 D10
Delaware 42 E4
Delaware □ 42 F8
Delaware B. 42 F8
Delegate 32 C4
Delgado, C. 28 G8
Delhi, *India* 25 C6
Delhi, *U.S.A.* 41 J9
Delicias 44 B3
Déline 36 C7
Dell City 39 L11
Dell Rapids 40 D6
Deloraine 32 D4
Delphi 42 E2
Delphos 42 E3
Delray Beach 43 M5
Delta, *Colo., U.S.A.* 39 G9
Delta, *Utah, U.S.A.* 38 G7
Delta Junction 36 C5
Deltona 43 L5
Delungra 32 A5
Deming 39 K10
Demopolis 43 J2
Den Haag = 's-Gravenhage 16 B2
Den Helder 16 B2
Denali = McKinley, Mt. 36 C4
Denbigh 8 D4
Denbighshire □ 8 D4
Denham, Mt. 44 a
Denial B. 32 B1
Deniliquin 32 C3
Denison, *Iowa, U.S.A.* 40 E7
Denison, *Tex., U.S.A.* 41 J6
Denizli 17 C3
Denmark ■ 7 F6
Denmark Str. 6 C5
Dennery 45 f
Denny 10 E5
Denpasar 23 D3
Denton, *Mont., U.S.A.* 38 C9
Denton, *Tex., U.S.A.* 41 J6
D'Entrecasteaux, Îs. 31 D11
D'Entrecasteaux Is. 30 B9
Denver 40 F2
Denver City 41 J3
Dera Ismail Khan 25 B6
Derby, *Australia* 30 D3
Derby, *U.K.* 8 E6
Derby, *U.S.A.* 41 G6
Derbyshire □ 8 D6
Dereham 9 E8
Derg → 11 B4
Derg, L. 11 D3
Deridder 41 K8
Dermott 41 J9
Derry = Londonderry 11 B4
Derryveagh Mts. 11 B3
Derwent →, *Cumb., U.K.* 8 C4
Derwent →, *Derby, U.K.* 8 E6
Derwent →, *N. Yorks., U.K.* 8 D7
Derwent Water 8 C4
Des Moines, *Iowa, U.S.A.* 40 E8
Des Moines, *N. Mex., U.S.A.* 41 G3
Des Moines → 40 E9
Deschutes → 38 D3
Dese 24 D2
Desert Center 39 K6
Dessau 16 C6
D'Estrees B. 32 C2
Detour, Pt. 42 C2
Detroit 42 D4
Detroit Lakes 40 B7
Deutsche Bucht 16 A4
Deventer 16 B3
Deveron → 10 D6
Devils Lake 40 A5
Devils Tower 40 C2
Devils Tower △ 40 C2
Devine 41 L5
Devizes 9 F6
Devon □ 9 G4
Devon I. 37 B10
Devonport, *Australia* 32 D4
Devonport, *N.Z.* 33 G5
Dewey 45 d
Dexter, *Maine, U.S.A.* 43 C11
Dexter, *Mo., U.S.A.* 41 G10
Dexter, *N. Mex., U.S.A.* 41 J2
Dezfūl 24 B3
Dezhneva, Mys 19 C19
Dhahran = Az Zahrān 24 C4
Dhaka 25 C8
Dhamār 24 D3
Dhanbad 25 C7
Dharwad 25 D6
Dhaulagiri 25 C7
Dhule 25 C6
Diamantina → 32 A2
Diamond Mts. 38 G6
Dibrugarh 25 C8
Dickens 41 J4
Dickinson 40 B3
Dickson 43 G2
Diefenbaker, L. 36 D9
Dieppe 12 B4
Dierks 41 H8
Digby 37 E13
Dighton 40 F4
Digne-les-Bains 12 D7
Dijlah, Nahr → 24 B3
Dijon 12 C6
Dili 23 D4
Dilley 41 L5
Dillingham 36 D4
Dillon, *Mont., U.S.A.* 38 D7
Dillon, *S.C., U.S.A.* 43 H6
Dimashq 24 B2
Dimboola 32 C3
Dimitrovgrad 15 C11
Dimmitt 41 H3
Dinan 12 B2
Dinant 16 C2
Dinara Planina 14 C7
Dingle 11 D1
Dingle B. 11 D1
Dingwall 10 D4
Dinin → 11 D4
Dinosaur △ 38 F9
Dinuba 39 H4
Dipolog 23 C4
Dire Dawa 24 E3
Dirranbandi 32 A4
Disappointment, C. 38 C2
Disappointment, L. 30 E3
Disaster B. 32 C4
Discovery B., *Australia* 32 C3
Discovery B., *China* 21 G11
Diss 9 E9
District of Columbia □ 42 F7
Divide 38 D7
Dixon 40 E10
Dixon Entrance 36 D6
Diyarbakır 17 C6
Djakarta = Jakarta 23 D2
Djerid, Chott 26 B7
Djibouti 24 D3
Djibouti ■ 24 D3
Dnepr = Dnipro → 17 A4
Dnestr = Dnister → 18 E4
Dnipro → 17 A4
Dniprodzerzhynsk 17 A4
Dnipropetrovsk 17 A5
Dnister → 18 E4
Doberai, Jazirah 23 D5
Dobrich 15 C12
Dodecanese 15 F12
Dodge City 41 G5
Dodgeville 40 D9
Dodoma 28 F7
Dodson 38 B9
Doha = Ad Dawḥah 24 C4
Dolbeau-Mistassini 37 E12
Dole 12 C6
Dolgellau 8 E4
Dolo 24 E3
Dolomiti 14 A4
Dolores 39 H9
Dolores → 39 G9
Dolphin and Union Str. 36 C8
Dominica ■ 45 D12
Dominican Rep. ■ 45 D10
Domville, Mt. 32 A5
Don →, *Russia* 18 E4
Don →, *Aberds., U.K.* 10 D6
Don →, *S. Yorks., U.K.* 8 D7
Don Figuerero Mts. 44 a
Donaghadee 11 B6
Donaghmore 11 D4
Donald 32 C3
Donaldsonville 41 K9
Donalsonville 43 K3
Doncaster 8 D6
Dondra Head 25 E7
Donegal 11 B3
Donegal □ 11 B4
Donegal B. 11 B3
Donetsk 17 A5
Dong Hoi 23 B2
Dongbei 21 B7
Dongchuan 20 D5
Dongting Hu 21 D6
Donington, C. 32 B2
Doniphan 41 G9
Donna 41 M5
Donnelly's Crossing 33 F4
Donostia-San Sebastián 13 A5
Doon → 10 F4
Dorchester 9 G5
Dorchester, C. 37 C12
Dordogne → 12 D3
Dordrecht 16 C2
Dorking 9 F7
Dornie 10 D3
Dornoch 10 D4
Dornoch Firth 10 D4
Döröö Nuur 20 B4
Dorrigo 32 B5
Dorris 38 F3
Dorset □ 9 G5
Dortmund 16 C3
Dothan 43 K3
Douai 12 A5
Douala 28 D1
Double Island Pt. 32 A5
Double Mountain Fork → 41 J4
Doubs → 12 C6
Doubtful Sd. 33 L1
Doubtless B. 33 F4
Douglas, *I. of Man* 8 C3
Douglas, *Ariz., U.S.A.* 39 L9
Douglas, *Ga., U.S.A.* 43 K4
Douglas, *Wyo., U.S.A.* 40 D2
Douglas Apsley △ 32 D4
Douglasville 43 J3
Dounreay 10 C5
Dourados 47 H8
Douro → 13 B1
Dove → 8 E6
Dove Creek 39 H9
Dover, *Australia* 32 D4
Dover, *U.K.* 9 F9
Dover, *Del., U.S.A.* 42 F8
Dover, *N.H., U.S.A.* 42 D10
Dover, *Ohio, U.S.A.* 42 E5
Dover, Str. of 9 G9
Dover-Foxcroft 43 C11
Dovrefjell 7 E5
Dowagiac 42 E2
Down □ 11 B5
Downey 38 E7
Downham Market 9 E8
Downieville 38 G3
Downpatrick 11 B6
Downpatrick Hd. 11 B2
Draguignan 12 E7
Drain 38 E2
Drake 40 B4
Drake Passage 6 B
Drakensberg 29 L5
Drammen 7 F6
Drava → 15 B8
Dresden 16 C6
Dreux 12 B4
Driffield 8 C7
Driggs 38 E8
Drina → 15 B8
Drobeta-Turnu Severin 15 B10
Drogheda 11 C5
Droichead Nua 11 C5
Droitwich 9 E5
Dromedary, C. 32 C5
Dromore 11 B4
Dromore West 11 B3
Dronfield 8 D6
Dronning Maud Land 6 E7
Drumcliff 11 B3
Drumheller 36 D8
Drummond 38 C7
Drummond I. 42 C4
Drummond Pt. 32 B2
Drumright 41 H6
Dry Harbour Mts. 44 a
Dryden 36 E10
Drygalski I. 6 D11
Du Quoin 40 G10
Dubai = Dubayy 24 C4
Dubawnt → 36 C9
Dubawnt L. 36 C9
Dubayy 24 C4
Dubbo 32 B4
Dublin, *Ireland* 11 C5
Dublin, *Ga., U.S.A.* 43 J4
Dublin, *Tex., U.S.A.* 41 J5
Dublin □ 11 C5
Dublin (DUB) 11 C5
Dubois, *Idaho, U.S.A.* 38 D7
Dubois, *Pa., U.S.A.* 42 E6
Dubrovnik 15 C8
Dubuque 40 D9
Duchesne 38 F8
Ducie I. 35 K15
Duck → 43 G2
Dudinka 19 C9
Dudley 9 E5
Duff Is. 31 B12
Dufftown 10 D5
Duisburg 16 C3
Dulce 39 H10
Duluth 40 B8
Dumaguete 23 C4
Dumas, *Ark., U.S.A.* 41 J9
Dumas, *Tex., U.S.A.* 41 H4
Dumbarton 10 F4
Dumfries 10 F5
Dumfries & Galloway □ 10 F5
Dumyât 27 B12
Dún Laoghaire 11 C5
Dunărea → 15 B13
Dunback 33 L3
Dunbar 10 E6
Dunblane 10 E5
Duncan, *Ariz., U.S.A.* 39 K9
Duncan, *Okla., U.S.A.* 41 H6
Duncansby Head 10 C5
Dundalk, *Ireland* 11 B5
Dundalk, *U.S.A.* 42 F7
Dundalk Bay 11 C5
Dundas 42 D6
Dundee 10 E6
Dundrum 11 B6
Dundrum B. 11 B6
Dunedin, *N.Z.* 33 L3
Dunedin, *U.S.A.* 43 L4
Dunfanaghy 11 A4
Dunfermline 10 E5
Dungannon 11 B5
Dungarvan 11 D4
Dungarvan Harbour 11 D4
Dungeness 9 G8
Dunglow 11 B3
Dungog 32 B5
Dunhuang 20 B4
Dunkeld, *Australia* 32 B4
Dunkeld, *U.K.* 10 E5
Dunkerque 12 A5
Dunkery Beacon 9 F4
Dunkirk = Dunkerque 12 A5
Dunkirk 42 D6
Dunleer 11 C5
Dunmanus B. 11 E2
Dunmanway 11 E2
Dunmore 42 E8
Dunmore East 11 D5
Dunmore Hd. 11 D1
Dunn 43 H6
Dunnellon 43 L4
Dunnet Hd. 10 C5
Dunning 40 E4
Dunolly 32 C3
Dunoon 10 F4
Duns 10 F6
Dunseith 40 A4
Dunshaughlin 11 C5
Dunsmuir 38 F2
Dunstable 9 F7
Dunstan Mts. 33 L2
Dunvegan 10 D2
Dupree 40 C4
Dupuyer 38 B7
Durance → 12 E6
Durand 40 C9
Durango, *Mexico* 44 C4
Durango, *U.S.A.* 39 H10
Durant, *Miss., U.S.A.* 41 J10
Durant, *Okla., U.S.A.* 41 J6
Durban 29 K6
Düren 16 C3
Durham, *U.K.* 8 C6
Durham, *U.S.A.* 43 H6
Durham □ 8 C6
Durness 10 C4
Durrës 15 D8
Durrow 11 D4
Dursey I. 11 E1
Dursley 9 F5
D'Urville I. 33 J4
Dushanbe 18 F7
Dusky Sd. 33 L1
Düsseldorf 16 C3
Dutch Harbor 36 D3
Duyun 20 D5
Dvina, Severnaya → 18 C5
Dwight 42 E1
Dyce 10 D6
Dyer, C. 37 C13
Dyersburg 41 G10
Dyfi → 9 E3
Dzhugdzur, Khrebet 19 D14
Dzungarian Gate 20 B3
Dzuumod 20 B5

E

Eads 40 F3
Eagar 39 J9
Eagle, *Alaska, U.S.A.* 36 C5
Eagle, *Colo., U.S.A.* 38 G10
Eagle Butte 40 C4
Eagle Grove 40 D8
Eagle L., *Calif., U.S.A.* 38 F3
Eagle L., *Maine, U.S.A.* 43 B11
Eagle Lake, *Maine, U.S.A.* 43 B11
Eagle Lake, *Tex., U.S.A.* 41 L6
Eagle Nest 39 H11
Eagle Pass 41 L4
Eagle River, *Mich., U.S.A.* 42 B1
Eagle River, *Wis., U.S.A.* 40 C10
Eaglehawk 32 C3
Ealing □ 9 F7
Earle 41 H9
Earlimart 39 J4
Earn → 10 E5
Earn, L. 10 E4
Earnslaw, Mt. 33 L2
Earth 41 H3
Easley 43 H4
East Anglia 8 E9
East Ayrshire □ 10 F4
East C. 33 G7
East Caroline Basin 34 G6
East Chicago 42 E2
East China Sea 21 D7
East Dunbartonshire □ 10 F4
East Falkland 48 G5
East Grand Forks 40 B6
East Grinstead 9 F8
East Helena 38 C8
East Kilbride 10 F4
East Lamma Channel 21 G11
East Lansing 42 D3
East Liverpool 42 E5
East London 29 L5
East Lothian □ 10 F6
East Mariana Basin 34 F7
East Orange 42 E8
East Pacific Rise 35 J17
East Point 43 J3
East Pt. 45 e
East Renfrewshire □ 10 F4
East Riding of Yorkshire □ 8 D7
East St. Louis 40 F9
East Sea = Japan, Sea of 22 D4
East Siberian Sea 19 B17
East Stroudsburg 42 E8
East Sussex □ 9 G8
East Tasman Plateau 34 M7
East Tawas 42 C4
East Timor ■ 23 D4
East Toorale 32 B4
Eastbourne, *N.Z.* 33 J5
Eastbourne, *U.K.* 9 G8
Easter Fracture Zone 35 K16
Easter I. = Pascua, I. de 35 K17
Eastern Ghats 25 D6
Eastland 41 J5
Eastleigh 9 G6
Eastmain 37 D12
Eastmain → 37 D12
Eastman 43 J4
Easton, *Md., U.S.A.* 42 F7
Easton, *Pa., U.S.A.* 42 E8
Eastport 43 C12
Eaton 40 E2
Eatonton 43 J4
Eau Claire 40 C9
Eau Claire, L. à l' 37 D12
Eauripik Rise 34 G6
Ebbw Vale 9 F4
Ebro → 13 B6
Ech Chéliff 26 A6
Echo Bay 36 C8
Eclipse Sd. 37 B12
Ecuador ■ 46 D3
Eday 10 B6
Eddrachillis B. 10 C3
Eddystone 9 G3
Eddystone Pt. 32 D4
Eden, *Australia* 32 C4
Eden, *N.C., U.S.A.* 43 G6
Eden, *Tex., U.S.A.* 41 K5
Eden → 8 C4
Edenderry 11 C4
Edenton 43 G7
Edgar 40 E6
Edge Hill 9 E6
Edgefield 43 J5
Edgeley 40 B5
Edgemont 40 D3
Edievale 33 L2
Edina 40 E8
Edinburg 41 M5
Edinburgh 10 F5
Edinburgh (EDI) 10 F5
Edithburgh 32 C2
Edmond 41 H6
Edmonds 38 C2
Edmonton 36 D8
Edmundston 37 E13
Edna 41 L6
Edson 36 D8
Edward → 32 C3
Edward, L. 28 E5
Edward VII Land 6 F17
Edwards Plateau 41 K4
Efate, I. 31 D12
Effigy Mounds △ 40 D9
Effingham 42 F1
Egan Range 38 G6
Eglinton I. 37 A10
Egmont △ 33 H5
Egmont, C. 33 H4
Egypt ■ 27 C12
Eidsvold 32 A5
Eifel 16 C3
Eigg 10 E2
Eil 24 E3
Eil, L. 10 E3
Eildon, L. 32 C4
Eindhoven 16 C2
Eire = Ireland ■ 11 C4
Eivissa 13 C6
Ekalaka 40 C2
Eketahuna 33 J5
El Aaiún 26 C3
El Cajon 39 K5
El Campo 41 L6
El Centro 39 K6
El Djouf 26 D4
El Dorado, *Ark., U.S.A.* 41 J8
El Dorado, *Kans., U.S.A.* 41 G6
El Dorado Springs 41 G8
El Faiyûm 27 C12
El Fâsher 27 F11
El Fuerte 44 B3
El Gîza 27 C12
El Iskandarîya 27 B11
El Jadida 26 B4
El Khârga 27 C12
El Khartûm 27 E12
El Khartûm Bahrî 27 E12
El Mahalla el Kubra 27 B12
El Malpais △ 39 J10
El Mansûra 27 B12
El Minyâ 27 C12
El Obeid 27 F12
El Paso 39 L10
El Qâhira 27 B12
El Salvador ■ 44 E7
El Suweis 27 C12
Elâzığ 17 C5
Elba, *Italy* 14 C4
Elba, *U.S.A.* 43 K2
Elbasan 15 D9
Elbe → 16 B4
Elbert, Mt. 39 G10
Elberton 43 H4
Elbeuf 12 B4
Elbląg 16 A9
Elbrus 18 E5
Elche 13 C5
Eldon 40 F8
Eldora 40 D8
Eldorado, *Ill., U.S.A.* 42 G1
Eldorado, *Tex., U.S.A.* 41 K4
Eldoret 28 D7
Elefantes → 29 J6
Elephant Butte Res. 39 K10
Elephant I. 6 D4
Eleuthera 45 C9
Elgin, *U.K.* 10 D5
Elgin, *Ill., U.S.A.* 42 D1
Elgin, *N. Dak., U.S.A.* 40 B4
Elgin, *Oreg., U.S.A.* 38 D5
Elgin, *Tex., U.S.A.* 41 K6
Elgon, Mt. 28 D6
Elizabeth, *Australia* 32 B2
Elizabeth, *U.S.A.* 42 E8
Elizabeth City 43 G7
Elizabethton 43 G4
Elizabethtown 42 G3
Elk → 43 H2
Elk City 41 H5
Elk River, *Idaho, U.S.A.* 38 C5
Elk River, *Minn., U.S.A.* 40 C8
Elkhart, *Ind., U.S.A.* 42 E3
Elkhart, *Kans., U.S.A.* 41 G4
Elkhorn → 40 E6
Elkin 43 G5
Elkins 42 F6
Elko 38 F6
Ellef Ringnes I. 37 B10
Ellendale 40 B5
Ellensburg 38 C3
Ellenville 42 E8
Ellerton 45 g
Ellery, Mt. 32 C4
Ellesmere, L. 33 M4
Ellesmere I. 37 B10
Ellesmere Port 8 D5
Ellice Is. = Tuvalu ■ 31 B14
Elliot Lake 37 E11
Ellis 40 F5
Elliston 32 B1
Ellisville 41 K10
Ellon 10 D6
Ellsworth, *Kans., U.S.A.* 40 F5
Ellsworth, *Maine, U.S.A.* 43 C11
Ellsworth Land 6 E2
Elma 38 C2
Elmhurst 42 E2
Elmira 42 D7
Elmore 32 C3
Eloy 39 K8
Eltham 33 H5
Eluru 25 D7
Elwood, *Ind., U.S.A.* 42 E3
Elwood, *Nebr., U.S.A.* 40 E5
Ely, *U.K.* 9 E8
Ely, *Minn., U.S.A.* 40 B9
Ely, *Nev., U.S.A.* 38 G6
Elyria 42 E4
Emāmrūd 24 B4
Emden 16 B3
Emerald 30 E8
Emmen 16 B3
Emmetsburg 40 D7
Emmett 38 E5
Emmonak 36 C3
Empalme 44 B2
Empangeni 29 K6
Emperor Seamount Chain 34 D9
Emperor Trough 34 C9
Emporia, *Kans., U.S.A.* 40 F6
Emporia, *Va., U.S.A.* 43 G7
Emporium 42 E6
Ems → 16 B3
Enard B. 10 C3
Encampment 38 F10
Encino 39 J11
Encounter B. 32 C2
Ende 23 D4
Enderbury I. 31 A16
Enderby Land 6 D9
Enderlin 40 B6
Endicott 42 D7
Enewetak Atoll 34 F8
Enfer, Pte. d' 44 c
Enfield 43 G7
Engadin 12 C9
Engels 18 D5
Enggano 23 D2
England 41 H9
England □ 9 E5
Englewood 40 F2
English → 36 D10
English Channel 9 G6
Enid 41 G6
Ennadai L. 36 C9
Enngonia 32 A4
Ennis, *Ireland* 11 D3
Ennis, *Mont., U.S.A.* 38 D8
Ennis, *Tex., U.S.A.* 41 J6
Enniscorthy 11 D5
Enniskillen 11 B4
Ennistimon 11 D2
Enns → 16 D7
Enschede 16 B3
Ensenada 44 A1
Entebbe 28 D6
Enterprise, *Ala., U.S.A.* 43 K3
Enterprise, *Oreg., U.S.A.* 38 D5
Enugu 26 G7
Enumclaw 38 C3
Épernay 12 B5
Ephraim 38 G8
Ephrata 38 C4
Epi 31 D12
Épinal 12 B7
Epsom 9 F7
Equatorial Guinea ■ 28 D1
Erdenet 20 B5
Erebus, Mt. 6 E15
Erfurt 16 C5
Eriboll, L. 10 C4
Erie 42 D5
Erie, L. 42 D5
Erigavo 24 D3
Eriskay 10 D1
Eritrea ■ 24 D2
Erlangen 16 D5
Erne → 11 B3
Erne, Lower L. 11 B4
Erne, Upper L. 11 B4
Eromanga 32 A3
Errigal 11 A3
Erris Hd. 11 B1
Erromango 31 D12
Erskine 40 B7
Erwin 43 G4
Erzgebirge 16 C6
Erzurum 17 C6
Es Sahrâ' Esh Sharqîya 27 C12
Esbjerg 7 F5
Escalante 39 H8
Escalante → 39 H8
Escambia → 43 K2
Escanaba 42 C2
Esch-sur-Alzette 12 B6
Escondido 39 K5
Escuinapa de Hidalgo 44 C3
Escuintla 44 E6
Eşfahān 24 B4
Esha Ness 10 A7
Esher 9 F7
Esk →, *Cumb., U.K.* 10 G5
Esk →, *N. Yorks., U.K.* 8 C7
Esker 37 D13
Eskilstuna 7 F7
Eskişehir 17 C4
Esmeraldas 46 C3
Espanola 39 H10
Esperance 30 G3
Esperance Harbour 45 f
Esperanza 45 d
Espinhaço, Serra do 47 G10
Espírito Santo 31 D12
Espoo 7 E8
Essen 16 C3
Essequibo → 46 B7
Essex □ 9 F8
Estancia 39 J10
Estevan 36 E9
Estherville 40 D7
Estrela, Serra da 13 B2
Etawah 25 C6
eThekwini = Durban 29 K6
Ethiopia ■ 28 B7
Ethiopian Highlands 3 D12
Etive, L. 10 E3
Etna 14 F6
Etowah 43 H3
Etrek 24 B4
Ettrick Water → 10 F6
Eua 31 E16
Euclid 42 E5
Eucumbene, L. 32 C4
Eudora 41 J9
Eufaula, *Ala., U.S.A.* 43 K3
Eufaula, *Okla., U.S.A.* 41 H7
Eufaula L. 41 H7
Eugene 38 E2
Eugowra 32 B4
Eulo 32 A4
Eunice, *La., U.S.A.* 41 K8
Eunice, *N. Mex., U.S.A.* 41 J3
Euphrates = Furāt, Nahr al → 24 B3
Eureka, *Canada* 37 B10
Eureka, *Calif., U.S.A.* 38 F1
Eureka, *Kans., U.S.A.* 41 G6
Eureka, *Mont., U.S.A.* 38 B6
Eureka, *Nev., U.S.A.* 38 G5
Eureka, *S. Dak., U.S.A.* 40 C5
Euroa 32 C4
Europe 3 B11
Eustis 43 L5
Evans 40 E2
Evans Head 32 A5
Evanston, *Ill., U.S.A.* 42 E2
Evanston, *Wyo., U.S.A.* 38 F8
Evansville 42 G2
Eveleth 40 B8
Everard, L. 32 B2
Everest, Mt. 25 C7
Everett 38 C2
Everglades △ 43 N5
Everglades, The 43 N5
Everglades City 43 N5
Evergreen, *Ala., U.S.A.* 43 K2
Evergreen, *Mont., U.S.A.* 38 B6
Evesham 9 E6
Evia 15 E11
Évora 13 C2
Évreux 12 B4
Ewe, L. 10 D3
Ewing 40 D5
Excelsior Springs 40 F7
Exe → 9 G4
Exeter, *U.K.* 9 G4
Exeter, *U.S.A.* 39 H4
Exmoor 9 F4
Exmoor △ 9 F4
Exmouth 9 G4
Exmouth Plateau 34 J3
Expedition △ 32 A4
Extremadura □ 13 C2
Eye Pen. 10 C2
Eyemouth 10 F6
Eyre (North), L. 32 A2
Eyre (South), L. 32 A2
Eyre, L. 30 F6
Eyre Mts. 33 L2
Eyre Pen. 32 B2

F

F.Y.R.O.M. = Macedonia ■ 15 D9
Fabens 39 L10
Færoe Is. = Føroyar ⊠ 4 A9
Fair Haven 42 D9
Fair Hd. 11 A5
Fairbanks 36 C5
Fairbury 40 E6
Fairfield, *Ala., U.S.A.* 43 J2
Fairfield, *Calif., U.S.A.* 38 G2
Fairfield, *Idaho, U.S.A.* 38 E6
Fairfield, *Ill., U.S.A.* 42 F1
Fairfield, *Iowa, U.S.A.* 40 E9
Fairfield, *Tex., U.S.A.* 41 K7
Fairhope 43 K2
Fairlie 33 L3
Fairmont, *Minn., U.S.A.* 40 D7
Fairmont, *W. Va., U.S.A.* 42 F5
Fairmount 42 D7
Fairplay 39 G11
Fairport 42 D7
Fairview, *Mont., U.S.A.* 40 B2
Fairview, *Okla., U.S.A.* 41 G5
Fairweather, Mt. 36 D6
Faisalabad 25 B6
Faith 40 C3
Fajardo 45 d
Fakaofo 31 B16
Fakenham 8 E8
Fakfak 23 D5
Falcon Res. 41 M5
Falfurrias 41 M5
Falkirk 10 F5
Falkland 10 E5
Falkland Is. ⊠ 48 G5
Fall River 42 E10
Fallon 38 G4
Falls City 40 E7
Falmouth, *Jamaica* 44 a
Falmouth, *U.K.* 9 G2
Falun 7 E7
Fanad Hd. 11 A4
Fanling 21 F11
Fannich, L. 10 D4
Farāh 24 B5
Farāh → 24 B5
Farasān, Jazā'ir 24 D3
Fareham 9 G6
Farewell, C. 33 J4
Farghona 18 E8
Fargo 40 B6
Faribault 40 C8
Faridabad 25 C6
Farina 32 B2
Farmerville 41 J8
Farmington, *Maine, U.S.A.* 43 C10
Farmington, *Mo., U.S.A.* 41 G9
Farmington, *N. Mex., U.S.A.* 39 H9
Farmington, *Utah, U.S.A.* 38 F8
Farmville 42 G6
Farne Is. 8 B6
Faro 36 C6
Farson 38 E9
Fartak, Ra's 24 D4
Farwell 41 H3
Fastnet Rock 11 E2
Fataka 31 C12
Faulkton 40 C5
Fayette, *Ala., U.S.A.* 43 J2
Fayette, *Mo., U.S.A.* 40 F8
Fayetteville, *Ark., U.S.A.* 41 G7
Fayetteville, *N.C., U.S.A.* 43 H6
Fayetteville, *Tenn., U.S.A.* 43 H2
Fdérik 26 D3
Feakle 11 D3
Feale → 11 D2
Fear, C. 43 J7
Feather → 38 G3
Featherston 33 J5
Fécamp 12 B4
Feilding 33 J5
Feira de Santana 47 F11
Felipe Carrillo Puerto 44 D7
Felixstowe 9 F9
Fens, The 8 E7
Fenton 42 D4
Fenyang 21 C6
Ferbane 11 C4
Fergus 42 D5
Fergus Falls 40 B6
Fermanagh □ 11 B4
Fermont 37 D13
Fermoy 11 D3
Fernandina Beach 43 K5
Fernando Póo = Bioko 28 D1
Ferndale 38 B2
Fernley 38 G4
Ferrara 14 B4
Ferret, C. 12 D3
Ferriday 41 K9
Ferron 39 G8
Fertile 40 B6
Fès 26 B5
Fessenden 40 B5
Festus 40 F9
Fetlar 10 A8
Feuilles → 37 D12
Feyẕābād 25 B6
Fez = Fès 26 B5
Fezzan 27 C8
Fianarantsoa 29 J9
Fife △, *U.K.* 10 E5
Fife □, *U.K.* 10 E5
Fife Ness 10 E6
Figeac 12 D5
Fiji ■ 33 C8
Filey 8 C7
Filey B. 8 C7
Fillmore 39 G7
Findhorn → 10 D5
Findlay 42 E4
Finisterre, C. = Fisterra, C. 13 A1
Finland ■ 7 E9
Finland, G. of 7 F9
Finlay → 36 D7
Finley, *Australia* 32 C4
Finley, *U.S.A.* 40 B6
Finn → 11 B4
Finniss, C. 32 B1
Fiordland △ 33 L1
Firenze 14 C4
Fish → 29 K3
Fishguard 9 E3
Fisterra, C. 13 A1
Fitchburg, *Mass., U.S.A.* 42 D10
Fitchburg, *Wis., U.S.A.* 40 D10
Fitzgerald 43 K4
Flagstaff 39 J8
Flagstaff L. 43 C10
Flambeau → 40 C9
Flamborough Hd. 8 C7
Flaming Gorge △ 38 F9
Flaming Gorge Res. 38 F9
Flandre 12 A5
Flandreau 40 C6
Flannan Is. 10 C1
Flathead L. 38 C7
Flattery, C. 38 B1
Flatwoods 42 F4
Fleetwood 8 D4
Flensburg 16 A4
Flers 12 B3
Fleurieu Pen. 32 C2
Flin Flon 36 D9
Flinders → 30 D7
Flinders I., *S. Austral., Australia* 32 B1
Flinders I., *Tas., Australia* 32 D4
Flinders Ranges 32 B2
Flint, *U.K.* 8 D4
Flint, *U.S.A.* 42 D4
Flint → 43 K3
Flint I. 35 J12
Flintshire □ 8 D4
Flodden 8 B5
Floodwood 40 B8
Flora 42 F1
Florala 43 K2
Florence = Firenze 14 C4
Florence, *Ala., U.S.A.* 43 H2
Florence, *Ariz., U.S.A.* 39 K8
Florence, *Colo., U.S.A.* 40 F2
Florence, *Oreg., U.S.A.* 38 E1
Florence, *S.C., U.S.A.* 43 H6
Florence, L. 32 A2
Flores 23 D4
Flores Sea 23 D4
Floresville 41 L5
Florianópolis 48 B7
Florida □ 43 L5
Florida, Straits of 45 C9
Florida Is. 31 B11
Florida Keys 43 N5
Florissant 40 F9
Florø 7 E5
Floydada 41 J4
Fly → 30 B7
Fochabers 10 D5
Focşani 15 B12
Fóggia 14 D6
Foix 12 E4
Foley 43 K2
Folkestone 9 F9
Folkston 43 K5
Fond-du-Lac, *Canada* 36 D9
Fond du Lac, *U.S.A.* 40 D10
Fongafale 31 B14
Fontainebleau 12 B5
Fontenay-le-Comte 12 C3
Fontenelle Res. 38 E8
Forbes 32 B4
Fords Bridge 32 A4
Fordyce 41 J8
Forel, Mt. 6 C5
Forest 41 J10
Forest City, *Iowa, U.S.A.* 40 D8
Forest City, *N.C., U.S.A.* 43 H5
Forest Grove 38 D2
Forestier Pen. 32 D4
Forfar 10 E6
Forks 38 C1
Forlì 14 B5
Forman 40 B6
Formby Pt. 8 D4
Føroyar ⊠ 4 A9
Forres 10 D5
Forrest City 41 H9
Forsayth 30 D7
Forsyth 38 C10
Fort Albany 37 D11
Fort Augustus 10 D4
Fort Beaufort 29 L5
Fort Benton 38 C8
Fort Bragg 38 G2
Fort Bridger 38 F8
Fort Chipewyan 36 D8
Fort Collins 40 E2
Fort Davis 41 K3
Fort-de-France 44 c
Fort Defiance 39 J9
Fort Dodge 40 D7
Fort Fairfield 43 B12
Fort Garland 39 H11
Fort Good Hope 36 C7
Fort Hancock 39 L11
Fort Kent 43 B11
Fort Klamath 38 E3
Fort Laramie 40 D2
Fort Lauderdale 43 M5
Fort Liard 36 C7
Fort Lupton 40 E2
Fort MacKay 36 D8
Fort Macleod 36 E8
Fort McMurray 36 D8
Fort McPherson 36 C6
Fort Madison 40 E9
Fort Meade 43 M5
Fort Morgan 40 E3
Fort Myers 43 M5
Fort Nelson 36 D7
Fort Nelson → 36 D7
Fort Payne 43 H3
Fort Peck 38 B10
Fort Peck Dam 38 C10
Fort Peck L. 38 C10
Fort Pierce 43 M5
Fort Pierre 40 C4
Fort Providence 36 C8
Fort Resolution 36 C8
Fort St. John 36 D7
Fort Scott 41 G7
Fort Simpson 36 C7
Fort Smith, *Canada* 36 D8
Fort Smith, *U.S.A.* 41 H7
Fort Stockton 41 K3
Fort Sumner 41 H2
Fort Thompson 40 C5
Fort Union △ 41 H2
Fort Valley 43 J4
Fort Walton Beach 43 K2
Fort Wayne 42 E3
Fort William 10 E3
Fort Worth 41 J6
Fort Yates 40 B4
Fort Yukon 36 C5
Fortaleza 47 D11
Forth → 10 E5
Forth, Firth of 10 E6
Fortrose 10 D4
Fortuna, *Calif., U.S.A.* 38 F1
Fortuna, *N. Dak., U.S.A.* 40 A3
Foshan 21 D6
Fossil 38 D3
Fossil Butte △ 38 F8
Fostoria 42 E4
Fougères 12 B3
Foula 10 A6
Foulness I. 9 F8
Fountain 40 F2
Fountain Hills 39 K8
Fouta Djallon 26 F3
Foveaux Str. 33 M2
Fowey 9 G3
Fowler 40 F3
Foxe Basin 37 C12
Foxe Chan. 37 C12
Foxe Pen. 37 C12
Foxford 11 C2
Foxton 33 J5
Foyle, Lough 11 A4
Foynes 11 D2
Franca 47 H9
France ■ 12 C5
Frances 32 C3
Franche-Comté □ 12 C6
Francis Case, L. 40 D5
Francistown 29 J5
François L. 36 D7
Francs Pk. 38 E9
Frankfort, *Ind., U.S.A.* 42 E2
Frankfort, *Kans., U.S.A.* 40 F6
Frankfort, *Ky., U.S.A.* 42 F3
Frankfurt, *Brandenburg, Germany* 16 B7
Frankfurt, *Hessen, Germany* 16 C4
Franklin, *Ky., U.S.A.* 43 G2
Franklin, *La., U.S.A.* 41 L9
Franklin, *N.H., U.S.A.* 42 D10
Franklin, *Nebr., U.S.A.* 40 E5
Franklin, *Pa., U.S.A.* 42 E6
Franklin, *Va., U.S.A.* 43 G7
Franklin, *W. Va., U.S.A.* 42 F6
Franklin B. 36 C7
Franklin D. Roosevelt L. 38 B4
Franklin-Gordon Wild Rivers △ 32 D4
Franklin L. 38 F6
Franklin Mts. 36 C7
Franklin Str. 36 B10
Franklinton 41 K9
Frankston 32 C4
Frantsa Iosifa, Zemlya 18 A6
Fraser → 36 E7
Fraser I. 32 A5
Fraserburgh 10 D6
Frederick, *Md., U.S.A.* 42 F7
Frederick, *Okla., U.S.A.* 41 H5
Frederick, *S. Dak., U.S.A.* 40 C5
Fredericksburg, *Tex., U.S.A.* 41 K5
Fredericksburg, *Va., U.S.A.* 42 F7
Fredericktown 41 G9
Fredericton 37 E13
Frederikshavn 7 F6
Fredonia, *Ariz., U.S.A.* 39 H7
Fredonia, *Kans., U.S.A.* 41 G7
Fredonia, *N.Y., U.S.A.* 42 D6
Fredrikstad 7 F6
Free State □ 29 K5
Freeman 40 D6
Freeport, *Bahamas* 45 B9
Freeport, *Ill., U.S.A.* 40 D10
Freeport, *N.Y., U.S.A.* 42 E9
Freeport, *Tex., U.S.A.* 41 L7
Freetown 26 G3
Freiburg 16 E3
Fremont, *Calif., U.S.A.* 39 H2
Fremont, *Mich., U.S.A.* 42 D3
Fremont, *Nebr., U.S.A.* 40 E6
Fremont, *Ohio, U.S.A.* 42 E4
Fremont → 39 G8
French Guiana ⊠ 47 C8
French Polynesia ⊠ 35 K13
Frenchman Cr. →, *N. Amer.* 38 B10
Frenchman Cr. →, *U.S.A.* 40 E4
Fresnillo 44 C4
Fresno 39 H4
Fresno Res. 38 B9
Freycinet △ 32 D4
Freycinet Pen. 32 D4
Fria, C. 29 H2
Frio → 41 L5
Friona 41 H3
Fritch 41 H4
Frobisher B. 37 C13
Frobisher L. 36 D9
Frome 9 F5
Frome →, *Australia* 32 A2
Frome →, *U.K.* 9 G5
Frome, L. 32 B2
Front Royal 42 F6
Frostburg 42 F6
Frýdek-Místek 16 D9
Fuchū 22 F3
Fuerte → 44 B3
Fuhai 20 B3
Fuji 22 F6
Fuji-San 22 F6
Fujian □ 21 D6
Fukui 22 E5
Fukuoka 22 G2
Fukushima 22 E7
Fukuyama 22 F3
Fulda 16 C4
Fulda → 16 C4
Fullerton 40 E6
Fulton, *Mo., U.S.A.* 40 F9
Fulton, *N.Y., U.S.A.* 42 D7
Funabashi 22 F7
Funafuti 31 B14
Fundy, B. of 37 E13
Furāt, Nahr al → 24 B3
Furneaux Group 32 D4
Fürth 16 D5
Fury and Hecla Str. 37 C11
Fushun 21 B7
Fustic 45 g
Futian 21 F11
Futuna 33 B8
Fuxin 21 B7
Fuyong 21 F10
Fuyu 21 B7
Fuzhou 21 D6
Fylde 8 D5
Fyn 7 F6
Fyne, L. 10 F3

G

Gabès, G. de 27 B8
Gabon ■ 28 E2
Gaborone 29 J5
Gābrīk 24 C4
Gabrovo 15 C11
Gadag 25 D6
Gadsden 43 H3
Gaffney 43 H5
Gagnon 37 D13

Gail 41 J4
Gainesville, Fla., U.S.A. 43 L4
Gainesville, Ga., U.S.A. 43 H4
Gainesville, Mo., U.S.A. 41 G8
Gainesville, Tex., U.S.A. 41 J6
Gainsborough 8 D7
Gairdner, L. 32 B2
Gairloch 10 D3
Gairloch, L. 10 D3
Galápagos = Colón, Arch. de 35 H18
Galapagos Fracture Zone 35 G17
Galapagos Rise 35 J18
Galashiels 10 F6
Galați 15 B13
Galax 43 G5
Galcaio 24 E3
Galdhøpiggen 7 E5
Galela 23 C4
Galena 36 C4
Galesburg 40 E9
Galicia □ 13 A2
Galina Pt. 44 a
Galiuro Mts. 39 K8
Gallan Hd. 10 C1
Gallatin 43 G2
Galle 25 E7
Galley Hd. 11 E3
Gallipoli = Gelibolu 15 D12
Gallipolis 42 F4
Gällivare 7 D8
Galloway 10 F4
Galloway △ 10 F4
Galloway, Mull of 10 G4
Gallup 39 J9
Galty Mts. 11 D3
Galtymore 11 D3
Galva 40 E9
Galveston 41 L7
Galveston B. 41 L7
Galway 11 C2
Galway □ 11 C2
Galway B. 11 C2
Gambia ■ 26 F2
Gambia → 26 F2
Gambier, Îs. 35 K14
Gambier Is. 32 C2
Gammon Ranges △ 32 B2
Gan Jiang → 21 D6
Ganado 39 J9
Gäncä 17 B7
Gander 37 E14
Ganga → 25 C8
Ganges = Ganga → 25 C8
Gani 23 D4
Gannett Peak 38 E9
Gansu □ 20 C5
Gantheaume, C. 32 C2
Ganzhou 21 D6
Gao 26 E5
Gap 12 D7
Gar 20 C2
Gara, L. 11 C3
Garagum 18 F6
Garah 32 A4
Garberville 38 F2
Garda, L. di 14 B4
Garden City, Ga., U.S.A. 43 J5
Garden City, Kans., U.S.A. 41 G4
Garden City, Tex., U.S.A. 41 K4
Gardēz 25 B5
Gardiner, Maine, U.S.A. 43 C11
Gardiner, Mont., U.S.A. 38 D8
Gardnerville 38 G4
Gardo 24 E3
Garfield 38 C5
Garforth 8 D6
Gargantua, C. 42 B3
Garland, Tex., U.S.A. 41 J6
Garland, Utah, U.S.A. 38 F7
Garner 40 D8
Garnett 40 F7
Garoe 24 E3
Garonne → 12 D3
Garrison, Mont., U.S.A. 38 C7
Garrison, N. Dak., U.S.A. 40 B4
Garron Pt. 11 A6
Garry → 10 E5
Garry, L. 36 C9
Garstang 8 D5
Garvie Mts. 33 L2
Gary 42 E2
Garzê 20 C5
Gascogne 12 E4
Gascogne, G. de 12 D2
Gaspé 37 E13
Gaspésie, Pén. de la 37 E13
Gastonia 43 H5
Gatehouse of Fleet 10 G4
Gateshead 8 C6
Gatesville 41 K6
Gatineau 42 C8
Gatton 32 A5
Gatwick, London (LGW) 9 F7
Gau 33 D8
Gaua 31 C12
Gävle 7 E7
Gawler 32 B2
Gaxun Nur 20 B5
Gaya 25 C7
Gaylord 42 C3
Gayndah 32 A5
Gaza 17 D4
Gaza Strip ■ 24 B2
Gaziantep 17 C5
Gcuwa 29 L5
Gdańsk 16 A9
Gdańska, Zatoka 16 A9
Gdynia 16 A9
Gebe 23 C4
Gedser 7 G6
Geelong 32 C3
Gejiu 20 D5
Gelib 24 E3
Gelibolu 15 D12
Gelsenkirchen 16 C3
General Santos 23 C4
Genesee 38 C5
Genesee → 42 D7
Geneseo, Ill., U.S.A. 40 E9
Geneseo, N.Y., U.S.A. 42 D7
Geneva = Genève 12 C7
Geneva, Ala., U.S.A. 43 K3
Geneva, N.Y., U.S.A. 42 D7
Geneva, Nebr., U.S.A. 40 E6
Geneva, Ohio, U.S.A. 42 E5
Genève 12 C7
Gennargentu, Mti. del 14 D3
Genoa = Génova 12 D8
Genoa, Australia 32 C4
Genoa, U.S.A. 40 E6
Génova 12 D8
Gent 16 C1
George 29 L4
George → 37 D13
George, L., N.S.W., Australia 32 C4
George, L., S. Austral., Australia 32 C3
George, L., Fla., U.S.A. 43 L5
George, L., N.Y., U.S.A. 42 D9
George Sound 33 L1
George Town, Australia 32 D4
George Town, Malaysia 23 C2
George V Land 6 D14
George West 41 L5
Georgetown, Guyana 46 B7
Georgetown, Colo., U.S.A. 38 G11
Georgetown, Ky., U.S.A. 42 F3
Georgetown, Ohio, U.S.A. 42 F4
Georgetown, S.C., U.S.A. 43 J6
Georgetown, Tex., U.S.A. 41 K6
Georgia □ 43 K5
Georgian B. 37 E11
Gera 16 C6
Geraldine 38 C8
Geraldton 30 F1
Gereshk 24 B5
Gering 40 E3
Gerlach 38 F4
Germantown 41 M10
Germany ■ 16 C5
Germiston 29 K5
Gerona = Girona 13 B7
Getafe 13 B4
Gettysburg, Pa., U.S.A. 42 F7
Gettysburg, S. Dak., U.S.A. 40 C5
Geyser 38 C8
Ghana ■ 26 G5
Ghanzi 29 J4
Ghats, Eastern 25 D6
Ghats, Western 25 D6
Ghazâl, Bahr el → 27 G12
Ghaziabad 25 C6
Ghaznī 24 B5
Ghent = Gent 16 C1
Giant Sequoia △ 39 J4
Giants Causeway 11 A5
Gibbon 40 E5
Gibraltar ⧄ 13 D3
Gibraltar, Str. of 13 E3
Gibraltar Range △ 32 A5
Gibson Desert 30 E4
Giddings 41 K6
Gifu 22 F5
Gigha 10 F3
Gijón 13 A3
Gila → 39 K6
Gila Bend 39 K7
Gila Bend Mts. 39 K7
Gila Cliff Dwellings △ 39 K9
Gilbert Is. 31 A14
Gilgandra 32 B4
Gilgit 25 B6
Gillam 36 D10
Gilles, L. 32 B2
Gillette 40 C2
Gillingham 9 F8
Gilmer 41 J7
Gilroy 39 H3
Gimie, Mt 45 f
Gin Gin 32 A5
Giohar 24 E3
Girard 41 G7
Girdle Ness 10 D6
Girona 13 B7
Gironde → 12 D3
Girraween △ 32 A5
Girvan 10 F4
Gisborne 33 H7
Giuba → 24 E3
Giza = El Gîza 27 C12
Gizhiga 19 C17
Gjoa Haven 36 C10
Glace Bay 37 E14
Glacier △ 38 B7
Glacier Peak 38 B3
Gladewater 41 J7
Gladstone, Queens., Australia 30 E9
Gladstone, S. Austral., Australia 32 B2
Gladstone, U.S.A. 42 C2
Gladwin 42 D3
Glamorgan, Vale of □ 9 F4
Glasco 40 F6
Glasgow, U.K. 10 F4
Glasgow, Ky., U.S.A. 42 G3
Glasgow, Mont., U.S.A. 38 B10
Glasgow Int. (GLA) 10 F4
Glastonbury 9 F5
Glen Affric 10 D3
Glen Canyon 39 H8
Glen Canyon △ 39 H8
Glen Canyon Dam 39 H8
Glen Coe 10 E3
Glen Garry 10 D3
Glen Innes 32 A5
Glen Mor 10 D4
Glen More △ 10 D5
Glen Moriston 10 D4
Glen Spean 10 E4
Glen Ullin 40 B4
Glenallen 36 C5
Glenariff △ 11 A5
Glenbeigh 11 D2
Glencoe 40 C7
Glencolumbkille 11 B3
Glendale, Ariz., U.S.A. 39 K7
Glendale, Calif., U.S.A. 39 J4
Glendive 40 B2
Glendo 40 D2
Glenelg → 32 C3
Glengad Hd. 11 A4
Glengarriff 11 E2
Glenmorgan 32 A4
Glennamaddy 11 C3
Glenns Ferry 38 E6
Glenreagh 32 B5
Glenrock 38 E11
Glenrothes 10 E5
Glens Falls 42 D9
Glenties 11 B3
Glenveagh △ 11 A3
Glenville 42 F5
Glenwood, Ark., U.S.A. 41 H8
Glenwood, Iowa, U.S.A. 40 E7
Glenwood, Minn., U.S.A. 40 C7
Glenwood Springs 38 G10
Glin 11 D2
Gliwice 16 C9
Globe 39 K8
Głogów 16 C8
Glomma → 7 F6
Glossop 8 D6
Gloucester, Australia 32 B5
Gloucester, U.K. 9 F5
Gloucester Point 42 G7
Gloucestershire □ 9 F5
Gniezno 16 B8
Goa □ 25 D6
Goalen Hd. 32 C5
Goat Fell 10 F3
Gobabis 29 J3
Gobi 21 B5
Godalming 9 F7
Godavari → 25 D7
Gods → 36 D10
Gods L. 36 D10
Gogebic, L. 40 B10
Goiânia 47 G9
Goio-Erê 48 A6
Golconda 38 F5
Gold Beach 38 E1
Gold Coast, Australia 30 F9
Gold Coast, W. Afr. 26 H5
Gold Hill 38 E2
Golden B. 33 J4
Golden Gate 38 H2
Golden Spike △ 38 F7
Golden Vale 11 D3
Goldendale 38 D3
Goldfield 39 H5
Goldsboro 43 H7
Goldsmith 41 K3
Goldthwaite 41 K5
Goliad 41 L6
Golspie 10 D5
Gómez Palacio 44 B4
Gonābād 24 B4
Gonaïves 45 D10
Gongbei 21 G10
Gongga Shan 25 C9
Gonghe 20 C5
Gongming 21 F10
Gongolgon 32 B4
Gonzales, Calif., U.S.A. 39 H3
Gonzales, Tex., U.S.A. 41 L6
Good Hope, C. of 29 L3
Gooding 38 E6
Goodland 40 F4
Goodooga 32 A4
Goole 8 D7
Goolgowi 32 B4
Goomeri 32 A5
Goondiwindi 32 A5
Goose Creek 43 J5
Goose L. 38 F3
Gorakhpur 25 C7
Gordon 40 D3
Gordon → 32 D4
Gore 33 M2
Gorey 11 D5
Gorgān 24 B4
Gorleston 9 E9
Görlitz 16 C7
Gorontalo 23 C4
Gort 11 C3
Gorzów Wielkopolski 16 B7
Gosford 32 B5
Goshen 42 E3
Gosport 9 G6
Göta kanal 7 F7
Göteborg 7 F6
Gotha 16 C5
Gothenburg = Göteborg 7 F6
Gothenburg 40 E4
Gotland 7 F7
Göttingen 16 C4
Gouda 16 B2
Gouin, Rés. 37 E12
Goulburn 32 B4
Gourock 10 F4
Gouverneur 42 C8
Governador Valadares 47 G10
Gowanda 42 D6
Gower 9 F3
Gowna, L. 11 C4
Goyder Lagoon 32 A2
Gozo 14 F6
Graaff-Reinet 29 L4
Gracias a Dios, C. 45 E8
Grady 41 H3
Grafham Water 9 E7
Grafton, Australia 32 A5
Grafton, N. Dak., U.S.A. 40 A6
Grafton, W. Va., U.S.A. 42 F5
Graham 41 J5
Graham, Mt. 39 K9
Graham Land 6 D3
Grahamstown 29 L5
Grain Coast 26 H3
Grampian Mts. 10 E5
Grampians, The 32 C3
Gran Canaria 26 C2
Gran Chaco 48 B4
Gran Sasso d'Itália 14 C5
Granada, Nic. 44 E7
Granada, Spain 13 D4
Granada, U.S.A. 41 F3
Granard 11 C4
Granbury 41 J6
Granby, Canada 37 E12
Granby, U.S.A. 38 F11
Grand →, Mo., U.S.A. 40 F8
Grand →, S. Dak., U.S.A. 40 C4
Grand Bahama I. 45 B9
Grand-Bourg 44 b
Grand Canyon 39 H7
Grand Canyon △ 39 H7
Grand Canyon-Parashant △ 39 H7
Grand Cayman 45 D8
Grand Coulee 38 C4
Grand Coulee Dam 38 C4
Grand Falls 37 E13
Grand Falls-Windsor 37 E14
Grand Forks 40 B6
Grand Haven 42 D2
Grand I. 42 B2
Grand Island 40 E5
Grand Isle 41 L9
Grand Junction 39 G9
Grand L. 41 L8
Grand Lake 38 F11
Grand Marais 42 B3
Grand Portage 40 B10
Grand Prairie 41 J6
Grand Rapids, Canada 36 D10
Grand Rapids, Mich., U.S.A. 42 D2
Grand Rapids, Minn., U.S.A. 40 B8
Grand St-Bernard, Col du 12 D7
Grand Staircase-Escalante △ 39 H8
Grand Teton 38 E8
Grand Teton △ 38 D8
Grand Union Canal 9 E7
Grand-Vigie, Pte. de la 44 b
Grande, Rio → 41 N6
Grande Baleine, R. de la → 37 D12
Grande Prairie 36 D8
Grande-Terre 44 b
Grandfalls 41 K3
Grandview 38 C4
Grangemouth 10 E5
Granger 38 F9
Grangeville 38 D5
Granite City 40 F9
Granite Falls 40 C7
Granite Pk. 38 D9
Granity 33 J3
Grant 40 E4
Grant, Mt. 38 G4
Grant City 40 E7
Grant Range 39 G6
Grantham 8 E7
Grantown-on-Spey 10 D5
Grants 39 J10
Grants Pass 38 E2
Grantsville 38 F7
Granville, N. Dak., U.S.A. 40 A4
Granville, N.Y., U.S.A. 42 D9
Grass Range 38 C9
Grass Valley, Calif., U.S.A. 38 G3
Grass Valley, Oreg., U.S.A. 38 D3
Grasse 12 E7
Grassy 32 D3
Graulhet 12 E4
's-Gravenhage 16 B2
Gravesend, Australia 32 A5
Gravesend, U.K. 9 F8
Grayling 42 C3
Grays 9 F8
Grays Harbor 38 C1
Grays L. 38 E8
Graz 16 E7
Great Australian Bight 30 G5
Great Bahama Bank 44 B4
Great Barrier I. 33 G5
Great Barrier Reef 30 D8
Great Basin 38 G5
Great Basin △ 38 G6
Great Bear → 36 C7
Great Bear L. 36 C8
Great Bend 40 F5
Great Blasket I. 11 D1
Great Camanoe 45 e
Great Channel 25 E8
Great Dividing Ra. 30 E8
Great Exuma I. 45 C9
Great Falls 38 C8
Great Inagua I. 45 C10
Great Karoo 29 L4
Great Lake 32 D4
Great Malvern 9 E5
Great Miami → 42 F3
Great Ormes Head 8 D4
Great Ouse → 8 E8
Great Pedro Bluff 44 a
Great Pee Dee → 43 J6
Great Plains 2 C5
Great Salt L. 38 F7
Great Salt Lake Desert 38 F7
Great Salt Plains L. 41 G5
Great Sand Dunes △ 39 H11
Great Sandy △ 32 A5
Great Sandy Desert 30 E3
Great Skellig 11 E1
Great Slave L. 36 C8
Great Smoky Mts. △ 43 H4
Great Snow Mt. 36 D7
Great Victoria Desert 30 F4
Great Wall 21 C5
Great Whernside 8 C6
Great Yarmouth 9 E9
Greater Antilles 45 D10
Greater London □ 9 F7
Greater Manchester □ 8 D5
Greater Sunda Is. 23 D3
Greece ■ 15 E9
Greeley, Colo., U.S.A. 40 E2
Greeley, Nebr., U.S.A. 40 E5
Greely Fd. 37 B10
Greem-Bell, Ostrov 18 A7
Green →, Ky., U.S.A. 42 G2
Green →, Utah, U.S.A. 39 G9
Green B. 42 C2
Green Bay 42 C2
Green C. 32 C5
Green Cove Springs 43 L5
Green River, Utah, U.S.A. 39 G8
Green River, Wyo., U.S.A. 38 F9
Green Valley 39 L8
Greenbush 40 A6
Greencastle 42 F2
Greeneville 43 G4
Greenfield, Ind., U.S.A. 42 F3
Greenfield, Iowa, U.S.A. 40 E7
Greenfield, Mass., U.S.A. 42 D9
Greenfield, Mo., U.S.A. 41 G8
Greenland ⧄ 6 C4
Greenland Sea 6 B6
Greenock 10 F4
Greenore 11 B5
Greenore Pt. 11 D5
Greensboro, Ga., U.S.A. 43 J4
Greensboro, N.C., U.S.A. 43 G6
Greensburg, Ind., U.S.A. 42 F3
Greensburg, Kans., U.S.A. 41 G5
Greensburg, Pa., U.S.A. 42 E6
Greenstone Pt. 10 D3
Greenville, Ala., U.S.A. 43 K2
Greenville, Calif., U.S.A. 38 F3
Greenville, Maine, U.S.A. 43 C11
Greenville, Mich., U.S.A. 42 D3
Greenville, Miss., U.S.A. 41 J9
Greenville, Mo., U.S.A. 41 G9
Greenville, N.C., U.S.A. 43 H7
Greenville, Ohio, U.S.A. 42 E3
Greenville, Pa., U.S.A. 42 E5
Greenville, S.C., U.S.A. 43 H4
Greenville, Tex., U.S.A. 41 J6
Greenwich □ 9 F8
Greenwood, Ark., U.S.A. 41 H7
Greenwood, Ind., U.S.A. 42 F2
Greenwood, Miss., U.S.A. 41 J9
Greenwood, S.C., U.S.A. 43 H4
Gregory 40 D5
Gregory, L. 32 A2
Grenada 41 J10
Grenada ■ 45 E12
Grenfell 32 B4
Grenoble 12 D6
Gresham 38 D2
Gretna, U.K. 10 F5
Gretna, U.S.A. 41 L9
Grey → 33 K3
Grey Ra. 32 A3
Greybull 38 D9
Greymouth 33 K3
Greystones 11 C5
Greytown 33 J5
Gridley 38 G3
Griffin 43 J3
Griffith 32 B4
Grimsay 10 D1
Grimsby 8 D7
Grinnell 40 E8
Gris-Nez, C. 12 A4
Grise Fiord 37 B10
Groesbeck 41 K6
Groningen 16 B3
Groom 41 H4
Groote Eylandt 30 C6
Gros Islet 45 f
Gros Piton 45 f
Gros Piton Pt. 45 f
Grossglockner 16 E6
Groton 40 C5
Grove Hill 43 K2
Groves 41 L8
Groveton 42 C10
Groznyy 17 B7
Grudziądz 16 B9
Gruinard B. 10 D3
Grundy Center 40 D8
Gruver 41 G4
Guadalajara, Mexico 44 C4
Guadalajara, Spain 13 B4
Guadalcanal 31 B11
Guadalete → 13 D2
Guadalquivir → 13 D2
Guadalupe 39 J3
Guadalupe → 41 L6
Guadalupe Mts. △ 41 K2
Guadalupe Peak 41 K2
Guadarrama, Sierra de 13 B4
Guadeloupe ⧄ 44 b
Guadiana → 13 D2
Guadix 13 D4
Guam ⧄ 34 F6
Guamúchil 44 B3
Guana I. 45 e
Guanajuato 44 C4
Guane 45 C8
Guangdong □ 21 D6
Guangxi Zhuangzu Zizhiqu □ 21 D5
Guangyuan 25 B9
Guangzhou 21 D6
Guanica 45 d
Guantánamo 45 C9
Guaporé → 46 F5
Guarapuava 48 B6
Guatemala 44 E6
Guatemala ■ 44 D6
Guatemala Basin 35 F18
Guatemala Trench 35 F18
Guaviare → 46 C5
Guayama 45 d
Guayaquil 46 D3
Guayaquil, G. de 46 D2
Guaymas 44 B2
Guéret 12 C4
Guernsey, U.K. 9 H5
Guernsey, U.S.A. 40 D2
Guildford 9 F7
Guilin 21 D6
Guinea ■ 26 F3
Guinea, Gulf of 4 D10
Guinea-Bissau ■ 26 F3
Güines 45 C8
Guingamp 12 B2
Guiyang 20 D5
Guizhou □ 20 D5
Gujarat □ 25 C6
Gujranwala 25 C6
Gulbarga 25 D6
Gulf Islands △ 43 E2
Gulfport 41 K10
Gulgong 32 B4
Gunnbjørn Fjeld 6 C5
Gunnedah 32 B5
Gunnewin 32 A4
Gunningbar Cr. → 32 B4
Gunnison, Colo., U.S.A. 39 G10
Gunnison, Utah, U.S.A. 38 G8
Gunnison → 39 G9
Guntersville 43 H2
Guntur 25 D7
Gurdon 41 J8
Gurley 32 A4
Gusinoozersk 19 D11
Gustine 39 H3
Guthrie, Okla., U.S.A. 41 H6
Guthrie, Tex., U.S.A. 41 J4
Guttenberg 40 D9
Guwahati 20 D4
Guy Fawkes River △ 32 A5
Guyana ■ 46 C7
Guyenne 12 D4
Guymon 41 G4
Guyra 32 B5
Gwabegar 32 B4
Gwādar 24 C5
Gwalior 25 C6
Gwangju 21 C7
Gweebarra B. 11 B3
Gweedore 11 A3
Gweru 29 H5
Gwinn 42 B2
Gwydir → 32 A4
Gwynedd □ 8 E3
Gyaring Hu 20 C4
Gympie 32 A5
Győr 16 E8
Gyumri 17 B6

H

Ha Tinh 23 B2
Ha'apai Group 31 D16
Haarlem 16 B2
Haast → 33 K2
Hachinohe 22 C7
Ḥadd, Ra's al 24 C4
Haddington 10 F6
Ḥaḍramawt 24 D3
Hadrian's Wall 8 B5
Haeju 21 C7
Hafar al Bāṭin 24 C3
Hagen 16 C3
Hagerman 41 J2
Hagerman Fossil Beds △ 38 E6
Hagerstown 42 F7
Hagondange 12 B7
Hags Hd. 11 D2
Hague, C. de la 12 B3
Hague, The = 's-Gravenhage 16 B2
Haguenau 12 B7
Haifa = Ḥefa 17 D5
Haikou 21 D6
Ḥā'il 24 C3
Hailar 21 B6
Hailey 38 E6
Hainan □ 21 E5
Haines 38 D5
Haines City 43 L5
Haines Junction 36 C6
Haiphong 20 D5
Haiti ■ 45 D10
Ḥajjah 24 D3
Hakodate 22 C7
Ḥalab 24 B2
Halberstadt 16 C5
Halcombe 33 J5
Halden 7 F6
Halesowen 9 E5
Halesworth 9 E9
Haleyville 43 H2
Halfmoon Bay 33 M2
Halifax, Canada 37 E13
Halifax, U.K. 8 D6
Ḥalīl → 24 C4
Halkirk 10 C5
Hall Pen. 37 C13
Hallāniyat, Jazā'ir al 24 D4
Halle 16 C5
Hallett 32 B2
Hallettsville 41 L6
Hallock 40 A6
Halls Creek 30 D4
Halmahera 23 C4
Halmstad 7 F6
Halstead 9 F8
Halton □ 8 D5
Haltwhistle 8 C5
Hamadān 24 B3
Ḥamāh 24 B2
Hamamatsu 22 F5
Hamar 7 E6
Hamburg, Germany 16 B4
Hamburg, Ark., U.S.A. 41 J9
Hamburg, N.Y., U.S.A. 42 D6
Hämeenlinna 7 E8
Hameln 16 B4
Hamersley Ra. 30 E2
Hami 20 B4
Hamilton, Australia 32 C3
Hamilton, Canada 37 E12
Hamilton, N.Z. 33 G5
Hamilton, U.K. 10 F4
Hamilton, Ala., U.S.A. 43 H1
Hamilton, Mont., U.S.A. 38 C6
Hamilton, N.Y., U.S.A. 42 D8
Hamilton, Ohio, U.S.A. 42 F3
Hamilton, Tex., U.S.A. 41 K5
Hamilton → 32 A2
Hamlet 43 H6
Hamley Bridge 32 B2
Hamlin 41 J4
Hamm 16 C3
Hammerfest 7 C8
Hammond, Ind., U.S.A. 42 E2
Hammond, La., U.S.A. 41 K9
Hammonton 42 F8
Hampden 33 L3
Hampshire □ 9 F6
Hampshire Downs 9 F6
Hampton, Ark., U.S.A. 41 J8
Hampton, Iowa, U.S.A. 40 D8
Hampton, S.C., U.S.A. 43 J5
Hampton, Va., U.S.A. 42 G7
Hancock 40 B10
Handan 21 C6
Hanford 39 H4
Hanford Reach △ 38 C4
Hangayn Nuruu 20 B4
Hangzhou 21 C7
Hangzhou Wan 21 C7
Hankinson 40 B6
Hankö 7 F8
Hanksville 39 G8
Hanmer Springs 33 K4
Hanna, Canada 36 D8
Hanna, U.S.A. 38 F10
Hannibal 40 F9
Hannover 16 B4
Hanoi 20 D5
Hanover, N.H., U.S.A. 42 D9
Hanover, Pa., U.S.A. 42 F7
Hans Lollik I. 45 e
Hanson, L. 32 B2
Hanzhong 20 C5
Haora 25 C7
Haparanda 7 D8
Happy 41 H4
Happy Camp 38 F2
Happy Valley-Goose Bay 37 D13
Har Hu 20 C4
Har Us Nuur 20 B4
Ḥaraḍ 24 C3
Harare 29 H6
Harbin 21 B7
Harbor Beach 42 D4
Hardangerfjorden 7 E5
Hardin 38 D10
Hardy, Pte. 45 f
Harer 24 E3
Hargeisa 24 E3
Hari → 23 D2
Haridwar 25 C6
Harīrūd → 24 B5
Harlan, Iowa, U.S.A. 40 E7
Harlan, Ky., U.S.A. 43 G4
Harlech 8 E3
Harlem 38 B9
Harlingen 41 M6
Harlow 9 F8
Harlowton 38 C9
Harney Basin 38 E4
Harney L. 38 E4
Harney Peak 40 D3
Härnösand 7 E7
Haroldswick 10 A8
Harricana → 37 D12
Harriman 43 H3
Harris 10 D2
Harris, L. 32 B2
Harris, Sd. of 10 D1
Harrisburg, Ill., U.S.A. 41 G10
Harrisburg, Nebr., U.S.A. 40 E3
Harrisburg, Pa., U.S.A. 42 E7
Harrison, Ark., U.S.A. 41 G8
Harrison, Nebr., U.S.A. 40 D3
Harrison, C. 37 D14
Harrisonburg 42 F6
Harrisonville 40 F7
Harrisville 42 C4
Harrodsburg 42 G3
Harrogate 8 C6
Harrow □ 9 F7
Harry S. Truman Res. 40 F7
Hart 42 D2
Hart, L. 32 B2
Hartford, Conn., U.S.A. 42 E9
Hartford, Ky., U.S.A. 42 G2
Hartford, S. Dak., U.S.A. 40 D6
Hartford, Wis., U.S.A. 40 D10
Hartford City 42 E3
Hartland Pt. 9 F3
Hartlepool 8 C6
Hartselle 43 H2
Hartshorne 41 H7
Hartsville 43 H5
Hartwell 43 H4
Harvey, Ill., U.S.A. 42 E2
Harvey, N. Dak., U.S.A. 40 B5
Harwich 9 F9
Haryana □ 25 C6
Harz 16 C5
Hasa 24 C3
Haskell 41 J5
Haslemere 9 F7
Hastings, N.Z. 33 H6
Hastings, U.K. 9 G8
Hastings, Mich., U.S.A. 42 D3
Hastings, Minn., U.S.A. 40 C8
Hastings, Nebr., U.S.A. 40 E5
Hastings Ra. 32 B5
Hat Yai 23 C2
Hatay 17 C4
Hatch 39 K10
Hatfield P.O. 32 B3
Hatgal 20 A5
Hattah 32 B3
Hatteras, C. 43 H8
Hattiesburg 41 K10
Haugesund 7 F5
Hauraki G. 33 G5
Haut Atlas 26 B4
Havana = La Habana 44 B3
Havana 40 E9
Havant 9 G7
Havasu, L. 39 J6
Havel → 16 B6
Havelock, N.Z. 33 J4
Havelock, U.S.A. 43 H7
Haverfordwest 9 F3
Haverhill, U.K. 9 E8
Haverhill, U.S.A. 42 D10
Havre 38 B9
Havre-St.-Pierre 37 D13
Haw → 43 H6
Hawaiian Is. 35 E12
Hawaiian Ridge 35 E11
Hawarden 40 D6
Hawea, L. 33 L2
Hawera 33 H5
Hawick 10 F6
Hawke B. 33 H6
Hawker 32 B2
Hawkinsville 43 J4
Hawley 40 B6
Hawthorne 38 G4
Hay 32 B3
Hay → 36 C8
Hay-on-Wye 9 E4
Hay River 36 C8
Hay Springs 40 D3
Hayden 38 F10
Hayes 40 C4
Hayes → 36 D10
Hayle 9 G2
Hayling I. 9 G7
Haymā' 24 D4
Hays 40 F5
Hayward, Calif., U.S.A. 39 G2
Hayward, Wis., U.S.A. 40 B9
Haywards Heath 9 G7
Hazard 42 G4
Hazelton 40 B4
Hazen 40 B4
Hazlehurst, Ga., U.S.A. 43 K4
Hazlehurst, Miss., U.S.A. 41 K9
Hazleton 42 E8
Healdsburg 38 G2
Healdton 41 H6
Healesville 32 C4
Heard I. 5 G14
Hearne 41 K6
Hearst 37 E11
Heart → 40 B4
Heathrow, London (LHR) 9 F7
Heavener 41 H7
Hebbronville 41 M5
Hebei □ 21 C6
Hebel 32 A4
Heber Springs 41 H9
Hebgen L. 38 D8
Hebrides, Sea of the 10 D2
Hebron, Canada 37 D13
Hebron, N. Dak., U.S.A. 40 B3
Hebron, Nebr., U.S.A. 40 E6
Hecate Str. 36 D6
Hechi 20 D5
Hechuan 20 C5
Hecla 40 C5
Heerlen 12 A6
Ḥefa 17 D5
Hefei 21 C6
Hegang 21 B8
Hei Ling Chau 21 G11
Heidelberg 16 D4
Heilbronn 16 D4
Heilongjiang □ 21 B7
Hejaz = Ḥijāz 24 C3
Hekou 20 D5
Helena, Ark., U.S.A. 41 H9
Helena, Mont., U.S.A. 38 C7
Helensburgh 10 E4
Helensville 33 G5
Helgoland 16 A3
Hells Canyon △ 38 D5
Helmand → 24 B5
Helmsdale 10 C5
Helmsdale → 10 C5
Helper 38 G8
Helsingborg 7 F6
Helsinki 7 E9
Helston 9 G2
Helvellyn 8 C4
Hemel Hempstead 9 F7
Hemet 39 K5
Hemingford 40 D3
Hempstead 41 K6
Henan □ 21 C6
Henderson, Ky., U.S.A. 42 G2
Henderson, N.C., U.S.A. 43 G6
Henderson, Nev., U.S.A. 39 H6
Henderson, Tenn., U.S.A. 43 H1
Henderson, Tex., U.S.A. 41 J7
Henderson I. 35 K15
Hendersonville, N.C., U.S.A. 43 H4
Hendersonville, Tenn., U.S.A. 43 G2
Henggang 21 F11
Hengmen 21 F10
Hengqin Dao 21 G10
Hengyang 21 D6
Henley-on-Thames 9 F7
Henlopen, C. 42 F8
Hennessey 41 G6
Henrietta 41 J5
Henrietta Maria, C. 37 D11
Henry 40 E10
Henryetta 41 H7
Hentiyn Nuruu 21 B5
Henty 32 C4
Henzada 25 D8
Heppner 38 D4
Herāt 24 B5
Hereford, U.K. 9 E5
Hereford, U.S.A. 41 H3
Herefordshire □ 9 E5
Herford 16 B4
Herington 40 F6
Herkimer 42 D8
Herm 9 H5
Hermann 40 F9
Hermidale 32 B4
Hermiston 38 D4
Hermosillo 44 B2
Hernando 41 H10
Herne Bay 9 F9
Herreid 40 C4
Herrin 41 G10
Hertford 9 F7
Hertfordshire □ 9 F7
's-Hertogenbosch 16 C2
Hesperia 39 J5
Hessen □ 16 C4
Hettinger 40 C3
Hewitt 41 K6
Hexham 8 C5
Heysham 8 C5
Heywood 32 C3
Hialeah 43 N5
Hiawatha 40 F7
Hibbing 40 B8
Hibbs B. 32 D4
Hickman 41 G10
Hickory 43 H5
Hicks, Pt. 32 C4
Hidalgo del Parral 44 B3
Higashiōsaka 22 F4
Higgins 41 G4
High Island Res. 21 G11
High Level 36 D8
High Point 43 H6
High Prairie 36 D8
High River 36 D8
High Wycombe 9 F7
Highland □ 10 D4
Highland Park 42 D2
Highmore 40 C5
Ḥijāz 24 C3
Hiko 39 H6
Hikurangi, Gisborne, N.Z. 33 H6
Hikurangi, Northland, N.Z. 33 F5
Hildesheim 16 B4
Hill City, Idaho, U.S.A. 38 E6
Hill City, Kans., U.S.A. 40 F5
Hill City, Minn., U.S.A. 40 B8
Hill City, S. Dak., U.S.A. 40 D3
Hillaby, Mt. 45 g
Hillcrest 45 g
Hillsboro, Kans., U.S.A. 40 F6
Hillsboro, N. Dak., U.S.A. 40 B6
Hillsboro, Ohio, U.S.A. 42 F4
Hillsboro, Tex., U.S.A. 41 J6
Hillsborough 42 D10
Hillsdale 42 E3
Hillston 32 B4
Hilton Head Island 43 J5
Hilversum 16 B2
Himachal Pradesh □ 25 B6
Himalaya 25 C7
Himeji 22 F4
Ḥimş 24 B2
Hinckley, U.K. 9 E6
Hinckley, U.S.A. 40 B8
Hindmarsh, L. 32 C3
Hindu Kush 25 B6
Hinesville 43 K5
Hingham 38 B8
Hinton 42 G5
Hios 15 E12
Hirosaki 22 C7
Hiroshima 22 F3
Hispaniola 45 D10
Hitachi 22 E7
Hitchin 9 F7
Hiva Oa 35 H14
Hjälmaren 7 F7
Hoa Binh 23 A2
Hoare B. 37 C13
Hobart, Australia 32 D4
Hobart, U.S.A. 41 H5
Hobbs 41 J3
Hobe Sound 43 M5
Hodgson 36 D10
Höfu 22 F2
Hogan Group 32 C4
Hohenwald 43 H2
Hohhot 21 B6
Hoisington 40 F5
Hokianga Harbour 33 F4
Hokitika 33 K3
Hokkaidō □ 22 B8
Holbrook, Australia 32 C4
Holbrook, U.S.A. 39 J8
Holden 38 G7
Holdenville 41 H6
Holdrege 40 E5
Holetown 45 g
Holguín 45 C9
Holland 42 D2
Hollandale 41 J9
Hollidaysburg 42 E6
Hollis 41 H5
Hollister, Calif., U.S.A. 39 H3
Hollister, Idaho, U.S.A. 38 E6
Holly Hill 43 L5
Holly Springs 41 H10
Hollywood 43 N5
Holman 36 B8
Holmen 40 D9
Holsworthy 9 G3
Holton 40 F7
Holtville 39 K6
Holy I., Anglesey, U.K. 8 D3
Holy I., Northumberland, U.K. 8 B6
Holyhead 8 D3
Holyoke, Colo., U.S.A. 40 E3
Holyoke, Mass., U.S.A. 42 D9
Home B. 37 C13
Homedale 38 E5
Homer, Alaska, U.S.A. 36 D4
Homer, La., U.S.A. 41 J8
Homestead 43 N5
Homestead △ 40 E6
Homs = Ḥimş 24 B2
Homyel 18 D4
Hondo 41 L5
Honduras ■ 44 E7
Honduras, G. de 44 D7
Honey L. 38 F3
Hong → 20 D5
Hong Gai 23 A2
Hong Kong □ 21 G11
Hong Kong I. 21 G11
Hong Kong Int. (HKG) 21 G10
Hongjiang 21 D5
Hongshui He → 21 D5
Hongze Hu 21 C6
Honiara 31 B10
Honiton 9 G4
Honolulu 35 E12
Honshū 22 F6
Hood, Mt. 38 D3
Hood River 38 D3
Hoodsport 38 C2
Hook Hd. 11 D5
Hooker 41 G4
Hooper Bay 36 C3
Hoopeston 42 E2
Hoorn 16 B2
Hoover 43 J2
Hoover Dam 39 J6
Hope 41 J8
Hope, L. 32 A2
Hopedale 37 D13
Hopetoun 32 C3
Hopewell 42 G7
Hopkinsville 43 G2
Hopland 38 G2
Hoquiam 38 C2
Horlivka 17 A5
Hormuz, Str. of 24 C4
Horn, Cape = Hornos, C. de 48 H3
Horn, Is. 31 C15
Horn Head 11 A3
Hornavan 7 D7
Hornbeck 41 K8
Hornbrook 38 F2
Horncastle 8 D7
Hornell 42 D7
Hornos, C. de 48 H3
Hornsea 8 D7
Horqin Youyi Qianqi 21 B7
Horse Cr. → 40 E3
Horsham, Australia 32 C3
Horsham, U.K. 9 F7
Horton 40 F7
Horton → 36 C7
Hot Creek Range 38 G6
Hot Springs, Ark., U.S.A. 41 H8
Hot Springs, S. Dak., U.S.A. 40 D3
Hot Springs △ 41 H8
Hotan 20 C2
Hotchkiss 39 G10
Hou Hai 21 F10
Houghton 40 B10
Houghton L. 42 C3
Houghton-le-Spring 8 C6
Houhora Heads 33 F4
Houlton 43 B12
Houma 41 L9
Houston, Mo., U.S.A. 41 G9
Houston, Tex., U.S.A. 41 L7
Hovd □ 20 B4
Hove 9 G7
Hovenweep △ 39 H9
Hövsgöl Nuur 20 A5
Howard, Australia 32 A5
Howard, U.S.A. 40 C6
Howe 38 E7
Howe, C. 32 C5
Howell 42 D4
Howitt, L. 32 A2
Howland I. 34 G10
Howrah = Haora 25 C7
Howth 11 C5
Howth Hd. 11 C5
Hoy 10 C5
Høyanger 7 E5
Hoylake 8 D4
Hradec Králové 16 C7
Hrodna 18 D3
Hron → 16 E9
Hsinchu 21 D7
Hua Hin 23 B1
Huahine, Î. 35 J12
Huai He → 21 C6
Huainan 21 C6
Huaiyin 21 C6
Hualapai Peak 39 J7
Huambo 29 G3
Huancayo 46 F3
Huang He → 21 C6
Huangshan 21 D6
Huangshi 21 C6
Huánuco 46 E3
Huascarán, Nevado 46 E3
Huatabampo 44 B3
Hubbard 41 K6
Hubei □ 21 C6
Hubli 25 D6
Hucknall 8 D6
Huddersfield 8 D6
Hudiksvall 7 E7
Hudson, N.Y., U.S.A. 42 D9
Hudson, Wis., U.S.A. 40 C8
Hudson, Wyo., U.S.A. 38 E9
Hudson → 42 E8
Hudson Bay 37 D11
Hudson Falls 42 D9
Hudson Str. 37 C13
Hue 23 B2
Huelva 13 D2
Huesca 13 A5
Hughenden 30 E7
Hugo, Colo., U.S.A. 40 F3
Hugo, Okla., U.S.A. 41 H7
Hugoton 41 G4
Huize 20 D5
Hull 37 E12
Hull → 8 D7
Hulun Nur 21 B6
Humacao 45 d
Humber → 8 D7
Humboldt, Canada 36 D9
Humboldt, Iowa, U.S.A. 40 D7
Humboldt, Tenn., U.S.A. 41 H10
Humboldt → 38 F4
Hume, L. 32 C4
Humen 21 F10
Humphreys Peak 39 J8
Hunan □ 21 D6
Hungary ■ 16 E9
Hungerford 32 A3
Hŭngnam 21 C7
Hunsrück 16 D3
Hunstanton 8 E8
Hunter I. 32 D3
Hunter Ra. 32 B5
Hunterville 33 H5
Huntingburg 42 F2
Huntingdon, U.K. 9 E7
Huntingdon, U.S.A. 42 E7
Huntington, Ind., U.S.A. 42 E3
Huntington, Oreg., U.S.A. 38 D5
Huntington, Utah, U.S.A. 38 G8
Huntington, W. Va., U.S.A. 42 F4
Huntington Beach 39 K5
Huntly, N.Z. 33 G5
Huntly, U.K. 10 D6
Huntsville, Canada 37 E12
Huntsville, Ala., U.S.A. 43 H2
Huntsville, Tex., U.S.A. 41 K7
Huonville 32 D4
Hurghada 24 C2
Hurley, N. Mex., U.S.A. 39 K9
Hurley, Wis., U.S.A. 40 B9
Huron 40 C5
Huron, L. 42 C4
Hurricane 39 H7
Hurunui → 33 K4
Hutchinson, Kans., U.S.A. 41 F6
Hutchinson, Minn., U.S.A. 40 C7
Hutton, Mt. 32 A4
Huzhou 21 C7
Hwang Ho = Huang He → 21 C6
Hyannis, Mass., U.S.A. 42 E10
Hyannis, Nebr., U.S.A. 40 E4
Hyargas Nuur 20 B4
Hyderabad, India 25 D6
Hyderabad, Pakistan 24 C5
Hyères 12 E7
Hyères, Îs. d' 12 E7
Hyndman Peak 38 E6
Hyrum 38 F8
Hysham 38 C10
Hythe 9 F9

I

Ialomița → 15 B12
Iași 17 A3
Ibadan 26 G6
Ibagué 46 C3
Ibb 24 D3
Iberian Peninsula 2 B9
Ibiza = Eivissa 13 C6
'Ibrī 24 C4
Ica 46 F3
İçel 17 C4
Iceland ■ 7 B2
Ichihara 22 F7
Ichinomiya 22 F5
Ida Grove 40 D7
Idabel 41 J7
Idaho □ 38 D7
Idaho City 38 E6
Idaho Falls 38 E7
Idar-Oberstein 16 D3
Ife 26 G6
Igarka 18 C9
Iglésias 14 E3
Igloolik 37 C11
Iguaçu, Cat. del 48 B6
Iguala 44 D5
Iisalmi 7 E9
IJsselmeer 16 B2
Ikaluktutiak 36 C9
Ikeda 22 F3
Ilagan 23 B4
Ile → 18 E8
Île-de-France □ 12 B5
Ilesha 26 G6
Ilfracombe 9 F3
Ilhéus 47 F11
Iliamna L. 36 D4
Iligan 23 C4
Ilkeston 8 E6
Ilkley 8 D6
Iller → 16 D4
Illinois □ 40 E10
Illinois → 40 F9
Iloilo 23 B4
Ilorin 26 G6
Imabari 22 F3
Imbil 32 A5
imeni Ismail Samani, Pik 18 F8
Imi 24 E3
Imlay 38 F4
Immingham 8 D7
Immokalee 43 M5
Imperatriz 47 E9
Imperial 40 E4
Imperial Dam 39 K6
Imphal 25 C8
Inangahua 33 J3
Inari 7 D9
Inarijärvi 7 D9
Incheon 21 C7
Incline Village 38 G4
Incomáti → 29 K6
Indalsälven → 7 E7
Independence, Calif., U.S.A. 39 H4
Independence, Iowa, U.S.A. 40 D9
Independence, Kans., U.S.A. 41 G7
Independence, Ky., U.S.A. 42 F3
Independence, Mo., U.S.A. 40 F7
Independence Mts. 38 F5
India ■ 25 C6
Indian → 43 M5
Indian Ocean 3 E14
Indian Springs 39 G6
Indiana 42 E6
Indiana □ 42 F3
Indianapolis 42 F2
Indianola, Iowa, U.S.A. 40 E8
Indianola, Miss., U.S.A. 41 J9
Indigirka → 19 B15
Indio 39 K5
Indo-China 23 B2
Indonesia ■ 23 D3
Indore 25 C6
Indravati → 25 D7
Indre → 12 C4
Indulkana 32 A1
Indus → 24 C5
Indus, Mouths of the 24 C5
Ingleborough 8 C5
Inglewood, Queens., Australia 32 A5
Inglewood, Vic., Australia 32 C3
Inglewood, N.Z. 33 H5
Inglewood, U.S.A. 39 K4
Ingolstadt 16 D5
Ingomar 38 C10
Inishbofin 11 C1
Inisheer 11 C2
Inishfree B. 11 A3
Inishkea North 11 B1
Inishkea South 11 B1
Inishmaan 11 C2
Inishmore 11 C2
Inishmurray I. 11 B3
Inishowen Pen. 11 A4
Inishshark 11 C1
Inishturk 11 C1
Inishvickillane 11 D1
Injune 32 A4
Inland Kaikoura Ra. 33 J4
Inn → 16 D6
Innamincka 32 A3
Inner Hebrides 10 E2
Inner Mongolia = Nei Monggol Zizhiqu □ 21 B6
Inner Sound 10 D3
Innsbruck 16 E5
Inny → 11 C4
Inowrocław 16 B9
Insein 25 D8
Interlaken 12 C7
International Falls 40 A8
Inukjuak 37 D12
Inuvik 36 C6
Inveraray 10 E3
Inverbervie 10 E6
Invercargill 33 M2
Inverclyde □ 10 F4
Inverell 32 A5
Invergordon 10 D4
Inverloch 32 C4
Inverness, U.K. 10 D4
Inverness, U.S.A. 43 L4
Inverurie 10 D6
Investigator Group 32 B1
Investigator Str. 32 C2
Inyo Mts. 39 H5
Inyokern 39 J5
Iola 41 G7
Iona 10 E2
Ione 38 G3
Ionia 42 D3
Ionian Is. = Ionioi Nisoi 15 E9
Ionian Sea 15 E7
Ionioi Nisoi 15 E9
Iowa □ 40 D8
Iowa → 40 E9
Iowa City 40 E9
Iowa Falls 40 D8
Iowa Park 41 J5
Ipatinga 47 G10
Ipoh 23 C2
Ipswich, Australia 32 A5
Ipswich, U.K. 9 E9
Ipswich, U.S.A. 40 C5
Iqaluit 37 C13
Iquique 46 H4
Iquitos 46 D4
Iraklio 15 G11
Iran ■ 24 B4
Irapuato 44 C4
Iraq ■ 24 B3
Ireland ■ 11 C4
Iringa 28 F7
Irish Republic ■ 11 C4
Irish Sea 8 D3
Irkutsk 19 D11
Iron Baron 32 B2
Iron Knob 32 B2
Iron Mountain 42 C1
Iron River 40 B10
Ironton, Mo., U.S.A. 41 G9
Ironton, Ohio, U.S.A. 42 F4
Ironwood 40 B9
Ironwood Forest △ 39 K8
Irrara Cr. → 32 A4
Irrawaddy → 25 D8
Irtysh → 18 C7
Irvine, U.K. 10 F4
Irvine, U.S.A. 42 G4
Irvinestown 11 B4
Irving 41 J6
Irymple 32 B3
Isabel 40 C4
Isabela 45 d
Isar → 16 D6
Isère → 12 D6
Isfahan = Eşfahān 24 B4
Ishim → 18 D8
Ishinomaki 22 D7
Ishpeming 42 B2
İskenderun 17 C5
Isla → 10 E5
Islamabad 25 B6
Island L. 36 D10
Island Lagoon 32 B2
Island Pond 42 C10
Islands, B. of 33 F5
Islay 10 F2
Isle of Wight □ 9 G6
Isle Royale △ 42 B1
Ismâ'ilîya 27 B12
Israel ■ 17 D4
Issoire 12 D5
İstanbul 15 D13
İstanbul Boğazı 15 D13
Istokpoga, L.
Istra
Istres
Istria = Istra
Itabuna
Itaipú, Represa
Italy ■
Itapipoca
Itchen →
Ithaca
Ivanhoe, Austr
Ivanhoe, U.S.A
Ivano-Frankivs
Ivanovo
Ivory Coast ■
Ivujivik
Ivybridge
Iwaki
Iwakuni
Iwo
Izhevsk
Izkī
İzmir

J

J. Strom Thurmond L.
Jabalpur
Jaboatão
Jackman
Jacksboro
Jackson, Barbados
Jackson, Ala., U.S.A.
Jackson, Calif., U.S.A.
Jackson, Ky., U.S.A.
Jackson, Mich U.S.A.
Jackson, Minn U.S.A.
Jackson, Miss. U.S.A.
Jackson, Mo., U.S.A.
Jackson, Ohio, U.S.A.
Jackson, Tenn. U.S.A.
Jackson, Wyo. U.S.A.
Jackson B.
Jackson L.
Jacksons
Jacksonville, A U.S.A.
Jacksonville, A U.S.A.
Jacksonville, F U.S.A.
Jacksonville, Ill U.S.A.
Jacksonville, N U.S.A.
Jacksonville, T U.S.A.
Jacksonville Be
Jacmel
Jacob Lake
Jaén
Jaffa = Tel Aviv Yafo
Jaffa, C.
Jaffna
Jagdalpur
Jahrom
Jaipur
Jakarta
Jal
Jalna
Jaluit I.
Jamaica ■
Jambi
James →, S. D U.S.A.
James →, Va., U.S.A.
James B.
Jamestown, Australia
Jamestown, N. Dak., U.S.
Jamestown, N. U.S.A.
Jammu
Jammu & Kashmir □
Jamnagar
Jamshedpur
Jan Mayen
Jandowae
Janesville
Japan ■
Japan, Sea of
Japan Trench
Japurá →
Jarvis I.
Jāsk
Jasper, Canada
Jasper, Ala., U.S.A.
Jasper, Fla., U.S.A.
Jasper, Ind., U.S.A.
Jasper, Tex., U.S.A.
Jaunpur
Java = Jawa
Java Sea
Java Trench
Jawa
Jaya, Puncak
Jayton
Jean
Jeanerette
Jebel, Bahr el →
Jedburgh
Jedda = Jiddah
Jefferson, Iowa U.S.A.
Jefferson, Tex., U.S.A.
Jefferson, Mt., Nev., U.S.A.
Jefferson, Mt., Oreg., U.S.A.
Jefferson City, Mo., U.S.A.
Jefferson City, Tenn., U.S.A.
Jeffersontown
Jeffersonville
Jeffrey City
Jeju-do
Jekyll I.
Jelenia Góra
Jena, Germany
Jena, U.S.A.
Jenkins
Jennings
Jeonju
Jeparit
Jequié
Jérémie
Jerez de la Frontera
Jerilderie
Jerome
Jersey
Jersey City
Jersey Shore
Jerseyville
Jerusalem
Jervis B.
Jesup
Jetmore
Jhansi
Jharkhand □
Jhelum →

Index (gazetteer), page 53. Entries are given as: Name — atlas page number, grid reference. Columns are transcribed left-to-right, top-to-bottom.

Column 1 (continuation fragments from preceding page, grid references only)

21 B8 · 21 D6 · 21 D6 · 21 C7 · 21 C7 · 24 C2 · 21 C6 · 21 B7 · 44 B4 · 21 C6 · 20 C5 · 32 C4 · 21 G10 · 20 D5 · 20 D7 · *ol Zizhiqu,* 21 B6 · *iong,* 21 C6 · 20 D5 · 21 D6 · 24 C5 · 21 B8 · 47 E12 · 25 D6 · 29 K5 · *ts.,* 38 D4 · 38 D3 · *ssil* 38 D4 · *Res.* 10 C5 · *A.* 41 G4 · *Tex.,* 41 K5 · 35 F11 · *eland* 11 D4 · *.Y.,* 42 D8 · *ia.,* 23 C2 · 42 E1 · 37 E12 · 23 C4 · 24 B3 · *k.,* 41 H9 · *.,* 41 J8 · 38 C9 · 37 E12 · 41 G7 · 24 C10 · 28 E5 · 26 E7 · *arte* 30 C4 · 23 C2 · *I.* 45 e · *n,* 41 L5 · *Str* · *lez,* 35 L20 · *orte* 47 E11 · 38 C9 · 48 A7 · 32 D4 · 32 B2 · 38 C8 · 40 F8 · 25 B6 · 27 C7 · 34 B3 · 41 K5 · 10 E4 · 11 D3 · 7 F8 · 29 H8 · 17 C5 · 33 J4 · 7 E9 · 11 B5 · 24 B4 · 38 C2 · 29 K4 · 38 D7 · 29 G5 · 25 C5 · 33 G6 · 33 G6 · 40 D2 · 41 G7 · 21 C7 · 33 J4 · 33 H5 · 36 B7 · 23 D7 · 16 D7 · 29 K4 · 16 A7 · 7 F7 · 33 H6 · 33 D7 · *'s,* 6 D7

Column 2 — Kanab … Kenton

Kanab 39 H7 · Kanab Cr. → 39 H7 · Kananga 28 F4 · Kanawha → 42 F4 · Kanazawa 22 E5 · Kandanghaur 23 D2 · Kandi 26 F6 · Kandy 25 E7 · Kane 42 E4 · Kane Basin 6 B3 · Kangaroo I. 32 C2 · Kangean, Kepulauan 23 D2 · Kangiqsualujjuaq 37 D13 · Kangiqsujuaq 37 C12 · Kangirsuk 37 D13 · Kanin, Poluostrov 18 C5 · Kankakee 42 E2 · Kankan 26 F3 · Kannapolis 43 H5 · Kano 26 F7 · Kanpur 25 C7 · Kansas □ 40 F7 · Kansas → 40 F7 · Kansas City, Kans., U.S.A. 40 F7 · Kansas City, Mo., U.S.A. 40 F7 · Kansk 19 D10 · Kanturk 11 D3 · Kanye 29 J5 · Kaohsiung 21 D7 · Kaolack 26 F2 · Kapiti I. 33 J5 · Kaposvár 16 E8 · Kapuas → 23 D2 · Kapuas Hulu, Pegunungan 23 C3 · Kapunda 32 E2 · Kapuni 33 H5 · Kaputar, Mt. 32 B5 · Kara Kum = Garagum 18 F6 · Kara Sea 18 B7 · Karachi 24 C5 · Karaganda = Qaraghandy 18 E8 · Karaj 24 B4 · Karakol 25 A6 · Karakoram Ra. 25 B6 · Karaman 20 B3 · Karamea Bight 33 J3 · Karasburg 29 K3 · Karbalā' 24 B3 · Karimata, Kepulauan 23 D2 · Karimata, Selat 23 D2 · Karimunjawa, Kepulauan 23 D3 · Karlskrona 7 F7 · Karlsruhe 16 D4 · Karlstad, Sweden 7 F6 · Karlstad, U.S.A. 40 A6 · Karnataka □ 25 D6 · Kärnten □ 16 E7 · Karonga 28 F6 · Karratha 30 C4 · Karsakpay 18 E7 · Karufa 23 D5 · Kasai → 28 E3 · Kasama 28 G6 · Kāshān 24 B4 · Kashi 20 C2 · Kaskaskia → 40 F10 · Kassalā 29 E12 · Kassel 16 C4 · Kasson 40 C8 · Kastamonu 20 A5 · Kasur 25 D6 · Katahdin, Mt. 43 C11 · Katanga □ 28 F4 · Katha 25 C8 · Katherine 30 B5 · Katmandu 25 C7 · Katoomba 32 E5 · Katrine, L. 10 E4 · Katsina 26 F7 · Kattegat 7 F6 · Kauai 45 e · Kaufman 41 J6 · Kaukauna 42 C1 · Kaunas 7 J20 · Kavala 15 D11 · Kavieng 30 A9 · Kavir, Dasht-e 24 B4 · Kawagoe 22 F6 · Kawaguchi 22 F6 · Kawawachikamach 37 D13 · Kawerau 33 H6 · Kawhia 33 H5 · Kawhia Harbour 33 H5 · Kayan → 23 C3 · Kaycee 40 F5 · Kayenta 45 J8 · Kayes 26 F2 · Kaysville 40 F8 · Kazakhstan ■ 18 E7 · Kazan 18 D8 · Kazan-Rettō 22 K18 · Käzerün 24 D4 · Keady 11 B5 · Kearney 39 K8 · Kearny 45 K7 · Kebnekaise 6 B7 · Kebri Dehar 24 N5 · Kebumen 23 D2 · Kecskemét 16 E9 · Kediri 23 D3 · Keeling Is. = Cocos Is. 23 C5 · Keene 42 D9 · Keeper Hill 11 D3 · Keetmanshoop 29 K3 · Kefalonia 15 E9 · Keflavík 6 D1 · Keighley 8 D6 · Keith, Australia 32 F3 · Keith, U.K. 10 D6 · Keizer 40 D2 · Kelang 23 D2 · Kellogg 40 C5 · Kelowna 36 D8 · Kelso, N.Z. 33 L2 · Kelso, U.K. 10 F6 · Kemerovo 18 D9 · Kemi 6 D7 · Kemijoki → 6 D7 · Kemmerer 40 F8 · Kemp Land 5 C5 · Kemp, L. 41 J5 · Kempsey 32 B5 · Kempten 16 E6 · Kenai 36 B4 · Kendal, Australia 32 B5 · Kendal, U.K. 8 C5 · Kendallville 42 E3 · Kenedy 41 L6 · Kenema 26 G3 · Kenhardt 29 K4 · Kenitra 26 B4 · Kenmare, Ireland 11 E2 · Kenmare, U.S.A. 40 A3 · Kenmare River 11 E2 · Kennebec 40 D5 · Kennebec → 43 D11 · Kennet → 9 F7 · Kennett 41 G9 · Kennewick 40 C4 · Kenora 36 D10 · Kenosha 42 D2 · Kent, Tex., U.S.A. 41 K2 · Kent, Wash., U.S.A. 40 C2 · Kent □ 9 F8 · Kent Group 32 F4 · Kent Pen. 36 B9 · Kentland 42 E2 · Kenton 42 E4

Column 3 — Kentucky … Kinvarra

Kentucky □ 42 G3 · Kentucky → 42 F3 · Kentucky L. 43 G2 · Kentville 37 E13 · Kenya ■ 28 D7 · Kenya, Mt. 28 E7 · Keokuk 40 E9 · Kerala □ 25 D6 · Kerch 17 A5 · Kerguelen 5 G14 · Kerinci 23 D2 · Kerkyra 15 E8 · Kermadec Is. 31 G15 · Kermadec Trench 31 G15 · Kermān 24 B4 · Kermānshāh 24 B3 · Kermit 41 K3 · Kern → 39 J4 · Kerrera 10 E3 · Kerrobert 36 D9 · Kerry □ 11 D2 · Kerry Hd. 11 D2 · Kerulen → 21 B6 · Keswick 8 C4 · Ketchenko 36 D6 · Ketchum 38 E6 · Kettering, U.K. 9 E7 · Kettering, U.S.A. 42 F3 · Kettle Falls 38 B4 · Kewanee 40 E10 · Kewaunee 42 C2 · Keweenaw B. 42 B1 · Keweenaw Pen. 42 B2 · Keweenaw Pt. 42 B2 · Key, L. 11 B3 · Key Largo 43 N5 · Keynsham 9 F5 · Keyser 42 F6 · Khabarovsk 19 E14 · Khambhat, G. of 25 C6 · Khamis Mushayṭ 24 D3 · Kharagpur 25 C7 · Kharkiv 18 E4 · Kharkov = Kharkiv 18 E4 · Khartoum = El Khartûm 27 E12 · Khaskovo 15 D11 · Khatanga 19 B11 · Kherson 17 A4 · Kholm 24 B5 · Khon Kaen 23 B2 · Khorramābād 24 B3 · Khorramshahr 24 B3 · Khorugh 25 B5 · Khouribga 26 B4 · Khújand 18 E7 · Khulna 25 C7 · Khvoy 24 B3 · Khyber Pass 25 B6 · Kiama 32 B5 · Kicking Horse Pass 36 D8 · Kidderminster 9 E5 · Kidnappers, C. 33 H6 · Kidsgrove 8 D5 · Kiel 16 A6 · Kiel Canal = Nord-Ostsee-Kanal 16 A4 · Kielce 16 C10 · Kielder Water 8 B5 · Kiev = Kyyiv 18 D5 · Kigali 28 E6 · Kigoma-Ujiji 28 E5 · Kikwit 28 E3 · Kilbeggan 11 C4 · Kilbirnie 10 F4 · Kildare 11 C5 · Kildare □ 11 C5 · Kilgarvan 11 E2 · Kilgore 41 J7 · Kilifi 28 E7 · Kilimanjaro 28 E7 · Kilkee 11 D2 · Kilkeel 11 B6 · Kilkenny 11 D4 · Kilkenny □ 11 D4 · Kilkieran B. 11 C2 · Killala 11 B2 · Killaloe 11 D3 · Killaloe 11 D3 · Killarney, Australia 32 A5 · Killarney, Ireland 11 D2 · Killarney △ 11 D2 · Killary Harbour 11 C2 · Killdeer 40 B3 · Killeen 41 K6 · Killin 10 E4 · Killiney 11 D5 · Killorglin 11 D2 · Kilmarnock 10 F4 · Kilmore 32 C3 · Kilosa 28 F7 · Kilrush 11 D2 · Kilwinning 10 F4 · Kim 41 G3 · Kimba 32 B2 · Kimball, Nebr., U.S.A. 40 E3 · Kimball, S. Dak., U.S.A. 40 D5 · Kimberley, Australia 30 C4 · Kimberley, S. Africa 29 K4 · Kimberly 40 C6 · Kimmirut 37 C13 · Kinabalu, Gunung 23 C3 · Kinder Scout 8 D6 · Kindersley 36 D9 · Kindu 28 E5 · King City 39 H3 · King George I. 5 C18 · King George Is. 37 D11 · King I. 32 F3 · King William I. 36 C10 · Kingaroy 32 A5 · Kingfisher 41 H6 · Kingman, Ariz., U.S.A. 39 J7 · Kingman, Kans., U.S.A. 41 G5 · Kings → 39 H4 · Kings Canyon △ 39 H4 · King's Lynn 9 E8 · Kingsbridge 9 G4 · Kingsburg 39 H4 · Kingscourt 11 C5 · Kingsland 43 K5 · Kingsport 43 G4 · Kingston, Canada 37 F8 · Kingston, Jamaica 44 a · Kingston, N.Y., U.S.A. 42 E8 · Kingston, Pa., U.S.A. 42 E8 · Kingston South East 32 C2 · Kingston upon Hull 8 D7 · Kingston-upon-Thames 9 F7 · Kingstown 45 E12 · Kingstree 43 J6 · Kingsville 41 M6 · Kingswood 9 F5 · Kington 9 E4 · Kingussie 10 D4 · Kinloch 33 D11 · Kinlochleven 10 E4 · Kinnairds Hd. 10 D6 · Kinross 10 E5 · Kinsale 11 E3 · Kinsale, Old Hd. of 11 F3 · Kinshasa 28 E3 · Kinsley 41 G5 · Kinston 43 H7 · Kintore 10 D6 · Kintyre 10 F3 · Kintyre, Mull of 10 F3 · Kinvarra 11 C3

Column 4 — Kiowa … Kudat

Kiowa, Kans., U.S.A. 41 G5 · Kiowa, Okla., U.S.A. 41 H7 · Kippure 11 C5 · Kirensk 19 D11 · Kirghizia = Kyrgyzstan ■ 18 E8 · Kiribati ■ 31 A15 · Kirkby 8 D5 · Kirkby-in-Ashfield 8 D6 · Kirkby Lonsdale 8 C5 · Kirkby Stephen 8 C5 · Kirkcaldy 10 E5 · Kirkcudbright 10 G4 · Kirkintilloch 10 F4 · Kirkland Lake 37 E11 · Kirksville 40 E8 · Kirkūk 24 B3 · Kirkwall 10 C6 · Kirov 18 D5 · Kirovohrad 17 A4 · Kirriemuir 10 E5 · Kirtland 39 H9 · Kiruna 6 C8 · Kiryū 22 E6 · Kisangani 28 D5 · Kishinev = Chișinău 17 A3 · Kislovodsk 17 A3 · Kissimmee 43 L5 · Kissimmee → 43 M5 · Kisumu 28 E6 · Kit Carson 40 F3 · Kitakyūshū 22 G2 · Kitami 22 D9 · Kitchener 37 E11 · Kitimat 36 C4 · Kittanning 42 E6 · Kittatinny Mts. 43 D10 · Kittery 43 D10 · Kitwe 28 E5 · Kivu, L. 28 E5 · Kizil Irmak → 17 B5 · Kladno 16 C7 · Klagenfurt 16 E7 · Klamath → 38 F1 · Klamath Falls 38 E3 · Klamath Mts. 38 F2 · Klang 23 C2 · Klarälven → 7 F6 · Klerksdorp 29 K5 · Klickitat 38 C3 · Kluane L. 36 C6 · Kluang 23 C2 · Klyuchevskaya, Gora 19 D17 · Knaresborough 8 C6 · Knighton 9 E4 · Knock 11 C3 · Knockmealdown Mts. 11 D4 · Knossós 15 G12 · Knox 42 E2 · Knoxville, Iowa, U.S.A. 40 E8 · Knoxville, Tenn., U.S.A. 43 H4 · Kōbe 22 F4 · København 7 E8 · Koblenz 16 C3 · Kocaeli 17 B3 · Kōchi 22 G3 · Kodiak 36 D4 · Kodiak I. 36 D4 · Kofiridua 26 G5 · Kōfu 22 F6 · Kokkola 7 E8 · Kokomo 42 E2 · Koksoak → 37 D13 · Kolaka 23 D2 · Kolar 25 D6 · Kolhapur 25 D6 · Kolkata 25 C7 · Köln 16 C3 · Kolomna 18 D4 · Kolskiy Poluostrov 7 D11 · Kolwezi 28 G5 · Kolyma → 19 C17 · Kolymskoye Nagorye 19 C16 · Komandorskiye Ostrova 19 D17 · Komatsu 22 E5 · Kompong Cham 23 B2 · Komsomolets, Ostrov 19 A10 · Komsomolsk 19 D14 · Konin 16 B9 · Konya 17 C4 · Koonibba, L. 32 B1 · Kooskia 40 C6 · Kootenay L. 36 D8 · Kopi 32 B2 · Korçë 15 D9 · Korea, North ■ 21 C7 · Korea, South ■ 21 C7 · Korea Bay 21 C7 · Korea Strait 21 C7 · Korinthiakos Kolpos 15 E10 · Kōriyama 22 E7 · Korla 20 B3 · Koro Sea 33 D9 · Körös → 16 E10 · Kortrijk 15 C1 · Kos 15 F12 · Kosciuszko, Mt. 32 C4 · Kosovo ■ 15 C9 · Košťi 27 F12 · Kostroma 18 D5 · Koszalin 16 A8 · Kota 25 C6 · Kota Bharu 23 C2 · Kota Kinabalu 23 C3 · Kotabumi 23 D2 · Kotka 7 E9 · Kotuy → 19 B11 · Kotzebue 36 B3 · Kouradsky 18 E8 · Kountze 41 K7 · Kowloon 21 G11 · Kra, Isthmus of = Kra, Kho Khot 23 B1 · Krakatau = Rakata, Pulau 23 D2 · Kraków 16 C10 · Kramatorsk 17 A5 · Krasnoyarsk 19 D10 · Krasnyy Luch 17 A5 · Krefeld 16 C3 · Kremenchuk 17 A4 · Krishna → 25 D7 · Kristiansand 7 G5 · Kristiansund 7 E5 · Kriti 15 G11 · Kroonstad 29 K5 · Krugersdorp 29 K5 · Krung Thep = Bangkok 23 B2 · Kruševac 15 C9 · Krymskyy Pivostriv 17 A4 · Kuala Lumpur 23 C2 · Kuala Terengganu 23 C2 · Kualakapuas 23 D3 · Kuantan 23 C2 · Kuching 23 C3 · Kudat 23 C3

Column 5 — La Barge … Lake Torrens (with L)

La Barge 38 E8 · La Belle 43 M5 · La Ceiba 44 b · La Coruña = A Coruña 13 A1 · La Crescent 40 D9 · La Crosse, Kans., U.S.A. 40 F5 · La Crosse, Wis., U.S.A. 40 D9 · La Désirade 44 b · La Fayette 43 H3 · La Follette 43 G3 · La Grande 38 D4 · La Grande → 37 D12 · La Grange, Ga., U.S.A. 43 J3 · La Grange, Ky., U.S.A. 42 F3 · La Grange, Tex., U.S.A. 41 L6 · La Habana 44 B3 · La Junta 41 F3 · La Loche 36 D9 · La Mancha 13 C4 · La Mesa 39 K10 · La Moure 40 B5 · La Paz, Bolivia 46 G5 · La Paz, Mexico 44 C2 · La Perouse Str. 21 B9 · La Plata 47 E5 · La Porte 41 L7 · La Push 38 C1 · La Rioja 47 B3 · La Roche-sur-Yon 12 C3 · La Rochelle 12 C3 · La Romana 45 D11 · La Ronge 36 C9 · La Salle 40 E10 · La Spézia 14 B3 · La Trinite 44 c · La Tuque 37 E12 · La Vega 45 D10 · La Vergne 43 G2 · Labasa 33 C9 · Laborie 45 f · Labrador 37 D13 · Labrador City 37 D13 · Labrador Sea 37 D14 · Labyrinth, L. 32 B2 · Lac La Biche 36 C8 · Lacepede B. 32 C2 · Lacey 38 C2 · Lachlan → 32 B4 · Lackagh Hills 11 B3 · Lacombe 36 C8 · Laconia 42 D10 · Ladakh → 25 B6 · Ladoga, L. = Ladozhskoye Ozero 7 E10 · Ladysmith, S. Africa 29 K5 · Ladysmith, U.S.A. 40 C9 · Lae 30 B8 · Lafayette, Ind., U.S.A. 42 E2 · Lafayette, La., U.S.A. 41 K9 · Lagan → 11 B6 · Lagos, Nigeria 26 G6 · Lagos, Portugal 13 D1 · Laguna 39 J10 · Lahad Datu 23 C3 · Lahat 23 D2 · Lahn → 16 C4 · Lahore 25 B6 · Lahti 7 E9 · Laidley 32 A5 · Lairg 10 C4 · Laizhou Bandao 21 C6 · Lajes 47 B5 · Lake Andes 40 D5 · Lake Arthur 41 K8 · Lake Bindegolly △ 32 A3 · Lake Cargelligo 32 B4 · Lake Charles 41 K8 · Lake City, Colo., U.S.A. 39 G10 · Lake City, Fla., U.S.A. 43 K4 · Lake City, Mich., U.S.A. 42 C3 · Lake City, Minn., U.S.A. 40 C8 · Lake City, S.C., U.S.A. 43 J6 · Lake District 8 C4 · Lake Eyre △ 32 A2 · Lake Harbour = Kimmirut 37 C13 · Lake Havasu City 39 J6 · Lake Jackson 41 L7 · Lake Meredith △ 41 H4 · Lake Mills 40 D8 · Lake Providence 41 J9 · Lake Roosevelt △ 38 B4 · Lake Torrens △ 32 B2

Column 6 — Lake Village … Lawrenceville

Lake Village 41 J9 · Lake Wales 43 M5 · Lake Worth 43 M5 · Lakeba 33 D9 · Lakeland 43 M5 · Lakeport 38 G2 · Lakes Entrance 32 C4 · Lakeview 38 E3 · Lakewood, Colo., U.S.A. 40 F2 · Lakewood, Ohio, U.S.A. 42 E5 · Lakin 41 G4 · Lakshadweep Is. 25 E6 · Lamar, Colo., U.S.A. 40 F3 · Lamberhurst 9 F8 · Lambesc 12 E6 · Lambley 8 B5 · Lame Deer 38 D10 · Lamego 13 B2 · Lameroo 32 C3 · Lamesa 41 J4 · Lamington △ 21 G11 · Lamon B. 23 B4 · Lampang 23 B1 · Lampasas 41 K5 · Lampeter 9 E3 · Lanai 45 e · Lanark 10 F5 · Lancang Jiang → 20 D5 · Lancashire □ 8 D5 · Lancaster, U.K. 8 C5 · Lancaster, Calif., U.S.A. 39 J4 · Lancaster, Ky., U.S.A. 42 G3 · Lancaster, N.H., U.S.A. 42 C10 · Lancaster, Ohio, U.S.A. 42 F4 · Lancaster, Pa., U.S.A. 42 E7 · Lancaster, S.C., U.S.A. 43 H5 · Lancaster, Wis., U.S.A. 40 D9 · Lancaster Sd. 37 B11 · Land Between the Lakes △ 43 G1 · Landen 13 B4 · Landes 12 D3 · Land's End 9 G2 · Lanett 43 J3 · Langdon 40 A5 · Langholm 10 F5 · Langres 12 C6 · Langres, Plateau de 12 C6 · Langsa 23 C1 · Langtry 41 L4 · Languedoc 12 E5 · Langwang 21 F9 · Lannion 12 B2 · Lansing 42 D3 · Lantau I. 21 G10 · Lanzhou 20 C5 · Lao Bao 23 B2 · Laoag 23 B4 · Laois □ 11 D4 · Laon 12 B5 · Laos ■ 23 B2 · Lapeer 42 D4 · Lappland 7 D8 · Laptev Sea 19 B13 · Laramie 40 E2 · Laramie Mts. 40 E2 · Laredo 41 M5 · Largo 43 M4 · Largs 10 F4 · Larisa 15 E10 · Larkana 24 C5 · Larne 11 B6 · Larned 41 F5 · Larose 41 L9 · Larrimah 30 B5 · Larvik 7 F6 · Las Animas 41 F3 · Las Anod 24 N4 · Las Cruces 39 K10 · Las Palmas 26 C2 · Las Tunas 45 C9 · Las Vegas, N. Mex., U.S.A. 39 J11 · Las Vegas, Nev., U.S.A. 39 J11 · Lashio 25 C8 · Lassen Pk. 38 F3 · Lassen Volcanic △ 38 F3 · Late 33 D16 · Latina 14 D5 · Latrobe 32 F4 · Lau Basin 31 E15 · Lau Fau Shan 21 F10 · Lau Group 33 C9 · Laughlin 39 J6 · Launceston, Australia 32 F4 · Launceston, U.K. 9 G3 · Laune → 11 D2 · Laurel, Miss., U.S.A. 41 K10 · Laurel, Mont., U.S.A. 38 D9 · Laurencekirk 10 E6 · Laurens 43 H4 · Laurentides 37 E13 · Laurinburg 43 H6 · Laurium 40 B10 · Lausanne 12 C7 · Laut, Pulau 23 D3 · Laut Kecil, Kepulauan 23 D3 · Lautoka 33 C8 · Lava Beds △ 38 F3 · Laval 12 B3 · Laverton 30 E4 · Lawas 23 C3 · Lawrence, N.Z. 33 L2 · Lawrence, Kans., U.S.A. 40 F7 · Lawrence, Mass., U.S.A. 42 D10 · Lawrenceburg, Ind., U.S.A. 42 F3 · Lawrenceburg, Tenn., U.S.A. 43 H2 · Lawrenceville 43 J4 · Lawton 41 H5 · Laxford, L. 10 C3 · Layla 24 C4 · Lazio □ 14 C5 · Le François 44 c · Le Gosier 44 b · Le Havre 12 B4 · Le Lamentin 44 c · Le Mans 12 C4 · Le Marin 44 c · Le Mars 40 D6 · Le Moule 44 b · Le Prêcheur 44 c · Le Puy-en-Velay 12 D5 · Le Robert 44 c · Le St-Esprit 44 c · Le Sueur 40 C8 · Lead 40 C3 · Leadville 39 G10 · Leaf → 41 K10 · Leamington 32 C2 · Leane, L. 11 D2 · Leatherhead 9 F7 · Leavenworth, Kans., U.S.A. 40 F7

Column 7 — Leavenworth, Wash. … Lodge Grass

Leavenworth, Wash., U.S.A. 38 C3 · Lebanon, Ind., U.S.A. 42 E2 · Lebanon, Kans., U.S.A. 40 F5 · Lebanon, Ky., U.S.A. 42 G3 · Lebanon, Mo., U.S.A. 41 G8 · Lebanon, N.H., U.S.A. 42 D9 · Lebanon, Oreg., U.S.A. 38 D2 · Lebanon, Pa., U.S.A. 42 E7 · Lebanon, Tenn., U.S.A. 43 G2 · Lebanon ■ 17 F5 · Lebec 39 J4 · Lecce 14 D8 · Lecco 14 B3 · Lech → 16 D6 · Leeds, U.K. 8 D6 · Leeds, U.S.A. 43 J2 · Leek 8 D5 · Leesburg 43 L5 · Leesville 41 K8 · Leeton 32 B4 · Leeuwarden 16 B3 · Leeuwin, C. 30 G2 · Leeward Is. 45 D12 · Lefkada 15 E9 · Leganés 13 B4 · Legazpi 23 B4 · Legnica 16 C8 · Leicester 9 E6 · Leicestershire □ 9 E6 · Leiden 16 B2 · Leine → 16 B5 · Leinster 11 C5 · Leinster, Mt. 11 D5 · Leipzig 16 C6 · Leith 10 F5 · Leith Hill 9 F7 · Leitrim 11 B3 · Leitrim □ 11 B4 · Lek → 16 C3 · Leland, Mich., U.S.A. 42 C3 · Leland, Miss., U.S.A. 41 J9 · Léman, L. 12 C7 · Lemhi Ra. 38 D7 · Lemmon 40 C3 · Lemoore 39 H4 · Lena → 19 B13 · Lenadoon Pt. 11 B2 · Leninogorsk 18 D9 · Leninsk-Kuznetskiy 18 D9 · Lennox 15 D9 · Lenoir 43 H5 · Lenoir City 43 H3 · Lens 12 B5 · Leola 40 C5 · Leominster, U.K. 9 E5 · Leominster, U.S.A. 42 D10 · León, Mexico 44 C4 · León, Nic. 44 E7 · León, Spain 13 A3 · Leon 40 E8 · Leonardtown 42 F7 · Leongatha 32 C4 · Leonora 30 F3 · Leoti 40 F4 · Lérida = Lleida 13 B6 · Lerwick 10 A7 · Les Cayes 45 D10 · Les Sables-d'Olonne 12 C3 · Leshan 20 D5 · Leskovac 15 C9 · Lesotho ■ 29 K5 · Lesser Antilles 45 D12 · Lesser Slave L. 36 C8 · Lesser Sunda Is. 23 D4 · Leszno 16 C8 · Letchworth 9 F7 · Lethbridge 36 D8 · Leti, Kepulauan 23 D4 · Letterkenny 11 B4 · Leuchars 10 E6 · Leuven 15 C2 · Levelland 41 J3 · Leven 10 E6 · Leven, L. 10 E5 · Lévis 37 E12 · Levittown 42 E8 · Lewes, U.K. 9 G8 · Lewes, U.S.A. 42 F8 · Lewis 10 C2 · Lewis Range 38 B7 · Lewisburg, Pa., U.S.A. 42 E7 · Lewisburg, W. Va., U.S.A. 42 G5 · Lewisporte 37 E14 · Lewiston, Idaho, U.S.A. 38 C5 · Lewiston, Maine, U.S.A. 43 C11 · Lewistown, Mont., U.S.A. 38 C9 · Lewistown, Pa., U.S.A. 42 E7 · Lexington, Ill., U.S.A. 40 E10 · Lexington, Ky., U.S.A. 42 F3 · Lexington, Mo., U.S.A. 40 F8 · Lexington, N.C., U.S.A. 43 H5 · Lexington, Nebr., U.S.A. 40 E5 · Lexington, Tenn., U.S.A. 43 H1 · Lexington, Va., U.S.A. 42 G6 · Lexington Park 42 F7 · Leyburn 8 C6 · Leyland 8 D5 · Leyte □ 23 B4 · Lhasa 20 D4 · Lianga 23 C4 · Lianyungang 21 C6 · Liaoning □ 21 B7 · Liaoyang 21 B7 · Liaoyuan 21 B7 · Liard → 36 C7 · Libby 38 B6 · Liberal 41 G4 · Liberec 16 C7 · Liberia ■ 26 G4 · Liberty, Mo., U.S.A. 40 F7 · Liberty, Tex., U.S.A. 41 K7 · Lībiya, Saḥrā' 27 C10 · Libourne 12 D3 · Libreville 28 D1 · Libya ■ 27 C9 · Lichfield 9 E6 · Lichinga 28 G7 · Liechtenstein ■ 16 E5 · Liège 15 D5 · Liepāja 7 F7 · Lifford 11 B4 · Lifou, I. 31 E12 · Lightning Ridge 32 A4 · Liguria □ 14 B3 · Ligurian Sea 14 C3 · Lijiang 20 D5 · Likasi 28 G5 · Lille 12 A5 · Lilongwe 29 G6 · Lima, Peru 46 F3 · Lima, Mont., U.S.A. 38 D7 · Lima, Ohio, U.S.A. 42 E4 · Limavady 11 A5 · Limbe 28 D1 · Limeira 47 H9 · Limerick 11 D3 · Limerick □ 11 D3 · Limfjorden 7 F5 · Limnos 15 E11 · Limoges 12 D4 · Limón, Costa Rica 45 F8 · Limoux 12 E5 · Limpopo → 29 K6 · Linares, Mexico 44 C5 · Linares, Spain 13 C4 · Lincoln, U.K. 8 D7 · Lincoln, Ill., U.S.A. 40 E10 · Lincoln, Kans., U.S.A. 40 F5 · Lincoln, Maine, U.S.A. 43 C11 · Lincoln, N. Mex., U.S.A. 39 K11 · Lincoln, Nebr., U.S.A. 40 E6 · Lincoln City 38 D1 · Lincoln Sea 6 A4 · Lincolnshire □ 8 D7 · Lincolnshire Wolds 8 D7 · Linden, Ala., U.S.A. 43 J2 · Linden, Tex., U.S.A. 41 J7 · Lindesnes 7 G5 · Lindsay, Calif., U.S.A. 39 H4 · Lindsay, Okla., U.S.A. 41 H6 · Lindsborg 40 F6 · Line Islands 35 H12 · Lingd18ng Yang 21 F10 · Lingga, Kepulauan 23 D2 · Lingle 40 E2 · Linhai 21 D7 · Linhares 47 G10 · Linköping 7 F7 · Linnhe, L. 10 E3 · Linton, Ind., U.S.A. 42 F2 · Linton, N. Dak., U.S.A. 40 B4 · Linxia 20 C5 · Linz 16 D7 · Lion, G. du 12 E6 · Lipetsk 18 D4 · Lippe → 16 C3 · Lippcomb 41 G4 · Liptrap, C. 32 C4 · Liquillo, Sierra de 45 d · Lisboa 13 C1 · Lisbon = Lisboa 13 C1 · Lisbon Falls 43 D10 · Lisburn 11 B5 · Liscannor B. 11 D2 · Lisdoonvarna 11 C2 · Lisianski I. 34 E10 · Lisieux 12 B4 · Lismore, Australia 32 A5 · Lismore, Ireland 11 D4 · Listowel 11 D2 · Litchfield, Ill., U.S.A. 40 F10 · Litchfield, Minn., U.S.A. 40 C7 · Lithgow 32 B5 · Little Andaman I. 25 D8 · Little Barrier I. 33 G5 · Little Belt Mts. 38 C8 · Little Bighorn Battlefield △ 38 D10 · Little Colorado → 39 H8 · Little Falls, Minn., U.S.A. 40 C7 · Little Falls, N.Y., U.S.A. 42 D8 · Little Fork → 40 A8 · Little Humboldt → 38 F5 · Little Minch 10 D2 · Little Missouri → 40 B3 · Little Ouse → 9 E9 · Little Red → 41 H9 · Little River 33 K4 · Little Rock 41 H8 · Little Sable Pt. 42 D2 · Little Sioux → 40 D6 · Little Snake → 38 F9 · Little Wabash → 42 G1 · Little White → 40 D4 · Littlefield 41 J3 · Littlehampton 9 G7 · Littleton 42 C10 · Liupanshui 20 D5 · Liuzhou 21 D5 · Live Oak 43 K4 · Livermore 39 H3 · Livermore, Mt. 41 K2 · Livermore Falls 43 C11 · Liverpool, Canada 37 E13 · Liverpool, U.K. 8 D4 · Liverpool Bay 8 D4 · Liverpool Ra. 32 B5 · Livingston, Ala., U.S.A. 43 J1 · Livingston, Mont., U.S.A. 38 D8 · Livingston, Tex., U.S.A. 41 K7 · Livingstone 29 H5 · Livonia 42 D4 · Livorno 14 C4 · Lizard Pt. 9 H2 · Ljubljana 14 A6 · Llandeilo 9 F4 · Llandovery 9 F4 · Llandrindod Wells 9 E4 · Llandudno 8 D4 · Llanelli 9 F3 · Llanfairfechan 8 D4 · Llangollen 8 E4 · Llanidloes 9 E4 · Llano 41 K5 · Llano → 41 K5 · Llano Estacado 41 J3 · Llanos 46 C4 · Llanwrtyd Wells 9 E4 · Lleida 13 B6 · Lleyn Peninsula 8 E3 · Llobregat → 13 B7 · Lloret de Mar 13 B7 · Lloydminster 36 C9 · Lobatse 29 K5 · Lobito 28 G2 · Loch Lomond and the Trossachs △ 10 E4 · Lochaber 10 E3 · Lochboisdale 10 D1 · Lochgilphead 10 E3 · Lochinver 10 C3 · Lochmaddy 10 D1 · Lochnagar 10 E5 · Lochy, L. 10 E4 · Lock 32 B2 · Lock Haven 42 E7 · Lockhart 41 L6 · Lockport 42 D6 · Lod 26 D3 · Lodge Grass 38 D10

Column 8 — Lillehammer … Luing

Lillehammer 7 E6 · Lima, Peru 46 F3 · Limavady 11 A5 · Limbe 28 D1 · Limeira 47 H9 · Limerick 11 D3 · Lüneburger Heide 16 B5 · Lüneburg 16 B5 · Lüni → 24 C4 · Lunéville 12 B7 · Luni → 24 C4 · Luohe 21 C6 · Luoyang 21 C6 · Luray 42 F6 · Lurgan 11 B5 · Lusaka 29 H5 · Lusk 40 D2 · Ľutselk'e 36 C8 · Lutsk 17 C7 · Luverne, Ala., U.S.A. 43 K2 · Luverne, Minn., U.S.A. 40 D6 · Luvua → 28 F5 · Luxembourg 15 E6 · Luxembourg ■ 15 E5 · Luxi 20 D4 · Luzern 16 E4 · Luzhou 20 D5 · Luzon 23 B4 · Lviv 17 C7 · Lyakhovskiye, Ostrova 19 B15 · Lybster 10 C5 · Lydenburg 29 K6 · Lyell 33 J4 · Lyme B. 9 G5 · Lyme Regis 9 G5 · Lymington 9 G6 · Lynchburg 42 G6 · Lynd Ra. 32 A4 · Lynden 38 B2 · Lyndhurst 32 E2 · Lynn 42 D10 · Lynn Haven 43 K3 · Lynn Lake 36 C9 · Lynton 9 F4 · Lyon 12 D6 · Lyonnais 12 D6 · Lyons, Ga., U.S.A. 43 J4 · Lyons, Kans., U.S.A. 40 F5 · Lysychansk 17 A5 · Lytham St. Anne's 8 D4 · Lyttelton 33 K4

Column 9 — Lodgepole Cr. … Luleå

Lodgepole Cr. → 40 E2 · Lodi 38 G3 · Łódź 16 C9 · Lofoten 7 D6 · Logan, Iowa, U.S.A. 40 E7 · Logan, Ohio, U.S.A. 42 F4 · Logan, Utah, U.S.A. 40 F8 · Logan, W. Va., U.S.A. 42 G5 · Logansport, Ind., U.S.A. 42 E2 · Logansport, La., U.S.A. 41 K8 · Loir → 12 C3 · Loire → 12 C2 · Loja 46 D3 · Lokan tekojärvi 6 C9 · Lom 15 C10 · Loma 38 C8 · Lombárdia □ 12 D8 · Lomblen 23 D4 · Lombok 23 D3 · Lomé 26 G6 · Lomond, L. 10 E4 · Lompoc 39 J3 · London, Canada 37 E11 · London, U.K. 9 F7 · London, Ky., U.S.A. 42 G3 · London, Ohio, U.S.A. 42 F4 · London Gatwick (LGW) 9 F7 · London Heathrow (LHR) 9 F7 · London Stansted (STN) 9 F8 · Londonderry □ 11 B4 · Londonderry, C. 30 B4 · Londrina 48 A6 · Lone Pine 39 H4 · Long Beach, Calif., U.S.A. 39 K4 · Long Beach, Wash., U.S.A. 38 C1 · Long Branch 42 E9 · Long Creek 38 D4 · Long I., Bahamas 45 C9 · Long I., U.S.A. 42 E9 · Long Island Sd. 42 E9 · Long Prairie 40 C7 · Long Xuyen 23 B2 · Longboat Key 43 M4 · Longford, Australia 32 F4 · Longford, Ireland 11 C4 · Longford □ 11 C4 · Longlac 37 E11 · Longmont 40 E2 · Longnawan 23 C3 · Longreach 30 E7 · Longtown 8 B5 · Longview, Tex., U.S.A. 41 J7 · Longview, Wash., U.S.A. 38 C2 · Longxue Dao 21 F10 · Lons-le-Saunier 12 C6 · Looc 23 B4 · Loop Hd. 11 D2 · Lop Nur 20 B4 · Lopez 42 E7 · Lopez, C. 28 E1 · Lora → 24 C4 · Lora del Rio 13 D3 · Lorain 42 E5 · Loralai 24 B5 · Lorca 13 D5 · Lord Howe I. 31 H12 · Lord Howe Rise / Seamount Chain 31 K9 · Lordsburg 39 K9 · Loreto 14 C5 · Lorient 12 C2 · Lorn 10 E3 · Lorn, Firth of 10 E3 · Lorne 32 C3 · Lörrach 16 E3 · Los Alamos 39 J10 · Los Andes 47 C2 · Los Angeles, Chile 47 D2 · Los Angeles, U.S.A. 39 K4 · Los Angeles Aqueduct 39 J5 · Los Banos 39 H3 · Los Lunas 39 J10 · Los Mochis 44 B3 · Lossiemouth 10 D5 · Lostwithiel 9 G3 · Loughborough 9 E6 · Loughrea 11 C3 · Louis XIV, Pte. 37 D12 · Louisa 42 F4 · Louisiade Arch. 30 C9 · Louisiana □ 41 K9 · Louisville, Ky., U.S.A. 42 F3 · Louisville, Miss., U.S.A. 41 J10 · Louisville Ridge 34 L10 · Louth, Australia 32 B4 · Louth, Ireland 11 C5 · Louth, U.K. 8 D7 · Louth □ 11 C5 · Lourdes 12 E3 · Lovech 15 C11 · Lovelock 38 F5 · Lovell 38 D9 · Loving 41 J2 · Lovington 41 J3 · Lower Alkali L. 38 F4 · Lower California = Baja California 44 A1 · Lower Hutt 33 J5 · Lower Red L. 40 B7 · Lower Saxony = Niedersachsen □ 16 B5 · Lowestoft 9 E9 · Loxton 32 E3 · Loyalty Is. = Loyauté, Îs. 31 F12 · Loyauté, Îs. 31 F12 · Lualaba → 28 D5 · Luanda 28 E2 · Luang Prabang 23 B2 · Luangwa → 28 G6 · Luanshya 28 G5 · Lubango 28 G2 · Lubbock 41 J4 · Lübeck 16 B6 · Lublin 16 C11 · Lubumbashi 28 G5 · Lucania, Mt. 36 C5 · Lucca 14 C4 · Lucena 23 B4 · Lucerne = Luzern 16 E4 · Lucknow 25 C7 · Lüda = Dalian 21 C7 · Lüderitz 29 K3 · Ludhiana 25 B6 · Ludington 42 D2 · Ludlow 9 E5 · Ludvika 7 F7 · Ludwigshafen 16 D4 · Lufkin 41 K7 · Luga 7 F9 · Lugano 14 A3 · Lugansk = Luhansk 17 A5 · Lugnaquilla 11 D5 · Lugo 13 A2 · Luhansk 17 A5 · Luing 10 E3 · Luleå 7 D8

Column 10 — Luleälven … Lyttelton / M — Ma'anshan …

Luleälven → 7 D8 · Luling 41 L6 · Lumberton 43 H6 · Lumsden 33 L2 · Lund 9 d · Lundy 9 F3 · Lune → 8 C5 · Lüneburger Heide 16 B5 · Lünen 28 D1 · Luni → 24 C4 · Luray 42 F6 · Lurgan 11 B5 · Lusaka 29 H5 · Lusk 40 D2 · Ľutselk'e 36 C8 · Lutsk 17 C7 · Luverne, Ala., U.S.A. 43 K2 · Luverne, Minn., U.S.A. 40 D6 · Luvua → 28 F5 · Luxembourg 15 E6 · Luxembourg ■ 15 E5 · Luzern 16 E4 · Luzhou 20 D5 · Luzon 23 B4 · Lviv 17 C7 · Lyakhovskiye, Ostrova 19 B15 · Lybster 10 C5 · Lydenburg 29 K6 · Lyell 33 J4 · Lyman 38 F8 · Lyme B. 9 G5 · Lyme Regis 9 G5 · Lymington 9 G6 · Lynchburg 42 G6 · Lynd Ra. 32 A4 · Lynden 38 B2 · Lyndhurst 32 E2 · Lynn 42 D10 · Lynn Haven 43 K3 · Lynn Lake 36 C9 · Lynton 9 F4 · Lyon 12 D6 · Lyonnais 12 D6 · Lyons, Ga., U.S.A. 43 J4 · Lyons, Kans., U.S.A. 40 F5 · Lysychansk 17 A5 · Lytham St. Anne's 8 D4 · Lyttelton 33 K4

M

Ma'anshan 21 C6 · Maas → 16 C2 · Maastricht 15 D5 · Mablethorpe 8 D8 · McAlester 41 H7 · McAllen 41 M5 · MacAlpine L. 36 C9 · Macapá 47 C8 · Macau 21 D6 · Macauley I. 31 G15 · McCall 38 D5 · McCamey 41 K3 · McCammon 40 E7 · Macclesfield 8 D5 · M'Clintock Chan. 36 A9 · M'Clure Str. 37 B10 · McClusky 40 B4 · McComb 41 K9 · McCook 40 E4 · McDermitt 38 F5 · Macdonald, L. 30 D4 · Macdonnell Ranges 30 D5 · Macduff 10 D6 · Macedonia ■ 15 D9 · Maceió 47 E12 · Macerata 14 C5 · Macfarlane, L. 32 B2 · McGehee 41 J9 · McGill 38 G6 · M'Gregor Ra. 32 A3 · Machakos 28 E7 · Machala 46 D3 · Machias 43 C12 · Machynlleth 9 E4 · McIntosh 40 C4 · Macintyre → 32 A5 · Mackay, Australia 30 E8 · Mackay, L. 30 D4 · McKeesport 42 E6 · Mackenzie 36 C7 · Mackenzie → 36 B6 · McKenzie 43 G1 · Mackenzie Mts. 36 B6 · McKinley, Mt. 36 B4 · McKinney 41 J6 · Macksville 32 B5 · McLaughlin 40 C4 · Maclean 32 A5 · McLean 41 H4 · McLeansboro 42 G1 · McLoughlin, Mt. 38 E2 · McMinnville, Oreg., U.S.A. 38 D2 · McMinnville, Tenn., U.S.A. 43 H3 · McMurdo Sd. 5 D11 · Mâcon, France 12 C6 · Macon, Ga., U.S.A. 43 J4 · Macon, Miss., U.S.A. 43 J1 · Macon, Mo., U.S.A. 40 F8 · Macquarie → 32 B4 · Macquarie Harbour 32 D4 · Macquarie Is. 34 N7 · Madadeni 29 K6 · Madagascar ■ 29 J9 · Madeira 26 B2 · Madeira → 46 D7 · Madha 24 C4 · Madhya Pradesh □ 25 C6 · Madill 41 H6 · Madinat ash Sha'b 24 E3 · Madison, Ind., U.S.A. 42 F3 · Madison, Nebr., U.S.A. 40 E6 · Madison, S. Dak., U.S.A. 40 D6 · Madison, Wis., U.S.A. 40 D10 · Madison → 38 D8 · Madison Heights 42 G6 · Madisonville, Ky., U.S.A. 42 G2 · Madisonville, Tex., U.S.A. 41 K7

Column 11 — Madisonville, Tex. … Manihiki Plateau

Madisonville, Tex., U.S.A. 41 K7 · Madiun 23 D3 · Madoc 42 D7 · Madrakah, Ra's al 24 D6 · Madras = Chennai 25 D7 · Madras 38 D3 · Madre, L. 41 M6 · Madre de Dios 46 F5 · Madre de Dios, I. 48 G1 · Madre Occidental, Sierra 44 B3 · Madre Oriental, Sierra 44 C5 · Madrid 13 B4 · Madura 13 B4 · Madurai 25 E6 · Maebashi 22 E6 · Maesteg 9 F4 · Mafeking = Mafikeng 29 K5 · Maff 32 C4 · Mafikeng 29 K5 · Magadan 19 D16 · Magallanes, Estrecho de 48 G2 · Magdalena 46 A4 · Magdeburg 16 B6 · Magee 41 K10 · Magelang 23 D3 · Magellan's Str. = Magallanes, Estrecho de 48 G2 · Maggiore, Lago 12 D8 · Maggotty 44 a · Magherafelt 11 B5 · Magnetic Pole (North) 37 B9 · Magnetic Pole (South) 5 D14 · Magnitogorsk 18 D6 · Magnolia, Ark., U.S.A. 41 J8 · Magnolia, Miss., U.S.A. 41 K9 · Mahabad 24 B3 · Mahajanga 29 J5 · Mahanadi → 25 C7 · Maharashtra □ 25 D6 · Maheno 33 L3 · Mahia Pen. 33 H6 · Mahilyow 17 B10 · Mahinerangi, L. 33 L2 · Maidenhead 9 F7 · Maidstone 9 F8 · Maiduguri 26 F8 · Main →, Germany 16 D4 · Main →, U.K. 11 B5 · Main Range △ 32 A5 · Maine 12 C3 · Maine □ 43 C11 · Maine → 11 D2 · Mainland, Orkney, U.K. 10 C5 · Mainland, Shet., U.K. 10 A7 · Mainz 16 C4 · Maitland, N.S.W., Australia 32 B5 · Maitland, S. Austral., Australia 32 B2 · Majorca = Mallorca 13 C7 · Majuro 34 G9 · Makale 23 D3 · Makasar = Ujung Pandang 23 D3 · Makasar, Selat 23 D3 · Makgadikgadi Salt Pans 29 J5 · Makhachkala 17 A8 · Makiyivka 17 A5 · Makkah 24 C2 · Malabar Coast 25 D6 · Malacca, Straits of 23 C1 · Malad City 38 E7 · Málaga 13 D3 · Malahide 11 C5 · Malaita 31 B11 · Malakal 29 G12 · Malang 23 D3 · Malanje 28 F3 · Malatya 17 F7 · Malawi ■ 28 G6 · Malawi, L. 28 G6 · Malay Pen. 23 C2 · Malaysia ■ 23 C3 · Malbooma 32 B1 · Malbork 16 A10 · Malden I. 35 H12 · Maldives ■ 25 E6 · Maldon 9 F8 · Malegaon 25 C6 · Malema 28 G7 · Malheur → 38 D5 · Mali ■ 26 E5 · Mali Kyun 23 B1 · Malik 23 D2 · Mallaig 10 D3 · Mallacoota Inlet 32 C4 · Mallorca 13 C7 · Mallow 11 D3 · Malmö 7 F6 · Malone 42 C8 · Malpelo, I. de 46 C2 · Malta, Idaho, U.S.A. 38 F7 · Malta, Mont., U.S.A. 38 B10 · Malta ■ 14 G6 · Malton 8 C7 · Maluku □ 23 D4 · Malvern, U.S.A. 41 H8 · Malvern Hills 9 E5 · Malvinas, Is. = Falkland Is. ☑ 48 G5 · Mammoth 39 K8 · Mammoth Cave △ 42 G3 · Mamoré → 46 F5 · Man 26 G4 · Man, I. of 8 C3 · Manado 23 C4 · Managua 44 E7 · Manapouri 33 L1 · Manapouri, L. 33 L1 · Manas 20 B3 · Manaus 46 D7 · Manawatu → 33 J5 · Manchester, U.K. 8 D5 · Manchester, Ga., U.S.A. 43 J3 · Manchester, Iowa, U.S.A. 40 D9 · Manchester, N.H., U.S.A. 42 D10 · Manchester, Ohio, U.S.A. 42 F4 · Manchester Intl. (MAN) 8 D5 · Manchuria = Dongbei 21 B7 · Mand → 24 C4 · Mandal 7 G5 · Mandalay 25 C8 · Mandan 40 B4 · Mandaue 23 B4 · Mandeville 44 a · Mandla 25 C7 · Mandsaur 25 C6 · Mandurah 30 G2 · Mandvi 24 C5 · Mandya 25 D6 · Maneroo Cr. → 30 E7 · Manfredónia 14 D6 · Mangalore 25 D6 · Mangaweka 33 H5 · Mangnai 20 C4 · Mango 33 C10 · Mangoky → 29 J8 · Mangole 23 D4 · Mangonui 33 F4 · Manhattan 40 F6 · Manicoré 46 E6 · Manicouagan → 37 D13 · Manicouagan, Rés. 37 D13 · Manihiki 35 J11 · Manihiki Plateau 35 K11